Praise for *Summons to Berlin*

T0007478

"Joanne Intrator's *Summons to Berlin* [is a] ... book. Spurred by unsettling deathbed questions, the writer restlessly searches for answers in order that her father, Gerhard, should one day rest easy. This memoir reads with intense imagery that is really the stuff of novels. I had to keep reminding myself that the entire narrative is all too real. A remarkable accomplishment that fully honors Intrator's family legacy while stimulating readers' minds and touching their hearts as well."

—Steven K. Baum, author of *Antisemitism Explained*
and *The Psychology of Genocide*

"In her captivating *Summons to Berlin*, Joanne Intrator skillfully interweaves an immense knowledge of Holocaust-era history into a vivid, complex, tragic narration of the restitution conflict that for many years possessed her heart and soul. A triumph!"

—Dr. Ava Siegler, author of *What Should I Tell the Kids?*

"Joanne Intrator's *Summons to Berlin* is a compelling confession full of intriguing questions and significant insights. In this absorbing book, the author is at once personal and objective, bringing together inner and outer realities in thoughtful, searching ways. Intrator rewards readers with a vivid feel for the complex, often disturbing events at the heart of her narrative."

—Dr. Michael Eigen, author of *The Sensitive Self*
and *The Psychoanalytic Mystic*

"Joanne Intrator's *Summons to Berlin* is a gripping story of loss and the struggle for restitution."

—William H. Weitzer, PhD, John H. Slade
Executive Director, Leo Baeck Institute

"With her *Summons to Berlin*, Joanne Intrator provides readers with rich, vibrant details of Mitte history that they simply will not find anywhere else. I hope and believe that Intrator's finely observed memoir, with its dramatic central conflict and upbeat ending, will make a significant contribution to continued good relations between Germany and the United States."

—Dr. Benedikt Goebel, Director, Office for City Research, Berlin, Büro für Stadtforschung

"What really strikes me about Joanne Intrator's remarkable *Summons to Berlin* is how compellingly the author—a practicing psychiatrist— decodes the emotional dimensions of her epic restitution drama. This stimulating, deeply moving book is sure to resonate."

—Dr. Frank Mecklenburg, Director of Research and Chief Archivist, Leo Baeck Institute

"As I finished Joanne Intrator's *Summons to Berlin,* I thought to myself, *What a harrowing, powerful read* . . . The author lets no amount of bureaucratic German cynicism, obfuscation, and foot-dragging deter her from her goals. In chilling detail, she recounts every step of her brave, often frustrating, yet ultimately successful mission. On his deathbed, Dr. Intrator's father asked whether she was 'tough enough' for this kind of complex, prolonged battle. *Summons to Berlin* leaves no doubt that she is."

—Peggy Taylor, photographer and author of *Streeteries: New York's Pandemic Outdoor Dining*

"Throughout her inspiring memoir *Summons to Berlin*, Dr. Joanne Intrator writes with her sharp, inquiring mind. Because she is a practicing psychiatrist and accomplished researcher, she is able to imbue her narrative with unique insights not just of the people involved in her case but also, more broadly, of history and its puzzlements. I find this book an exceptionally enriching read."

—Elisabeth von Haebler, Editor-in-Chief, *Ästhetik & Kommunikation*, Berlin

SUMMONS
TO BERLIN

SUMMONS TO BERLIN

Nazi Theft and A Daughter's
Quest for Justice

Joanne Intrator

SHE WRITES PRESS

Published 2023
Printed in the United States of America
Print ISBN: 978-1-64742-513-5
E-ISBN: 978-1-64742-514-2
Library of Congress Control Number: 2023901594

For information, address:
She Writes Press
1569 Solano Ave #546
Berkeley, CA 94707

Interior Design by Kiran Spees

She Writes Press is a division of SparkPoint Studio, LLC.

To Ben

FOREWORD

Robert D. Hare

In 1990, I had the pleasure of meeting Dr. Joanne Intrator at the San Diego meeting of the American Academy of Psychiatry and Law. For several years, we had been communicating about a common interest: The potency of words to manipulate and control others and the deceptive, callous, and devastating use of this power by psychopaths. My concern was primarily scientific—part of a long-standing investigation into the nature and manifestations of psychopathy. Joanne's interest in the crafty use of words resulted from her early experience as a victim of language used for manipulation and gaslighting, and the limitations of the commonly used Mental Status Exam used to assess perpetrators when she was at the Bronx Criminal Court clinic.

When we met, Joanne was a psychiatrist at the Mount Sinai School of Medicine and Bronx VA Medical Center, and I was a psychologist at the University of British Columbia (UBC). The outcome was two-fold. We planned the first neuroimaging study of psychopathy, and developed a conceptual framework subsequently used by Joanne to understand and deal with the personality and actions of those in the Nazi regime that stole her family's factory in the historic center of Berlin.

This book depicts the seemingly insurmountable obstacles she encountered during her deeply personal, soul-searing quest for justice from the German authorities. As she recently explained, our collaboration helped her to understand those who perpetrated the crimes against her family. It also helped her deal with a German bureaucratic system that did everything possible to block and bury her search for the truth. However, by 1990, Joanne was already well versed in psychopathic stratagems, as exemplified, for example, in her course on *The Psychopath in Fact and Film*. I suggest that my work provided empirical validation and encouragement for her clinical expertise and perspectives on human nature.

During our San Diego meeting, we discussed my recent development of the *Psychopathy Checklist-Revised* (PCL-R) and its publication in 1991 (with a second edition in 2003). The PCL-R is a rating scale in which trained clinicians and researchers use an interview and collateral information to rate offenders on items relevant to psychopathy. At the time, the instrument was relatively new, but now is an international standard for the clinical and forensic assessment of psychopathy.

Joanne and I also discussed a recent UBC lexical decision (LD) study in which we used the PCL-R to assess offenders for psychopathy. My students and I submitted the findings to *Science* in 1989. The editors declined to send it out for peer review because the data "could not have come from real people." However, *Psychophysiology* accepted the article in 1990 and published it the following year. Our study was the first to evaluate Hervey Cleckley's speculation, described in *The Mask of Sanity*, that psychopaths have a central and deep-seated semantic/affective disorder in which the words have semantic meaning but little emotional depth or coloring. Most words have semantic (dictionary) and affective meaning. But, the words of psychopaths are two-dimensional, having only dictionary meaning, making them an effective tool for glib and shallow persuasion, deception, and manipulation. In *Without Conscience*, I suggested that "inner speech" was influential in the development and operation of conscience. Emotionally charged thoughts, images, and internal dialogue give a 'bite' to conscience, account for its robust control over behavior, and generate guilt and remorse for transgressions. For psychopaths, conscience is little more than an intellectual awareness of the rules others make.

In the LD study, my students and I tested the hypothesis that psychopaths process and use all words as having few if any affective connotations. We recorded event-related brain potentials as offenders determined as rapidly as possible if a letter string flashed on a computer screen formed an actual word. The letter strings were words with emotional or neutral connotations, and pronounceable non-words, presented randomly in one session. Brain potentials in lexical decision tasks typically are speedy, measured in milliseconds following the presentation of the letter strings. Among the low psychopathy offenders, decisions (Is it a word?) were quicker to emotional than to neutral words, consistent with a general literature on lexical decision times. In sharp contrast, the decisions of the high psychopathy offenders were relatively slow and virtually the same for emotional and neutral words. The interpretation of this finding is that emotional words carry a lot of information that most people readily access, thus facilitating lexical decisions. However, psychopathic offenders were unable to access this information, and therefore "viewed" emotional words as if they were neutral words.

The group differences in brain potential responses recorded during the LD task were striking, and the reason for the skepticism about the data expressed by *Science*. Brain potentials evoked during a cognitive task are complex; they provide an insight into the depth, duration, and pattern of brain activity in response to the task. For low psychopathy offenders, components of the brain potential responses typically observed in an LD task were *larger and more prolonged to affective than neutral words*. In sharp contrast, the brain potentials of high psychopathy offenders were *short-lived* and virtually the same for emotional and neutral words. The brain potential and decision time data painted the same picture of psychopathic language. We concluded that psychopathic offenders conceptualize and process words in a cursory, shallow manner, and do little more than make a lexical decision with few semantic/affective associations.

Our LD study provided the first behavioral and electrocortical support for clinical impressions that psychopathic language lacks normal affect. The study, development of the PCL-R, and my meeting with Joanne in San Diego occurred at a time opportune for generating collaborative imaging research on psychopathy. Moreover, the Berlin Wall had fallen a year earlier, and the unification of East and West Germany took place in the year of our meeting, 1990. These geopolitical events were important for Joanne because she would not have to deal with the German Democratic Republic, where her family's factory was in the 1930s.

At the Bronx VA Medical Center, Joanne had access to its single-photon emission computed tomography (SPECT) brain imaging facility. SPECT measures regional cerebral blood flow while a patient is at rest or engaged in cognitive/behavioral activity. Joanne suggested we combine resources for a SPECT extension of the lexical decision protocol. Her proposal initially proved challenging to implement; the study of psychopathy was not within the Bronx VA Medical Center's area of interest. However, Joanne was able to, first, convince the administration and staff that a SPECT study of psychopathy was clinically and scientifically worthwhile; second, enlist and coordinate the talents and experience of experts and colleagues involved in research with imaging technology; and, finally, solicit male volunteers from substance abuse and psychiatric inpatient programs under VA Human Studies Committee guidelines. Obtaining permission for the study was quite an accomplishment. It also was a high-stakes professional gamble, for Joanne was advocating for the extensive use of valuable resources and personnel to conduct an innovative study with an uncertain outcome. Fortunately, she was resolute in her need to understand the nature and roots of psychopathic speech. She also had the support of several colleagues interested in moving from categorical psychiatric diagnoses (e.g., Antisocial Personality Disorder) to the dimensional psychological construct measured by the PCL-R.

With funding from the British Columbia Health Research Foundation and the Bronx VA Services, we put together a research team for a SPECT study of psychopathy, with Joanne as the principal investigator and lead author of the article, published in 1997 in *Biological Psychiatry*. Pairs of trained raters scored the PCL-R for inpatient volunteers, with high interrater reliability. We selected two groups of inpatients, one with high and the other with low PCL-R scores. We matched them on relevant variables, including age, education, and substance abuse. We also recruited a group of community volunteers. I note that my students and I collaborated with Joanne's team, but she and her team conducted the SPECT experimental procedures. In the previous LD study, we recorded trial-by-trial brain potentials in milliseconds. Because changes in cerebral blood flow are much slower than brain potentials, we blended blood flow data over ten-minute segments in two sessions. We presented the participant with a block of neutral words and nonwords in one session and a block of emotional words and nonwords in a second session a week later, with the order of sessions balanced across participants. These modifications made it unlikely to obtain the same reliable group differences in reaction times to letter strings found in the LD study. Still, the modifications were consistent with our primary goal, which was to determine if there is an association between psychopathy and cerebral blood flow in regions involved in processing neutral and emotional information.

Following the injection of a nuclear isotope, which allowed the SPECT scanner to track cerebral blood flow, the participant performed the lexical decision task. We found significant group differences in regional blood flow during the performance of the tasks. During both neutral and emotional sessions, brain activation was widespread among the low psychopathy inpatients and community sample, indicating that many regions of the brain were involved in making lexical decisions. In contrast, activation among the high psychopathy inpatients was much more limited, occurring primarily in the posterior (occipital) region of the brain. What did this mean? The answer lies in brain-imaging evidence that people can make lexical decisions early in cognitive processing, in occipital/extrastriate cortex. However, the higher-level processing of words and their semantic/affective meanings occurs in more anterior areas of the brain. The activation pattern among the psychopathic patients suggested they discriminated between words and nonwords, but this was the extent of their cognitive effort. Thus, both the LD and the SPECT study indicated that psychopathic language is cognitively and affectively superficial and involves little interaction among brain regions. The findings are consistent with clinical and research evidence that psychopathic language lacks deep meanings and subtle semantic and emotional nuances.

The SPECT study also produced another important and equally intriguing finding. The regional blood flow of psychopathic inpatients *increased more* during the emotional than the neutral condition of the lexical decision task. This effect did not occur with the other participants. However, this increase in cerebral blood flow occurred in frontal/temporal brain regions *related to language processing*. We interpreted this surprising finding in terms of a literature indicating that emotional meaning is an essential part of the language of ordinary individuals. For them, the neurophysiological processes involved in decoding the affective information contained in words are so overlearned and efficient that additional metabolic requirements are minimal. Psychopaths, however, seem to have difficulty fully understanding and using words that should refer to ordinary emotional events and feelings. Instead, they process and use them primarily in terms of denotative dictionary meaning. In this sense, emotion is like a second language to them, requiring a considerable amount of mental transformation and cognitive effort on their part. In the SPECT study, lexical decisions involving emotional words may have placed heavy demands on the psychopaths, thus requiring assistance from language-related regions.

This highly cited SPECT study preceded several functional magnetic resonance imaging (fMRI) investigations of psychopathy conducted at the University of British Columbia with the collaboration of the Departments of Psychology, Psychiatry, and Radiology. Unlike SPECT, fMRI is a noninvasive method (no injection of a radioactive tracer) for measuring regional cerebral blood flow during the performance of a task. In several studies, we found that some brain regions were relatively inactive in psychopathic offenders when they processed emotional words and pictures. These were regions of the paralimbic system involved with emotion. Importantly, these studies replicated the SPECT findings several times; psychopathic offenders showed reduced activity in limbic regions and increased activity in language-related regions. Since the SPECT article, there have been hundreds of brain-imaging studies of psychopathy, most finding structural and functional anomalies related to decision-making, inhibition, frontal-temporal-limbic connectivity, and cognitive/affective processes. I believe the SPECT finding that language-related brain regions facilitated emotional processing among psychopathic inpatients was an essential step in understanding psychopathy. The gamble taken by Joanne Intrator certainly has paid off.

While we were planning and conducting the SPECT study and during subsequent meetings, Joanne described the enormous legal, political, and disputatious obstacles she would have to overcome in her "mission," despite the recent fall of the Berlin Wall and the unification of Germany. (Anecdotally, my wife, Averil, our daughter, Cheryl, and I spent ten days in 1969 in a VW Westphalia, camped five feet from the Berlin Wall, near the Brandenburg Gate. We entered East Germany through Checkpoint Charlie, had several disturbing encounters with soldiers carrying machine guns, and likely walked by the former site of the Intrator factory.) Throughout her mission, Joanne often thought about the malignant narcissism and psychopathy of the Nazi leaders. She wondered about the millions of people who followed these leaders, many of whom once were ordinary citizens whose personalities and behaviors the leaders warped into those of cruel true believers. She knew others were willing candidates for a regime that promoted hate and cruelty toward its designated enemies.

Along these lines, my colleagues and I published an article in the *Journal of Criminal Justice* in 2022 about men convicted for crimes against humanity committed during the Pinochet junta in Chile. Not surprisingly, most had an extreme disposition for self-serving, callous, and ruthless treatment of others without guilt or remorse. As in Nazi Germany, many of these state actors were highly psychopathic, with the innate personality and attributes that seamlessly fit the junta's ideology and aims. Others were products of persuasion, indoctrination, or intimidation; they accepted that remorseless manipulation and violence were necessary and acceptable, not only for their own well-being but to protect the state from its declared scapegoats and "enemies."

Because of her training and experiences, Joanne was acutely aware of the diverse Nazi manipulations and avenues to brutality, but initially less prepared for the harsh machinations of a legal and political system determined to impede her relentless exposure of the injustice done to her family. However, the system was unprepared for her. Irony can be satisfying but sometimes informative and inspirational. Recently Joanne received an invitation to participate in the planning to redevelop the historic Berlin Mitte, the site of her family's factory.

Dr. Robert Hare is an Emeritus Professor of Psychology at the University of British Columbia. He has become recognized as the foremost authority on psychopaths with over 35 years of research at UBC. He has devoted most of his academic career to investigating psychopathy, its nature, assessment, and implications for mental health and criminal justice. He is the author of several books, including *Without Conscience: The Disturbing World of the Psychopaths Among Us*, and more than one hundred scientific articles on psychopathy. He is the developer of the *Hare Psychopathy Checklist-Revised* (PCL-R)

Prologue

A few days before my father died in 1993, I flew from New York City to Palm Beach, Florida, to be with him. Afternoon stretched into evening, and he dozed off as I sat beside his bed. Hearing his breathing ease, I thought he had fallen asleep. Suddenly my father bolted upright, his eyes meeting mine.

"Are you tough enough yet? Do they know who you are?"

It crossed my mind that he might be delirious, at the mercy of some hallucination, but his no-nonsense tone made me wonder. My father's voice once again sounded like that of the younger, healthier man I had known before a lifetime's accumulation of stress and illness led him to bodily collapse.

Was I *tough enough*? For what? I was mystified, but he never explained what he meant. The two enigmatic questions turned out to be the last words Gerhard Intrator would utter to me in our forty-seven years together on this earth. The effort knocked him out. Seconds later he slumped over, barely giving me time to catch him in my arms and settle him comfortably into his pillows.

My father fell soundly asleep and died two days later, leaving me to parse his words on my own.

I had an idea of where to start.

For about a year before his death, and despite terminal illness, my father tried to achieve restitution for the theft of 16 Wallstrasse, a commercial building in Berlin's Mitte district that his family co-owned in the 1930s. *Wallstrasse* means "Wall Street" in German; considered by many to be the heart of the city, bustling, cosmopolitan Mitte was a business center and central to Jewish life in Berlin before the Nazis took over. After World War II, between 1961 and 1990, this area fell under the control of Communist East Berlin. With the fall of the Berlin Wall in November 1989, restitution finally became possible for Nazi-era crimes committed in Mitte.

Though, I sensed that my father referred to the injustice done to our family as part of the Nazi's Aryanization program—the transfer of Jewish property to non-Jews from 1933 to 1945—I had no sense of what lay ahead of me when I joined his quest for justice. My experience would involve journeys both literal and figurative, extending over many years, and very nearly break me.

Part 1:

History

1 The Intrators

Like any Jewish child whose parents were refugees from Hitler's Third Reich, I had always known the broad outlines of my family's fraught history. But that did not mean we spoke much about it. On the contrary, from my earliest childhood, I had a sense that although the Nazis had committed unspeakable crimes against my European family, I had better not speak or ask about them.

As I grew through my teenage years into young adulthood, my interest in Holocaust history also grew—and as it did, I became increasingly conflicted about fully facing what the Nazis had done. Though I grew up hearing my Jewish mother and father speaking German with each other, almost all things German, including the language, made me feel intimidated and anxious. Despite this welter of emotions, I was driven to learn more and more about the Nazis. What I learned filled me with even more angst, which further intensified my compulsion. I was unable to push away these terror-filled thoughts, and they are among the reasons I was motivated to help other people by becoming a psychiatrist.

But that is getting ahead of my story.

The cabinets had been there forever, in my father's den in my childhood home in Forest Hills, Queens. I had never opened a single drawer, but now, following his death on April 24, 1993, I took a deep

15

breath, walked over, and removed a file. Eventually, I would open every drawer, each packed deep with letter-size files, all labeled in my father's strong, clear print. When I was growing up, my father would sometimes offhandedly relate something of his family's experiences under the Nazis when they lived in Berlin. However, it was only after my father died and I went through his files in New York, combing through the letters he meticulously collected and saved, that I fully understood his harrowing history.

More than a hundred years before my father's deathbed challenge, his family's story took shape against growing antisemitism in Europe. From the letters, I learned that my two paternal grandparents were born in 1875 in villages in what today is southeastern Poland—my grandfather, Jakob Intrator, in Śliwnica, and my grandmother, Rosa, in Dubiecko. At the time of their birth, the region, Galicia, was the "crown land" of the Austro-Hungarian Empire.[1]

In the attic of our house, I found photos of Jakob and Rosa taken on their wedding day in 1902. They were a striking couple, seeming to have every reason to be optimistic about their futures. Rosa's soft, full hair was swept luxuriously up into a chignon. She was dressed in a lovely bodice with soutache trim, a generous gold necklace falling gracefully on her full bosom. Jakob sported an impeccably trimmed mustache turned up at its sculptural edges. He wore a three-piece suit and a stiff-looking white stand-up collar with a bow tie. His pocket watch chain was draped over his vest.

Despite its oil reserves, Galicia was one of the poorest provinces of Europe. And despite that, my grandfather Jakob had success with his wholesale egg and poultry business. Around 1905, though, worsening conditions, widespread famine, and antisemitism led many members of the Intrator family to leave Galicia for Germany, which at the time had a thriving Jewish population. One of my father's uncles,

Alex Mersel, moved to the United States, where he found success as a commodities trader.

After Jakob and Rosa Intrator's first child, Alexander (my beloved uncle Alex), was born in 1905 in Dubiecko, my grandparents moved to Berlin. There was no information about their journey in the files, but they apparently settled into urban German life with little difficulty. My father, Gerhard, was born in Berlin in 1910. Aspiring to become part of the well-educated, culturally rich classes in the German capital, my grandfather—like a latter-day Moses Mendelssohn—made sure his two sons received a rigorous education in Greek and Latin, literature, philosophy, mathematics, and science, while preserving their identity as Jews.[2]

As was the case for many other similarly situated Jewish men, Jakob fought for Germany in World War I.[3] I remembered my father more than once saying that my grandfather had suffered mustard gas damage to his lungs. With my father gone, I hoped my uncle Alex—who was about twelve years old when my grandfather went to war—would be able to enlighten me about his father's experience. Accordingly, I visited him at his home in White Plains, New York.

"*Es war sehr schwierig*, Joanne. It was very, very tough," he told me, his voice ripe with emotion. "Papa was missing at the front for a long time. Going without news from him was unbearable. We simply had no way of knowing what had happened to him. Your Oma Rosa had real courage, though!"

Alex's eyes shone as he described his mother's bravery and initiative.

"She refused to believe our Jakob had perished. In the dead of winter, she left Berlin and took me and your father trekking across the war-ravaged landscape, far to the east in Poland, in hopes of finding him. She searched and searched, all the while taking care of us, lamentably though with no luck. But do you know what we found when we arrived home in Berlin?"

"What?" I asked.

"Mail! With a postcard photograph of your grandfather in a hospital bed. He was wasted away, but he was alive. After so much fear, to receive that injection of hope was like a miracle."

After he recovered from the brutality of his war experience, Jakob Intrator managed to build a business empire that included companies dealing with private banking, real estate, egg imports, textile imports and exports, and retail clothing. In 1919, the family moved to an exclusive address on what is the Champs-Élysées of Berlin, the Kurfürstendamm in the Charlottenburg district, famed for its cafés, elegant apartment houses, abundant parks, world-class shopping, and sophisticated theater.

It was in this cosmopolitan atmosphere that Uncle Alex thrived during the 1920s, planning to become a concert violinist, which set him at loggerheads against my grandfather, who wanted his eldest son to embrace a more conventional profession. Their long-running conflict over the issue was resolved after Jakob insisted that Alex be evaluated by the famed violinist Bronislaw Huberman, a personal friend of Albert Einstein and Arturo Toscanini.

Huberman thought Alex had potential, so Jakob yielded. His eldest son attended the Hochschule für Musik, today known as the Berlin University for the Arts. Later, Alex played professionally with the Rostal Quartet and the Edwin Fisher Orchestra. In 1930, he married Ilse Davidsohn, a daughter of the acclaimed opera singer and cantor Magnus Davidsohn, who worked with the Fasanenstrasse Synagogue, which my family in Berlin attended. Using the stage name Ilse Davis, Alex's wife performed in live theater and had parts in films including Fritz Lang's *Metropolis*. In 1932, Alex and Ilse had a son, Manfred, who became the joy of my grandparents' life.

∼

Their comfortable life in Berlin began to change in 1933. One of the first indications affected my uncle Alex. It was a query by the Nazi government to the leadership of the Edwin Fisher Orchestra: Was Alex Intrator Jewish? An affirmative answer forced my uncle out of a career in German classical music; he was restricted to playing with the Jüdischer Kulturbund, the Cultural Federation of German Jews.

My father took a more conventional path than his older brother. Going through his files, I found that in March 1928, Gerhard graduated from the Bismarck Gymnasium in Berlin. Next, I found my father's student ID, documenting his enrollment as a summer law student at the University of Freiburg. That autumn, he received an additional ID as a law student at the Friedrich Wilhelm University in Berlin (now the Humboldt University of Berlin). Finally, Gerhard passed the state's professional law examination in 1932, certified by the Prussian State Ministry. He therefore was eligible to begin a career in law, first as a legal clerk in the regional courts and then in Berlin's civil court.

How incredible to think of this all happening for my Jewish father in Germany in February of 1932! He was primed for a hope-filled, promising professional start—at the dawn of the end of time.

One set of letters I discovered in my father's files showed how good Germans did what they could to fight Nazi injustice, even as the situation grew more perilous for Jews. The letters were between my father and a Dr. Eduard Kern, his dissertation advisor as well as his criminal and procedural law professor at the University of Freiburg. For his dissertation topic, my father originally was assigned to research the shape that the Nazi Party's future criminal law code might take. In July 1932, he wrote to Kern, saying in a polite, carefully worded letter that not enough information was available on that topic and inquiring if he might be assigned an alternate subject. The Nazis were not yet in power, but my father knew that something monstrous was brewing. It was preposterous that he, as a Jewish student, had been assigned this dissertation topic.

I soon understood why my father had mentioned Professor Kern to me in so positive a light. In August 1932, Kern readily proposed different dissertation topics to my father, who selected an esoteric point of law from early twentieth-century German legal history.

On April 7, 1933—which happened to be my father's birthday—the Nazis initiated the Law for the Restoration of the Professional Civil Service—the first step towards throwing all Jews in Germany out of the legal profession. On his twenty-third birthday, my father received an official Nazi letter telling him to request a leave of absence from his position if he was Jewish. A follow-up letter that June repeated the demand, emphasizing that if Gerhard could not prove he was exempt from the ban, he would be dismissed from his position indefinitely. By September the Nazis succeeded in expelling my Jewish father from his clerkship and the legal profession.

My father and Kern corresponded again in 1934. This was the point where, had Kern been a hard-bitten Jew-hater, he could have ignored my father or deliberately harmed him. Instead, at a time when the Nazi Party had most German universities under its iron fist, and when barbaric book burnings had already scarred Freiburg, Kern meticulously instructed my father on how to get his accepted dissertation registered so that he would be considered a full university graduate, holder of a doctoral degree.

Kern is a complex historical figure. In April 1934, he replaced Martin Heidegger as rector at Freiburg. To be granted that position at that time would have been impossible for a person who did not express agreement with the Nazi Party's early politics, which Kern did. Yet there is no evidence of Kern ever harboring antisemitic prejudice or hate. And the best evidence I have of his character is that Kern was kind to my father when being kind to a Jew entailed considerable personal risk.

My father was reticent about discussing his past, but the few times he described what happened to him in Berlin were seared into my memory.

"After the Nazis banned me from continuing in law," he said, "I went to work in the Berglases' textile business. The company had representatives across Europe, in the Near East, and South America. I supervised the work of those people, coordinating our foreign trade relations."

My grandfather—Gerhard's father, Jakob—co-owned the building at 16 Wallstrasse that was, more than fifty years later, to so preoccupy my dying father. The co-owner was Jacques Berglas, my father's first cousin and Jakob's nephew. Jacques's mother, Fanny, was my grandmother Rosa's sister.

The Berglases owned a lavish villa near the Wannsee lake in Berlin. "On Sundays," my father would tell me, "we used to have family gatherings, alternately on Kurfürstendamm and at the Wannsee villa. They were like intellectual salons, with all six of the Berglas siblings there, discussing the best of books, sciences, and the arts. And the choicest of foods were served: in the summers, cold roasts, vichyssoise, poached salmon, chilled white wines, then cheeses, fruits, cakes and coffee . . . and . . ."

Invariably, as my father reminisced about these family Sundays, his expression grew brighter and more animated. Then he would catch himself, shadows of loss becoming visible on his face. I sensed I should not press him to talk further.

2 My Father Leaves Berlin

On September 15, 1935, the Nazis passed their antisemitic Nuremberg Laws, stripping my Jewish relatives of their German citizenship. My grandfather Jakob and his Berglas business partners were strategically positioned, though. With their international connections, they had access to foreign currency the Nazis needed to buy raw materials for Germany's rearmament.

"It was a trap," my father more than once explained to me. "The Nazis were exploiting the Intrators, Berglases, and other Jewish businesspeople to get what they needed, but I knew that in the end their businesses would be stolen from them, Aryanized, and they'd be left with nothing."

While Uncle Alex enjoyed a bohemian period in Berlin, even as life grew more ominous, my father had been more focused on the gathering menace. "I saw what the Nazis were going to do," he told me. "I read *Mein Kampf*. With my own eyes, even before Hitler came to power, I saw Nazis beating people in the streets."

My father knew the whole family had to flee, and his uncle Alex Mersel's emigration from Galicia to the United States in 1905 proved providential. As Mersel was a distinguished member of the New York Commodities Exchange, the Underwriters Trust Company was able to send a letter to the American Consul in Berlin attesting that Mersel would support my father in the United States. Accordingly, the US government issued an immigration visa for my father on September 3, 1935.

To his great frustration, Gerhard was unable to convince his parents to leave. "I did not have the heart to abandon them, and that is what it felt like, that I was abandoning them," he told me solemnly. "I let my US immigration visa expire, but then got another one that December. Mama and Papa were adamant they would not leave if there was no plan to get little Manfred out safely."

Finally, my father had seen enough. On April 7, 1937—his twenty-seventh birthday—he left for America on the SS *Normandie*. Whatever good he was going to be able to achieve for his family he would have to achieve from the New World. The family was close-knit; it was unspeakably stressful for my father to leave them.

From April through October 1937, after he arrived in New York, my father wrote thirty-three letters to his parents in Berlin. These were the only letters I found from him to them in the six years they corresponded. By contrast, I found hundreds of letters that Jakob wrote to his son. Tellingly, Jakob avoided mentioning or criticizing Hitler or the Nazis; he obviously knew that his letters were subject to review while going through the Reichspost. Indeed, of those hundreds of letters from Jakob, only one mentioned the Nazis, "these are awful people"— and *that* letter was written outside of Nazi oversight, sent from Romania during one of Jakob's last business trips in 1938.

My father's first letters were filled with worries about his parents and declarations of how much he missed them. After one week in the United States, he wrote that it felt like an eternity since he had seen his family.

In one letter, my father confessed to his parents that his émigré life was proving to be very difficult. Because his German law degree was based on Roman rather than British law, if Gerhard were to become an attorney in the United States, he would have to attend law school all over again. He did not have the money for that—or for much of anything else. And without money, he would not be able to sponsor for immigration any of his relatives stranded in Hitler's Europe. Pounding the pavement, he found jobs beneath his education and abilities: a ten-hour night shift as a textile laborer, a cashier in a restaurant, a movie theater employee.

Still, my father wrote to his parents about his diligence in becoming fluent in English by reading the daily papers, studying vocabulary on the subway between job interviews, and listening attentively to the radio at night to accustom himself to the pronunciation and cadences of the language.

Despite adverse conditions, for a while my grandfather, still living in Berlin, was able to conduct business while traveling through Europe as Nazi power grew. Jakob's obvious reluctance to give up his work fueled my father's pessimism about his parents' understanding of the imperative to leave. For six maddening years, as the Jewish situation grew ever more desperate, Gerhard begged his parents to join him. If Jakob was reluctant to leave, Rosa adamantly refused to, and the stubborn couple dragged their feet until it was nearly impossible for them to escape Germany.

Yad Vashem, the Holocaust remembrance center in Israel, has referred to 1938 as "the fateful year."

The Nazi regime was tightening its stranglehold on Germany's Jewish citizens. A January 1938 law forbade Jews from changing their names; its intent was to prevent Jews from camouflaging that they were Jewish, thus avoiding Nazi persecution. In August, an executive order, issued as a supplement to that law, required the name "Israel" to be added to the names of all Jewish men and "Sarah" to the names of all Jewish women; its intention was to erode individuals' personhood.

For those German Jews who had not yet been compelled to surrender their passports, each passport remaining with a Jewish holder had to be stamped with a large red *J*.

In 1938, the Aryanization of property was moving ahead far more aggressively, hastening the Nazi theft and takeover of what had been Jewish-owned businesses. The assets of Jewish people featured on an ever-increasing number of Nazi government lists. In resorts, theaters, and public parks, Jews were prohibited. In late March, my father received a letter from his cousin Alfred Intrator, who lived in London. Alfred—the son of Leo, Jakob's brother—described being in Vienna on business the very day, March 11, the Nazis marched in and took over. "What we experienced in Germany compares as paradise to what the Austrian Jews went through in a couple of days." Alfred describes a harrowing train journey out of Vienna, with periodic searches executed by the Hitler Youth. "Then, we reached the border. All Jews including me were taken off the train, all their luggage as well, regardless of nationality. Everybody was interrogated intensely, the luggage got investigated, and everybody was subjected to a body search. After an hour and a half, we were released; nobody was held back. I've never been so relieved to cross the Swiss border." [1]

For Jakob and Rosa, still nursing the delusion that the Nazi menace would somehow pass, 1938 was a most inauspicious year. On April 26, the Nazi government issued its Decree for the Reporting of Jewish-Owned Property. My grandfather had to submit a complete accounting of his assets, including his financial accounts and real-estate holdings, which included 16 Wallstrasse. My grandfather's dress business, Schott & Co., was still profitable, against all odds, which prompted him to write to my father, "As long as I can work here and make a living, it is difficult to decide to leave."[2]

Throughout May and June, there were violent attacks against Jews in my grandparents' district. All along the street where they lived—Kurfürstendamm—shops and restaurants either owned or frequented by Jews were picketed and boycotted by ordinary Germans and vandalized with antisemitic slogans across their windows. These actions often were referred to as a *cold pogrom*.[3] Increasingly, Jews in Berlin were being arrested and imprisoned in concentration camps, where they were beaten and tortured.

Jakob mentioned none of that in his letters to my father. He did, however, express alarm that his older brother Samuel had been falsely accused of a crime. Jakob reported that Samuel was menaced; if he did not leave Germany by a specific date, the Nazis would have him arrested.

Then, on June 18, Jakob told my father that he had been required to sell properties and conform to currency limits the Nazis were imposing. Still, he refused to accept reality: "Mama and I feel that . . . as long as it's possible to remain in Berlin, we will. The prospect of depending on others for charity for years on end is unbearable to us. As lonely as we are here, as discouraged as we may be, it seems to us that it would be even more unbearable having to live dependent on others in London before being able to join you in the US. Don't you agree with this?"[4]

In the immediate wake of Kristallnacht, which occurred on November 9 and 10, 1938, my father received three telegrams from relatives letting him know that my grandparents had survived. Though he was not born in Germany, because Jakob had served in the German Army during World War I he and Rosa thus were permitted to remain in their Berlin apartment. However, my father's brother Alex, having been born in Poland, was "sleeping out," which meant he was not staying in the same place for more than two days at a time in order to avoid getting arrested and deported from Berlin.

My grandfather wrote to Gerhard that he and Rosa were trapped in their apartment, with the streets too dangerous for them to venture out and the few public spaces in which they were still permitted tightly restricted. Their assets were under state control, putting them at the mercy of the Reich for the amounts they could use for daily living. As the Nazis began co-opting apartments and homes owned by Jews, redistributing them to Nazi Party members, my grandparents took in a neighbor, Frau Weiser, who remained living with them until she was granted a visa for South America. After Frau Weiser left, two other women took her place.

On November 13, 1938, Alfred Intrator wrote to Gerhard about the situation with obvious exasperation: "I'm horribly worried about your parents. Without passports, and so limited in their freedoms—how is one to help them? As of a week ago, your mother alas still believed it possible to stay safely in Germany. Your father is influenced by her stubborn denial of reality. And that is, in large part, why he continues to reject your practical suggestions."[5]

By 1939, it was clear that Jakob—at least, and at last—finally understood the significance of their plight. He wrote to Gerhard, "We failed to judge the situation correctly. We therefore have nobody but ourselves to blame. On our own, we must bear the consequences."[6] Jakob's letters to my father reveal his struggles with hopelessness as he began the formal emigration process.

Jakob and Rosa finally managed an unlikely escape in October 1941 on the last sealed train from Berlin, traveling to Lisbon, Portugal, and from there to Cuba, then to the United States. But their reunion with my father, six years after they had last seen one another, was not a happy one: Jakob died of a heart attack just hours after reuniting with his son in Manhattan. I would never meet my paternal grandfather.

Uncle Alex once told me how the Nazis financially trapped my grandfather. "One day in 1938," he said, "a businessman from Nuremberg showed up in Berlin, asking to buy Papa's clothing company for a fraction of its worth. The lowball offer was a galling insult, and he of course refused. Do you know how that Nazi reacted to his refusal?"

"How?"

"By saying, 'You can sell it to me now at the price I'm offering, or I can return in a few months and take it without giving you a thing.' So Papa sold it to him at the insulting price, only to have to pay every miserable penny he got for it to the Reich in punitive taxes." That example of the Aryanization process has a parallel in how my family was stripped of its property at 16 Wallstrasse.

3 The "Polish Action"

My father, Gerhard, never quite managed to fit in with his new American world. The American nickname "Jerry," which many people called him, didn't quite suit him. He never became as successful in New York as he had been in Berlin; unlicensed to work as an attorney in the United States, virtually penniless, with the fate of his European family in his hands, he took menial jobs before being drafted into the US Army in 1942. Later, he went into business, where two of his enterprises swiftly failed. From the age of forty-four, my father was plagued by kidney disease that prematurely aged and weakened him for the remaining four decades of his life.

As a psychiatrist, I never doubted the degree to which my father being stripped of his homeland, cultural identity, and livelihood negatively impacted his health. He also carried a great sadness that I couldn't fully appreciate while he was alive. At one point I came across a mysterious photo of twin boys in my father's files, which I recalled seeing as a young girl. As I began piecing together their story, I understood, finally, a significant reason for Gerhard's sadness. I was to learn the fate of these two boys, as well as that of my father's beloved cousin Max Karp, from the file letters. In both narratives, the Nazis were culpable, their victims were innocent, and my father—unable to help them—suffered terribly from their deaths.

The Twins

In the summer of 1938, Alfred Intrator wrote to my father in America about fears for his sister, Edith; her husband, Ignaz Brav; and their twin boys, Lothar and Max. So those were the twins I'd first glimpsed as a little girl! I had a flashback to the time when I came across the twins' photo tucked away in an elegant leather case in my father's desk drawer. When my father found me contemplating the photo, his mood so dramatically deflated that I knew I had crossed some line, even though I did not understand what it was. I sensed that I had better not ask any questions.

On October 28, 1938, the Nazi regime began its notorious "Polish Action." This declaration that all Jews born in Poland and currently holding German residency permits were to have their permits revoked and be deported back to border towns in Poland was in response to Hitler learning that the Polish government planned to prevent Polish-born Jews from reentering Poland. Thus Polish-born German Jews no longer had Polish or German citizenship.

In a letter dated December 18, 1938, Jakob reported that members of our family had been "violently" removed from Germany to Poland. Letters mentioned Samuel Intrator and Wolf Drücker, two of my father's uncles, and Ignaz Brav.[1]

The story of Edith Intrator Brav, her husband, Ignaz, and their twin sons has been difficult to piece together. Edith was born in Berlin and thus was not at immediate risk for being deported to Poland. Because Ignaz, Polish born, had no success arranging emigration in the preceding years, the family stayed in Germany until the Polish Action. Edith had freedom of movement, but Ignaz did not. She had time to go to their home in Iserlohn, Germany, to attempt selling their business and ship their belongings out of Germany. She brought her twin boys to my grandparents. Her mother, Anni, Leo's wife, came from London to join the twins, Lothar and Max, at my grandparents' home. Ignaz was thrown out of Germany and went to Lvov, Ukraine. Though his hometown was Tarnow, he feared the Poles would arrest him there for escaping Polish conscription in 1918. After Iserlohn, Edith went to Tarnow, hoping he would join her and she would then arrange to bring the boys to them. Not alert enough to the impending danger, Anni acceded to Edith's request to bring the twins to the border. A family friend in Tarnow arranged for the boys to be carried across to Poland.

The extended family scrambled to find a way to extricate Edith and her children, encountering hurdles that were frustrating and ultimately insurmountable. On May 10, 1940, Jakob reported hearing that the American Consulate in Warsaw could issue an affidavit Edith needed to escape but noted that the affidavit could only be issued in either Berlin or Vienna; there was no way for Edith, a Jew, to reach those cities from Nazi-occupied Poland. Jakob despaired of her being able to find a way out with the twins and noted that his brother Leo, Edith's father, was no longer able to get any money through to her.[2]

My father received a few letters from Edith postmarked Tarnow. Mainly, in those letters, she is stoic about her situation, recalling happier times with my father and describing her little twin sons' daily antics. From news reports that got through, however, everybody knew that Edith and her boys were in gravest danger.

Meanwhile, Edith's husband, Ignaz, along with thousands of Jewish refugees, was in Lvov—alone, without his wife and sons—when the Germans occupied the city in June 1941. His letters to my father were desperate. Ignaz's last letter to my father was dated June 12, 1941; he almost certainly perished shortly after, most likely during one of the pogroms in Lvov, as he was never heard from again. His words were chilling. "I live uneasier [*sic*] than at any time, as I do not know what could occur with me at every moment, and therefore spend terrible sleepless nights about my wife and children."[3]

I learned more about Edith's fate through tracking the dates of her letters to my father and to her brother Alfred, and from my research about the history of Tarnow's Jews. The Germans entered the town on September 7, 1939, just days after the invasion of Poland that marked the beginning of World War II. In May 1940, the Nazis organized the first deportations to Auschwitz. The Tarnow ghetto was established in March 1941, and the first widespread murders occurred during June 1942.

In September 1942, the Germans ordered all Tarnow ghetto residents to assemble in Targowica Square, where roughly 8,000 of them were deemed unessential and "selected" to be sent to extermination camps. As I read the history of Tarnow's destruction by the Nazis, I repeated the word "extermination" out loud, over and over again, as if hearing the horrible word would make me understand what had happened. The word at first sounded unreal, hollow, but then its meaning seeped in.

"Extermination" spoke of efficiency, the kind of efficiency one used to be rid of vermin. The final "liquidation" of the Jews of Tarnow occurred between August and September of 1943. I said the word "liquidation" aloud. Were they actually liquidated? Were they melted into liquid? How did one do that to human beings? Those Tarnow Jews who were not murdered in the town were sent to Auschwitz.

"Extermination," "liquidation": words that roll off the lips so easily, words I read over the years in history books, missing their true meaning because I defended myself, too afraid to grasp what had happened. Clearly, my psychological defenses for facing the Nazi meaning of the words were rapidly eroding. The letters in the black file cabinets changed everything.

Possessed of a heightened alertness to the abuses of language as a psychiatrist, I turned to an indispensable tool for understanding how the Nazis twisted language in order to achieve their ends: Victor Klemperer's *The Language of the Third Reich*, which he culled from diaries he kept while suffering at the hands of the Nazis. A trained scholar and linguist, Klemperer offered penetrating insights into how the Nazis manipulated the masses with perversions of language. He found that the main distinguishing feature of Third Reich language was its linguistic impoverishment. With the publication of *Mein Kampf* and its clichés, many German words were stripped of their precision and clarity. For example, instead of using the word *niedermachen*, a word for murder or massacre that maintained the concept of a human being, the Nazis instead used the word *liquidieren*, negating any human connection.[4]

After the war, my surviving family members inquired about the fate of Edith and her children. The International Red Cross found a Tarnow source, Max Blecher, a friend of our family who had fled Nazi Germany for Poland before the German invasion. Max Blecher managed to escape with his life, and he testified that in Tarnow he had witnessed the Nazis shooting Edith and her sons, Lothar and Max, to death.[5] We never learned the ultimate fate of Ignaz.

That is what my father knew when he found me looking at a photo of the twins.

Max Karp

Another victim of the Polish Action in 1939 was my father's beloved cousin Max Karp. When I was growing up, I knew nothing of Max. My father and my uncle would occasionally talk about very dark things that had happened to somebody in our family, but as though trying to protect me, they never provided a full explanation. And they had never mentioned Max's name around me.

Max was the only child of my grandmother Rosa's sister Anna. Like my uncle Alex, Max was an accomplished musician; as I learned from the letters, he was contemplating an escape from Nazi-controlled Europe, confident of being able to earn his living as a musician abroad.

Instead, he found himself abruptly deported to a fetid camp in Zbąszyń, a small town at the German–Polish border. Like Edith, he managed to send letters to my father, such as this one, written on November 17, 1938:

At six in the morning, straight out of our beds, we were arrested in Berlin [on October 28, 1938].

Inside the apartment, the police gave us a document ordering us to leave the Reich within twenty-four hours. However, we weren't in fact given that much time. We had to dress quickly and then immediately follow the arresting officers. They didn't allow us to take so much as a change of clothing or even underwear. I thus was forced to leave Germany with insufficient clothing and only a few marks.

Before entering the trains, we were divided into groups. We were forced to surrender our passports. And while that was going on, a battalion of German police made a show of marching around us, loading their guns. It was obviously done for effect. More and

more Jewish "refugees"—people being expelled from the Reich—
kept arriving from all over Germany.
Since there were some invalids among us, we had to carry them.
The police regiments accompanying us carried rifles with bayonets
attached. Now and again, we were illuminated with small search
lights so that no one could slip away. We were being driven like
hunted animals! Anyone who couldn't keep up was goaded forward
with painful strikes and blows to the ribs.[6]

Conditions in Zbąszyń were unbearable, Max wrote. He described dark, filthy barracks where prisoners, many of them sick and infecting others, were packed together. Eight months after being sent to Zbąszyń, Max was permitted to return to Germany—but told that he had to leave Germany within eight weeks or be imprisoned.

Desperate to escape, Max told my father in one letter that he might be safe if he could get to Shanghai. But he noted that Jacques Berglas warned him to wait on that, given the political instability in China. Jacques had made a proposal—the Berglas Plan—to settle Jewish refugees in the Chinese interior.[7] Another possibility was for him to get to England with the help of Alfred Berglas, who had immigrated there. None of these "outs" were sure things, though, and each one of them required a separate load of official documentation that was difficult if not impossible to obtain.

After three frantic weeks back in Germany, Max still did not have a solid escape plan. Though he managed to get a visa to China, he lacked the money required to secure transportation, which was part of the ticket price in foreign currency. He tried to get a loan but was refused. He considered taking a train to China through Siberia, but he would need a work contract with an official Chinese stamp to get a through-visa, and he didn't have one.

There was another option for Max, though: an Italian ship was regularly taking passengers from Italy to Shanghai. My father managed to purchase a ticket for his cousin on that ship. On August 8, 1939, Max wrote to Gerhard to thank him, adding, "I want to get out of Germany as soon as possible. I must underline that the situation here is <u>very</u> intense."[8]

I tried to imagine what Max Karp must have felt as he underlined the word "very." The tension in Berlin must have been nearly unbearable. As his eight-week limit decreased to seven, then six, then five weeks, with Nazi menace constantly around him, the panic, confusion, terror, and hopelessness must have been incalculable.

From my family's letters, I gathered that Max never was able to fully assemble all the paperwork he needed for either of his envisioned escape routes. Additionally, the door to China was closing inexorably.

The proposal made by Jacques was ultimately deemed aspirational and impractical. Moreover, the Shanghai Municipal Council shut down immigration except for refugees already en route.

In an August 17 letter, Jakob wrote to Gerhard that it was too late to help Max get to Shanghai, as just days before, entry to Shanghai without a visa had been terminated. In October 1939, Jakob's report to my father was brief and chilling: "Max Karp is no longer here. We have no idea where he went or where he might be. One day, he simply vanished. All of our inquiries have been in vain."[9]

Eventually, word reached my grandparents that their nephew had been arrested by the police in Berlin—on contrived grounds that he was a "stateless Eastern Jew"—and imprisoned in the Sachsenhausen concentration camp. Later I was to discover that at Sachsenhausen, Max Karp was given the Nazi concentration camp prisoner number 009060.

Sadistically, the Nazis would allow prisoners like Max rays of false hope. In a letter he sent from Sachsenhausen to Jakob on October 31, Max asked if there might be a possibility of changing the date of the Italian ship ticket my father had bought for him.[10] The Italian ship company denied that request.

In a January 8, 1940, letter to my father, Jakob reported that the situation for Max at Sachsenhausen had worsened, adding, "We are unable to do anything for him. We are in despair."[11] At the end of January, Jakob wrote to Gerhard that his cousin had died.

How Max Karp perished, we do not know with certainty. Conditions at Sachsenhausen were rampant with disease, and an epidemic among the prisoners may have killed him. But the German historian Götz Aly, who reviewed what is known regarding Max Karp, expressed serious skepticism that he died of an illness.[12] Aly told me that at this date, the Nazis still saw some value in trying to cover up what they were really doing in the concentration camps. As of the date of Max's death, Sachsenhausen had not yet installed a crematorium; Max was cremated elsewhere in Berlin. Then a box labeled as containing his ashes was delivered to my grandparents' apartment, prompting Rosa to faint.

I often wonder what it was like for my father in those years, while he struggled to adapt to American ways and worked long, hard, lonely hours, only to be greeted in his evenings by letter after despairing letter from European relatives either begging for their lives or for the lives of other loved ones.[13] And then to either strongly suspect or know that they were dead. My heart aches for the Gerhard of that time.

4 The Rothschilds

The loneliness my father felt as an immigrant to the United States eased as the years passed. Slowly Gerhard integrated into the culture, his stint in the military reinforcing to him that he was now in America, fighting for the Americans, and would become an American citizen in due time. He began dating, and eventually he met and married my mother, another Jewish immigrant from Germany.

My parents met during the summer of 1944 at a Catskills resort in Boiceville, New York, when my father was thirty-four and my mother, Lotte Rothschild, was twenty-five. At the time, Gerhard was dating another woman, but my mother, beautiful, smart, and charming, captivated him. They married less than a year later. I was born in 1946, and my brother, Jack, was born in 1948.

Prior to the 16 Wallstrasse case, I was not fully aware of the deeply damaging effects of religious persecution and forced immigration on my parents, or of the ominous consequences for my childhood. Like so many others, centered on thinking about the murder of six million people, I was unable to fully consider the plight of the relatively fortunate few who had succeeded in escaping their European homelands. In the hierarchy of Holocaust-era victimization, people like my parents simply got left off the charts.

Indeed, as a young woman and medical student, I forcibly rejected the concept that there *was* such a thing as a "second-generation Holocaust survivor." My parents had no understanding that their trauma could be passed down to us; their attitude was that we were safe in America with our immediate family intact. Had I indulged in any personal identification with the Shoah while growing up, my parents would have been contemptuous of me.

In my early thirties, searching after explanations for my lifelong, free-floating anxiety, I read Helen Epstein's book *Children of the Holocaust*, first published in 1979.[1] In 2018, I contacted the author, and Helen graciously responded. She said that my distressed emotions as well as my uncertainty surrounding the topic of second-generation Holocaust survivors were familiar phenomena. She pointed out that while my parents had not been in concentration camps, they were severely victimized, their promising lives wrecked. They may have escaped Nazi Germany alive, but the world as they knew it had been destroyed. Her perspective helped me to overcome my deeply internalized notion that if I acknowledged my specific relationship to the Holocaust, I would be exhibiting vanity, false pride, and weakness.

I regretted that I hadn't understood how the Nazis had altered not only my parents' lives but also my life and my brother's. I had a very fraught relationship with my mother, and I became who I am despite, not because, of her. Now, with the benefit of distance, I have developed empathy for what Lotte went through. Hers was not the story of 16 Wallstrasse, but she, too, was shaped by the horror of the Nazi past.

As a child, I knew far more about my father's early life than my mother's. In fact, I was all but in the dark when it came to Lotte's family. Ever since I can remember, she volunteered scant information and clearly was uninterested in dwelling on things past.

Here's some of the little I know. Much of it comes from testimony that my mother's sister Irma gave to the USC Shoah Foundation Institute for Visual History and Education in 1997.[2]

Three months after the end of the First World War, Lotte Rothschild was born on February 16, 1919, in Miltenberg—"the pearl of the Main River"—about fifty miles southeast of Frankfurt. Her paternal and maternal family tree branched back centuries in German territories.

Lotte was the middle of three sisters and had one brother she would never know. Selma, her older sister, was born in 1907; Irma, the youngest, in 1920. Their father, Leopold Rothschild, an infantry officer, was one of eight brothers who fought for Germany in World War I.

Leo returned from the war to find his wife, Rikka, and daughter Selma mourning the death of their only son, Hans, who had perished when another boy swung an ice skate at his head. Whether that was a schoolboy game gone wrong or a deliberate attack against a Jewish child can, apparently, never be known. My mother came into this world one year after Leo's return. I can only speculate about the expectations my grandparents visited on my mother as a little girl to fill the void left by Hans's death.

Until Hitler came to power in 1933, my mother's life was idyllic. Her parents owned a beautiful fabric, dress, and notions store—Kaufhaus Rothschild—in Miltenberg am Main. They lived above the store. Their building on the town's main street, Hauptstrasse, was built during the Middle Ages. One of thirty Jewish families in a total population of 5,600, the Rothschilds led lives seemingly well integrated with those of the other townspeople. They attended synagogue, studied Hebrew, and observed Jewish holidays. The sisters swam at a club on the river Main, played tennis, skied with other family members in the surrounding mountains, and attended private schools. My mother was even able to go to the boys' gymnasium to learn Latin and receive a classical education so—like one of her uncles in Frankfurt—she could become a doctor.

Then, in 1933, life changed drastically for the Rothschilds. Non-Jewish friends abandoned Lotte and Irma, many joining the Hitler Youth, parading through the small medieval town while screaming vicious antisemitic hate. The sisters were cast aside or virulently scorned. Lotte was banned from the gymnasium because she was Jewish; instead of studying sciences, she learned stenography in hopes it would be useful, should she be able to escape.

Among the three sisters, Selma escaped Germany first, departing for the United States in 1936 with her husband, Fritz Humpole. Like my father, Fritz received a Nazi government letter in April 1933 ending his career as a lawyer. With their daughter, Lore, they settled in Manhattan's Washington Heights, a neighborhood with many German Jewish refugees. Irma and my mother fled Germany separately in 1938.

Leo and Rikka believed that Hitler and the Nazis would be short-lived, until November 1938, when Nazis broke into their home during Kristallnacht, slashing paintings, smashing vases, destroying furniture, and smearing jam over their down quilts. The Nazis arrested the couple, took their passports, imprisoned them, and robbed them of their business, putting it in Aryan hands.

In 1940, my maternal grandparents finally escaped Germany. They did so through Italy, embarking from Genoa for the US, where my aunt Selma and uncle Fritz were able to sponsor them.

Settled in Washington Heights, my mother babysat and cleaned apartments. When satisfied that she was ready to debut her newfound American ways on a larger stage, Lotte worked at the flagship Gimbels store in Herald Square, first as a main floor salesgirl and then as a food demonstrator, cooking and engaging shoppers to taste her samples. Her dreams of becoming a doctor in Germany were crushed by the realities of her new life, but she carried on.

My grandfather Leo Rothschild died in early 1948 when my mother was pregnant with Jack. In Shoah Foundation testimony, Irma blamed the Nazis for his death—the stress, the agonizing escape, and starting over again all accumulated into a death sentence. Lotte's mother, Rikka, my last living grandparent, died in my bedroom in 1954, when I was seven. My attentive, devoted Oma had been my solace, an antidote to my mother's cruelty. I do not remember experiencing my Nazi terrors before her death.

My mother was in her early teens when the Nazis "otherized" her, alleging that she and her family were not part of the German culture into which she had been born and was being raised. This profound crisis of cultural identity followed my mother in her escape to the New World, coloring her perspective as well as the framework in which she raised her own children.

My parents fought frequently, *auf Deutsch*. The menacing sounds were at times hair-raising. When Lotte and Gerhard started in, my brother and I would disappear, Jack to his shortwave radio and I under the down quilt on my bed, hoping for a break in all the scary Teutonic yelling.

My mother would sometimes extend the fight to me, belittling her daughter and slapping me across the face. I can feel the sting of those slaps even now and hear her shrill voice labeling me "Spoiled!" or "Stupid!" or screaming "Shut up!" at me. And though I can recall countless times like these, I barely remember any time that Lotte hugged and kissed me. Was it just her nature? Had she read German child-rearing manuals advising against physical contact? Had Lotte's experience in Nazi Germany damaged her ability to be a nurturing mother? How is one to explain her failure of empathy for her own children, when her mother—my Oma—was so loving and kind?[3] When it came to seeing the destructive, frightening nature of my mother's explosiveness, my father had a blind spot. In part due to his own upbringing, he left the parenting mainly to Lotte. Also, between his lifelong illness and financial troubles, he was dependent on my mother to manage the household, which she did efficiently if at times ruthlessly.

Perhaps my mother wouldn't have been so frequently angry if she had developed a professional identity. Had she become a doctor, her story—*our* story—might have been very different. The *Merck Manual* rested on Lotte's bedside table, handy for ready reference during the phone consultations she often provided to girlfriends or her sisters. That was as far as life allowed my mother's professional dream to advance.

Sadly, Lotte lacked the emotional generosity to encourage me in my own goal of becoming a physician. "You could apply to nursing school, or study to earn a teaching certificate," she would suggest. Message received! I was not smart enough. Instead of becoming a doctor, I should marry one. I accepted her disparagement of me for years until, one day, I simply no longer did. And I did not tell my mother as I worked towards my goal until, in my first semester of a postbaccalaureate premed program at New York University, I earned straight As. Knowing to protect me, my father had kept my secret from her.

I was thirty years old during my first year at Columbia University's medical school—the oldest woman in a class that was 20 percent female. My mother was familiar with the neighborhood, as she'd lived in Washington Heights when she first arrived in the United States. I brought her to my laboratory and showed her the cadaver I was dissecting. She was fascinated, and I was relieved to see her take pleasure in my accomplishment.

In 1980, during my third year of medical school, I visited my parents in Palm Beach, Florida, where they had recently purchased a retirement home. It was the Martin Luther King Day weekend, and I had just finished a grueling rotation in medicine. Throughout the years of my father's illness, my mother had never been sick or even complained of discomfort, but, as if overnight, she was unable to go for her daily walk and swim.

Reluctantly, Lotte admitted to having had no appetite for days. She described her symptoms as sudden in onset, but I mistrusted that. Long ago, I had learned my mother tuned out all unpleasant somatic sensations so as not to feel or convey weakness. Her symptoms increased.

Having just finished eight weeks of a medicine rotation, I asked to examine her abdomen. To my horror, I felt her liver enlarged deep into her pelvis, studded hard with a pebble-like surface. It was clear Lotte had metastatic disease; I guessed by the heavy blood in the toilet she had colon cancer. Two days later, she was back in New York at LaGuardia Airport. My sixty-year-old mother, huddled in a wheelchair, had seemingly aged twenty years. I drove her to Lenox Hill Hospital for diagnosis and treatment.

Within five months, she was dead.

During the final days of my mother's life, when Lotte's body was ravaged by cancer, I washed her, changed her nightgown, combed her hair, and painted her fingernails. Through the night, I sat beside her, guarding her peace and quiet.

This was a radical change. My mother had spent years of my youth terrorizing me with her unpredictable rants, criticizing my appearance, telling me I was not smart enough. Now Lotte allowed me to care for her in ways that had been absent from her care for me. As she slept ever-longer periods during the day, I tried to prepare my father for what was coming, but he could not accept the reality.

Having relied so heavily on my mother, Gerhard could not fathom that she would die first. Lotte was nine years younger, and he was saddled with significant kidney and heart disease, so he had long assumed that he would predecease her. Only at the very end did my father secure a plot close to where their parents are buried, in a community of German Jews who fled the Nazis for the United States.

The same day Gerhard arranged for that burial plot, my mother's breathing transmogrified into the distinctive death rattle. I was so sad that the last years of my parents' lives together were finally calmer, perhaps even happy, and now my mother's premature death was to rip their time away from them.

Her face was calm and untroubled. As Lotte drew her final breath, I pressed her hand to my cheek. Odd as it might sound, I can still, forty years later, recall that sensation. That we had been speaking German in her last days was poignant yet eerie. In a primal last embrace, a Jewish mother and her daughter were bound together by the German language. In it, I rediscovered something of the love I felt as a little girl, while my mother, for her part, had returned to the language of her homeland. In my mind, the horrible associations connected with my mother melted away in the face of her death. And that day, I stopped speaking German.

I learned over time, with the benefit of my professional life as well as from the perspective of being a parent, that my mother loved me in her own limited way. Like many women of her day, Lotte saw me as an opportunity to fulfill her own shattered dreams. When I did not perform to her standards, she belittled me. Yet when I strove towards a goal once hers, she grew jealous and discouraged me. She grabbed pleasure where she could, even at the expense of her children and her husband, my dear father. That included a long-ago affair I witnessed as a child, which she denied, gaslighting me when I recalled the traumatic experience.

When my brother, Jack, and I arrived to dismantle our parents' long-time home in Queens after my father's death, we weren't emotionally prepared for the mournful reality of actually beginning. Opening the front door, I entered the foyer. Removing my shoes—as all good German children do—I stepped onto the plush beige living room carpeting. The blinds were closed; the house was tranquil, stuffy, and hot.

In the kitchen, out of curiosity, I opened the door to the refrigerator and then the freezer, just to see what, if anything, remained. With tears welling in my eyes, I had to smile over what I found inside the freezer. All these years since my mother's death, my father had preserved one of her legendary homemade *Baumkuchen*. Literally translated, *Baumkuchen* means "tree cake." One layer of batter after another is baked for a few moments, so that sliced, it looks like a cross section of a tree. My father had savored this sweet visual reminder of his Lotte.

5 The Inheritance

Until I inherited my father's 16 Wallstrasse restitution claim, I never had a concrete means of fully investigating our family's European background. One reason was the attitude the East German Communists had towards Nazism. After World War II, with the division of Berlin, our building in Mitte was behind the Iron Curtain. Through cunning exploitation of the shameless lie that Communist states were anti-fascist and thus had no connection to the Nazis' crimes, the East Germans excused themselves from indemnifying victims of the Third Reich, all the while co-opting for themselves properties that the Nazis had stolen from Jews. Unlike West Germany, East Germany neither made reparation payments nor permitted claims involving properties like 16 Wallstrasse.

Right up until the fall of the Berlin Wall on November 9, 1989, East Germany persisted with its self-serving propaganda that people in its territory never had the least association with the Nazi Party. With the reunification of Germany in 1990, though, 16 Wallstrasse fell within a more auspicious jurisdiction. The government of the newly expanded Federal Republic of Germany was open to helping people robbed by Nazis—and/or by the Communists—either by compensating them or by returning their properties.

To me, these recent historical shifts were less meaningful than the stark, irrevocable fact that everything my family came from had gotten wrenched away from them. For me, our building in Mitte would come to represent all of that unforgivable, embittering loss. Over the decade following my father's death, the restitution case consumed my attention. I was a dedicated mother, wife, and working psychiatrist, yet at times my relationship with 16 Wallstrasse swamped my world. The sheer Germanic thoroughness of my father's recordkeeping was, considered in the abstract, astounding. The file cabinet in Gerhard's study revealed a file full of letters that German banks sent to his father, my grandfather Jakob Intrator, between 1936 and 1941. At the bottom of each letter, next to the bank officials' signatures, were black-and-red-ink swastika stamps. While the minutiae of such letters sent by Nazi bank officials to German Jewish customers during that time varied, it wasn't hard to imagine that their common denominator conveyed devastating, unfair declarations that portended tragic consequences.

I was soon to learn what had transpired for my Berlin relatives during the Nazi property grab. In German, a land registry is called a *Grundbuch*. The relevant *Grundbuch* shows that on April 15, 1920, Realitas, a company owned by Jakob Intrator and his nephew Jacques Berglas, was registered as the owner of 16 Wallstrasse. On September 12, 1938, through what was called a "forced auction," Realitas's ownership of the property ended.

I learned that these forced auctions were common, an Aryanization technique. The Nazis stripped Jews of their business licenses, among other punitive legal measures, making it impossible for them to pay their mortgages. The Nazis would then grab the properties and sell them far below market value to "Aryans," leaving the Jewish owners robbed.

Until his property was seized, my grandfather had hoped to sell it for at least *some* badly needed money before emigrating. By that time, of course, he was familiar with the "special taxes" imposed on Jewish citizens fleeing Germany. On November 13, 1938, he wrote to my father, "I still have to put everything in order with the tax office. I must liquidate assets in order to be able to pay the special taxes imposed on those leaving the Reich. That entails selling off properties. I'm not the sole owner—and consensus among owners is needed for a sale—so the process can't go as quickly as I'd like."[1]

Ongoing letters from Jakob in 1938 and 1939 bear testimony that as his and Rosa's finances were drained by the Nazi government, their health suffered. Jakob continued to fear for the well-being of his only grandchild, Manfred, whose safe escape had not yet been secured. And after levying confiscatory taxes on the sale of my grandfather's real estate, the Nazis started hounding him over his access to foreign currency.

Writing on August 3, 1939, Jakob reported the good news that Ilse and Manfred had managed to set out for the United States from England. Manfred's father, my uncle Alex, had escaped to London earlier that year without his wife and son, as he was Polish born and the US quota for Poles was already filled. Alex was to remain with his cousin, Alfred, in London while tolerating what turned out to be a seven-year wait for a visa to the United States. Eventually, Alex was able to rejoin Ilse and Manfred—though his marriage would not survive the long separation and disruption to Alex's career. Jakob's letters, even when mentioning the positive news of Ilse's successful emigration, illustrate the punishing circles of hell Jews were having to endure.

On January 8, 1940, Jakob wrote that the Nazis had changed their legal travel requirements for leaving the Reich: "The passage out of here must now be paid entirely with foreign currency, and thus will cost significantly more. The absolute minimum? It amounts to $400. Where is one to find the money?"[2]

Another letter that spring detailed Jakob's struggles to obtain paperwork that would allow him and Rosa to escape from the Nazis. He had no solid idea of where they would be permitted to go. Shanghai? He mentioned that as a possibility. Imagine having Nazis steal everything you own, leaving you with no money, and then still breathing down your neck while you hope against hope that you might somehow find a way to get from Berlin to Shanghai.

My grandfather's last surviving letter sent from Berlin to my father is dated September 22, 1941. Amid a welter of snags, hitches, and errors that hindered his arrangements for escape, the one bright light was that the money for his and Rosa's tickets on a steamer from Germany to Cuba via Portugal had not been sacrificed. However, he describes all manner of nightmares, including transports out of Berlin routinely getting cancelled, first several days per week and then for two weeks solid. Jakob concludes by saying: "Today, we were supposed to be getting on the ship. We could have been looking forward to celebrating a joyous reunion with you in about two weeks. Instead, we sit here in the cold with next to nothing. . . . Nevertheless, we hope to reach Cuba safe and sound. . . . And we are fervently hoping to see you again as soon as possible. Mama and I both send you hugs, kisses, and all our love."[3]

My grandparents originally hoped to escape from Berlin to Lisbon without substantial interruption. En route, though, my grandfather became seriously ill with high blood pressure. In Bilbao, Spain, he had to discontinue his desperate voyage, stopping there for medical treatment and to convalesce, causing my grandparents to miss their scheduled ship from Lisbon to Havana, adding to my grandfather's fathomless stress, jeopardizing his recovery. In the meantime, the United States had entered the war.

Once Jakob was well enough, he and Rosa traveled on to Lisbon. "I'm healthy again," my Opa alleged in a January 7, 1942, letter to my father, "but I must be especially careful not to relapse. We don't know what's going to happen to us."[4]

Jakob and Rosa's two months of purgatory in Lisbon were marked by incalculable uncertainty. The city was crowded with other traumatized refugees scrambling to flee to safer end destinations. Obviously, all of the Jewish refugees in Lisbon were keenly aware of the ominous circumstances faced by their relatives left behind in other parts of Europe.

Passenger ships out of Lisbon were being incessantly cancelled and then rescheduled due to U-boat hostilities in the open ocean. Every agency was overcrowded and understaffed. Attempting to arrange for new travel plans was a ceaseless, ongoing nightmare.

Eventually, my grandparents were able to board the SS *Nyassa*, a refugee ship, on January 28, 1942. They arrived in Cuba on February 25. Four weeks might seem like a long time for a steamship ocean crossing, but with the Battle of the Atlantic raging, the *Nyassa*'s captain and crew doubtless carried out many maneuvers to deliver the boat and its passengers safely to the port of Havana. When Jakob filled out paperwork at the US Embassy in Havana, he wrote, "I am a citizen of no country, formerly of Germany."[5]

In Cuba, a devastating disappointment awaited my grandparents. They had been expecting my father there to greet them in Havana, but he was nowhere to be seen. Jakob addressed many pained letters to my father, asking where he was and why they had not heard from him.

Only recently, going through my family archives, did I understand what happened. My father was unable to obtain exit and reentry visas for himself from the United States to Cuba. And letters he attempted to send to my grandparents in Havana either got lost or were greatly delayed.

While Jakob was struggling in ill health to recover enough to leave for the United States—and still awaiting his visa to travel there—Jakob's younger brother, Leo, died of heart failure in London. Whatever the coroner's report might cite as the primary and secondary causes of his death, the most significant stress on Leo at the end of his life was the knowledge that his daughter and twin grandsons already had been—or were likely to be—murdered by Nazis in Poland. Colloquially, stress-induced cardiomyopathy is sometimes referred to as "broken heart syndrome."[6] I think about his unbearable suffering. I personally do not believe I could have survived such a loss.

In their letters, other family members debated whether to tell Jakob that his younger brother was dead. They feared the emotional blow might exacerbate his already weakened state.

Finally, my father's efforts to obtain visas for Jakob and Rosa to travel from Cuba to the United States bore fruit that April. The army granted my father a very short leave to meet his beloved parents in New York City. Jakob and Rosa entered the United States via Florida, then rode a train several days up the Eastern Seaboard. Then they checked into the Alden, at 225 Central Park West.

At the height of spring, Central Park—with its blossoming dogwoods, fragrant magnolias, and tender-leafed trees—can inspire a feeling that one is opening a door onto an infinity of golden new opportunities. But the 382 miles my father traveled from his military camp in Pennsylvania to meet his parents in New York was a doomed trip before he ever stepped onto the bus that brought him there.

Never did my father talk candidly and directly with me about what occurred in the Alden. Like the photo of Edith's twins Max and Lothar, that day inside the hotel represented events so unspeakably painful for my father that he could not bear to share them with me. In my mind's eye, I have tried to picture it. Did my father enter their rooms wearing his US Army private's uniform? Did he bring fresh-cut flowers for his Mutti? What was my Oma Rosa feeling? Surely, at first, if only fleetingly, she was overjoyed to see her son for the first time in six years, and he, equally overjoyed to be reunited with his beloved parents.

My Opa Jakob somehow had entered the hotel, and I like to assume he did so on his own two legs. Yet I am not certain whether he was able to rise out of a chair or bed to embrace my father.

The heartrending, pitiful reality is that through strength of will, my grandfather succeeded in clinging to life just long enough to deliver Rosa to their youngest son in New York. But then he died inside the Alden his first day there, my father a shattered witness to his death.

Fighting for Germany in World War I, my Jewish grandfather had suffered lung damage from poison gas. Was that lung damage among the causes of his hypertensive heart disease? I suspect so, just as I'm convinced that Hitler and the Nazis then finished him off with persecution and stress.

The more I learned about what the Nazis had inflicted on my Jewish family, the less I cared about the money involved in the 16 Wallstrasse case, and the more determined I grew to expose every detail of the Nazis' destruction of my family's livelihoods and their lives. I didn't know it in 1993, when I went for the first time to meet the German lawyer who had contacted my father, but my quest for justice was to extend beyond financial restitution. It was, in fact, to become the core tension in this restitution case as I sought the complete truth about what Hitler and his Nazi government did to my family.

Part 2

Restitution

6 Von Trott

The German attorney who communicated with my father about the 16 Wallstrasse case was Jost von Trott zu Solz, whom I thought of simply as "von Trott." I was scheduled to meet with von Trott, from Berlin, several weeks after Gerhard's death in 1993. Given von Trott's illustrious family, I imagined I would be in good legal hands.

Jost von Trott zu Solz hailed from German nobility, part of a family that traced its roots back to the year 1252. Over the centuries, the family in its various branches amassed magnificent holdings, including castles as well as immense *Fachwerk*-style compounds that resemble romantic storybook visions.

Von Trott family members served as military leaders for the Holy Roman Empire and as highly placed German government officials. For example, August von Trott zu Solz served as the minister of culture for the Kingdom of Prussia. In the 1500s, Eva von Trott zu Solz set off a scandal by faking her own burial in an attempt to avoid the social consequences of her very enthusiastic participation in an extramarital affair; that legendary scandal has featured in many works of German literature over centuries.

More relevant to my situation, on July 20, 1944, Adam von Trott zu Solz participated in a failed plot to assassinate Adolf Hitler, for which he was hanged in Berlin at the age of thirty-five. I vaguely knew, having heard it from more than one source, that Jost von Trott was related to Adam von Trott. Whereas the Nazis hanged Adam von

Trott and his co-conspirators as traitors, the official West German line was that von Trott and his co-conspirators were patriots and heroes (though some of Adam von Trott's co-conspirators, prior to plotting against Hitler, had participated in all manner of Nazi barbarity).[1]

Just as some postwar Germans relied on isolated figures like the heroic Adam von Trott to spare them indelible association with the evils of Nazism, I was engaging in my own form of what we psychiatrists call "magical thinking" by imagining this attorney, Jost von Trott, to be genetically infused with goodness through his relation to Adam.[2] My magical thinking drew nourishment from a *New York Times Magazine* feature article in which he told the reporter, "The return of properties is one of the few ways of making good on past wrongs."[3]

Von Trott was referring to *Wiedergutmachung*, or "restitution." The German word had comforted me when I first heard it as a child, after my father got his first pension check from the German government for the loss of his civil service position. *Wiedergutmachung* had a lilting, sweet sound, as if it came from a children's story. It was the word used when my father was invited back to Berlin in the 1970s. The possibility of *Wiedergutmachung* soothed me at the start of my family's case, and I thought von Trott was sincere when he used the precise English translation in the article. Later, given what was to transpire, I would change my mind.

Now, however, Jost von Trott, whom I had not yet met, was to be my Teutonic knight in shining legal armor.

Having dealings with a non-Jewish German attorney at this juncture was, for me, a formidable, disquieting prospect. And until the day before, I was unable to give the upcoming meeting the concentrated forethought it warranted. Still profoundly grief-stricken over losing my father, I found the notion that my family had once owned a large, center-city Berlin building phantasmagorical.

Yes, I was curious enough about the meeting to accept and attend it, but within myself I was up, I was down, I was all over the place. If my mother hadn't slapped the Yiddish out of me as a child, I might have labeled my feelings as verklempt: I was overcome with emotion—intensely missing my father, taking on *his* unfinished German Jewish business with non-Jewish Germans.

Stepping outside myself, though, I understood why I was finding that notion so unreal.

Derealization, as it is called in psychiatry, is a way for the brain to protect against destabilizing, overwhelming feelings. Outside conscious control, derealization helped me shield myself against feeling burdened with more than I could then handle.

"What in the *world* am I going to wear?" I wondered the day before the meeting. Trying on outfit after outfit, sizing myself up in a full-length mirror, I heard the internalized voice of my hypercritical mother mocking my appearance: "*Aren't you too fat for that dress?*" Though Lotte had died thirteen years earlier, my mother's specter hovered over me still, particularly when I was in a vulnerable state. And the recent death of my father had me feeling unmoored.

If one part of me was a scientific researcher making progress in the first-ever brain imaging study of well-defined psychopaths, another part of me was shaken—indeed, overpowered—by the prospect of meeting a German attorney in the matter of a Berlin building in which I had never set foot.

I reached into my closet for a black dress, trying it on in front of a mirror. It gave me a no-nonsense, businesslike profile while showing me thin enough. I had alternate options in mind, though, and intended to see how they looked in comparison, ever mindful that I wanted to be able to match my dress with the tallest heels possible while still looking appropriate for the meeting.

How tall is this von Trott? I wondered, looking over all five-foot-two-and-a-half inches of myself with trepidation. I recalled my mother saying, more than once, "You know, you'd be more of a beauty if you were taller."

The next day, as I boarded a train from Croton-on-Hudson to Manhattan for the meeting, then gazed through the windows at verdant, sun-kissed river valley landscapes, I found myself wishing I were on vacation, hanging out with my son, Ben. Maybe throwing sticks, watching our dogs run after them. Definitely relaxing, not fretting, on this warm June afternoon in 1993. Not doing . . . this. As my Metro-North train pulled into the Ardsley-on-Hudson station, the sunlight turned the river surface luminous.

I willed myself back to reality, reviewing the fragments of relevant information I could recall. Working on the restitution claim had been my father's thing; I was so busy with my profession and with home life that I had not been attentive to exactly what was involved, though I still had some back-of-envelope calculations Gerhard had done to figure out how the claim might work out financially. I remembered something my father had said last winter, when I had gone down to visit him in his little rental place in Palm Beach. Gerhard was talking with somebody else about the Berlin property, and I overheard him say with bitter finality, "We will *never* see a penny from those Germans."

That declaration of defeat, issued from my seriously ill father, had landed with a thud in my heart. It had given me something of a lift, knowing he had this restitution matter to work on, but his pessimistic statement regarding the outcome had made me heartsick for him. Gerhard should have been a top-flight attorney in a peaceful, prosperous Berlin fully accepting of its Jewish citizens, but instead he was driven out by rabid prejudice and hate. Who really knew all that he had suffered in the process?

The worst emotional trauma humans experience does not always leave a visible marker. Their signature is an unnatural silence, an emotional absence. Meanwhile the body acts as historian—sometimes with frantic activity, sometimes with paralysis, and sometimes with an occult disease process that surfaces long after the original injury. Our family was one such example. My father's sickness was part of my family's medical history, but only recently had I begun to truly understand it. In the words of renowned psychiatrist and author Bessel van der Kolk, himself the child of Dutch survivors, "The body keeps the score."[4]

And that—the question of exactly *what* my father and his family (and my mother and her family) had been through—was a mysterious phantom weight on my sense of history and self. Imagine nursing an acute awareness that unfathomable tragedies had felled some of your relatives but never asking your parents about their past, prevented by an inhibiting sense of doom, along with a feel for which types of questions were strictly verboten.

The memory of my father bitterly predicting defeat gave me pangs of anguish. Thankfully, by then the train was passing through the soul-steadying sight of the Palisades on the opposite side of the Hudson River.

Formed about 200 million years ago when molten magma moved up into sandstone, the Palisades tower, in their steep, rugged grandeur, many hundreds of feet above the river. Depending on how sunlight angles onto the cliffs, when traveling past them I can sometimes see emerald-toned glints of olivine or feldspar clusters glittering within darkest basalt. Atop and below the cliffs are mixed oak woodland habitats diversified by sugar maples, tulip trees, red cedar, and eastern hemlock. Meditating on the organic stateliness of the Palisades had a significant and welcome centering effect on me. I was not going to be *schwach*—German for weak. I was not going to show any outward signs of self-doubt, trepidation, neuroticism, or terror. I was to *be* a human palisade: strong, solid, inarguably present for this encounter.

As my train entered the Park Avenue Tunnel, the other passengers grew quiet in the relative darkness underground. Then the contagious energy from the crowds inside Grand Central Station propelled me up and over to Park Avenue, where I strode in warming sunshine to the Waldorf Astoria, its ornamental bronze lanterns and marquees glinting in the afternoon light. Inside the entryway, my brother, Jack, greeted me with a hug and a wry smile.

And then, there was von Trott.

Jost von Trott zu Solz: tell me if that name does not sound contrived to be more German than the Kaiser! And the non-Jewish German man we found waiting for us at the Waldorf Astoria on June 29, 1993, seemed to have come straight out of central casting. Wearing horn-rimmed glasses, not a blond hair out of place, tall, with a powerful, utterly poised body, von Trott was at once physically imposing yet disconcertingly aloof.

In minutes, we were seated inside the famed Peacock Alley lounge on comfortable leather chairs around a small table. Jack and I each came prepared with yellow legal pads and pens. Von Trott was businesslike to a fault, perfunctory and making almost no eye contact. He signaled the waiter, opened his briefcase, then laid out his documents without giving Jack or me more than a fleeting look. I was so unnerved by his brusque style that words seemed stuck in my mouth. *Careful, Joanne. You need to be alert. His offhand manner is reminding you more than a little of your mother.*

I registered that von Trott said nothing about our father's recent death. Was this lack of normal human consideration a harbinger of things to come?

According to a German expression cautioning against negativity, one should not paint the devil on the wall, but I was worried that a soulless bureaucratic "devil" had popped up here all by itself. In my mind, at this well-appointed table were not just a lawyer and his clients but also tortured phantoms demanding their due. And in the pit of my stomach, I sensed that the thoughtful, empathetic fellow portrayed in the *New York Times Magazine* article was gone. This real-life von Trott was clipped and efficient, informing us about the case at a rapid pace without seeming to care whether we were able to follow him. The crimes of the Holocaust were being minimized to a business transaction like any other.

Nevertheless, like the obedient German Jewish children we were in our youth, Jack and I feverishly scribbled down the gist of what von Trott said. At intervals, I gingerly lifted my hand to request that he slow down. I dared not risk reaching for the carafe of coffee.

My notes captured what von Trott told us. "You two are among a number of claimants to 16 Wallstrasse," he said. "Your portion of the claim is being held by the Conference on Jewish Material Claims Against Germany. That organization's involvement with the property will end once you are certified as your father's heirs and sign on to this case, joined with your uncle Alex Intrator, as well as various members of your grandfather's nephew's family, the Berglases."

My father's Berglas relatives still lived mainly in the United Kingdom or Europe, some in the United States as well. I had known an older generation of Berglases who often visited the United States when I was young, but over the decades I had not regularly been in touch with their children and grandchildren.

I continued writing as von Trott went on to explain how the

relevant *Grundbuch*, or land registry, showed that Realitas, a company owned by Jakob Intrator and his nephew Jacques Berglas, was registered as the owner of 16 Wallstrasse on April 15, 1920. He described how a forced auction resulted in the end of Realitas's ownership of the property on September 12, 1938.

My notes of von Trott's lecture continued. "As a result of the forced auction, the new owner of 16 Wallstrasse was the Heim & Gerken Furniture Company, headquartered in Birkenwerder, just north of Berlin. In the process of what was then called Aryanization, Heim & Gerken were known as the *Ariseurs*. Heim & Gerken remained the legally inscribed owner of the property until East Germany nationalized it on January 29, 1972. Germans whose property was nationalized in '72 are able to file restitution claims now."

Beginning to grasp the situation, aghast, I asked, "Do you mean to tell me we aren't the only family filing for restitution for this building?"

"No, you are not. The descendants of Heim & Gerken also filed for restitution for 16 Wallstrasse. They, too, maintain they are rightful owners of the building."

He paused to pour himself some water, then continued, "The Heim & Gerken heirs, furthermore, assert that your family lost the property because your grandfather and his nephew were bad businessmen."

I certainly knew what I was capable of saying in response to *that*, but at first I followed Jack's lead in not interrupting. Still, I knew that not a Jew in Nazi Germany could possibly be a good enough businessperson to maintain property under the Third Reich. I asked, "Who are these 'rightful owners,' and how can they be filing a restitution claim for our building?"

Von Trott held up one hand, the palm facing me.

"I will get to that," he said sharply.

I shifted around nervously in the leather chair, realizing that an opposing claim for 16 Wallstrasse would mean a fight, most likely one my father had worried I would chicken out on. Thinking of him in these circumstances, I experienced a flashback to 1967, when I was traveling to Europe but intensely anxious over the idea of going to Berlin, where there was something my father wanted me to do.

"For me," he had said. "Please do it for me."

Catching myself, distracted by those thoughts, I spoke up to von Trott. "In Hitler's time, when my grandparents were still living on Kurfürstendamm and things got very difficult for them, there was a non-Jewish porter in their building who took extra-good care of them. My father wanted me to go meet that man, that porter. And he wanted me to visit where he had once lived, so I'd see something of the kind of life he had." I did not add that I had been unable to bring myself to fulfill my father's wish.

Von Trott nodded politely, but did he care?

"Your Berglas family cousins filed their portion of the claim in 1991, but without your father and uncle, it was incomplete," he continued. "My associate added their two names just before a deadline last December. With your father's passing, the application is incomplete without your names."

Now recalling that the Berglases had put a lot of pressure on my desperately ill father to complete the paperwork, I felt a shiver of sadness.

"Is there a deadline now?"

"It's been extended twice already. Your two names have already been added, but details remain to be discussed. And then there's the question of documentation."

I silently wondered about these deadlines. Seeking restitution for properties in the former East Germany had only recently become possible, but Holocaust survivors were given tight deadlines to assemble whatever paperwork they could, and to complete inquiry forms about events more than fifty years past. What was the practical purpose of these deadlines, other than to intimidate and exclude claimants who failed to meet them?

The next thing von Trott said was, "Your claim has more merit than Heim & Gerken's."

Relieved, I poured myself some coffee and did not ask his reasoning, as it seemed self-evident that our claim had more merit.

Von Trott continued, "Nevertheless, your claim doesn't satisfy the requirements of the German Property Claims Law of 1990. That law specifies that properties within the former East Germany, taken during the Third Reich, must have been appropriated because of racism if they are to be returned."

"So why is that a problem? It's a fact. It's our history."

What was von Trott talking about? How could it be any plainer that our Jewish family was a victim of antisemitic Nazi hatred? Noticing that Jack and I were exchanging looks, von Trott attempted to explain.

"The Property Claims Law of 1990 is tricky. It doesn't include forced auctions because, in theory, buildings or land could conceivably have been foreclosed by the courts for reasons other than racism."

"Why were there so many forced auctions, then?"

I could see the "in theory" part of what von Trott had said, yet it was insufferable.

"What does this mean for us?" my brother asked.

Von Trott ignored my question and addressed my brother. "We must prove that the forced auction was a result of antisemitic measures designed to confiscate your family's wealth, making it impossible for them to pay the mortgage."

"How?" Jack asked. My brother was a banker, always interested in the practical side of things. Meanwhile, I was stewing. German Jews driven out of the Reich were having to prove they had been victims of antisemitism? It seemed too monstrously preposterous to be real. "Don't you think this requirement is, at the least, a little ludicrous?" Von Trott evaded the question by looking down at his plate, then neutrally beckoning a waitress for more coffee. Did *he* think our grandfather was an incompetent businessman?

Down into my seat I sank, believing this must be some dark farce. We would have to prove antisemitism in *this* case?

Yes, von Trott had a legal duty to inform us of the reality, yet my mind raced as I tried to grasp the absurdity of our predicament. The Germans who wrote this 1990 restitution law surely knew what Hitler exacted from Jews financially.

Hitler came to power early in 1933, and on April 1 of that same year my grandfather's clothing business and his wholesale egg business were officially boycotted only because my grandfather was Jewish. One week later, my father was forced out of his judicial clerkship because he was Jewish. By that September, my uncle Alex, a concert violinist, was forbidden to perform for non-Jewish audiences. All that, five years before the forced auction of 16 Wallstrasse!

Von Trott was oblivious to my turmoil. He rattled off facts with the clinical tone of a *Deutsche Welle* newsreader. I suspected that beyond whatever profit he stood to gain through this legal challenge, the case meant nothing to him. But why should it? He was not there as a delegate offering an olive branch; he was there describing steps towards a deal to compensate us for some of what was stolen from our family. The sense I had conjured of von Trott from reading the *New York Times Magazine* article—that we might have some noble commonality of purpose beyond money—was, clearly, unrealistic.

As I picked at the pound cake on my plate, crumbling it into bits, I felt a darkening shadow over my inner being. I knew the source of that shadow too. Though I had long feared Germans, despite my being one generation removed from Nazi terror, I also ached to be accepted by the most highly educated and cultured of them, and to have them respect my accomplishments and those of my family.

Why?

At some level, I had to admit, I was embarrassed about what had happened to our family. It was degrading—living as humbly as we did when I was growing up, while knowing that people such as von Trott likely dwelled in the very neighborhoods where our family once resided, enjoying full access to the society from which my family had been ousted. I felt a bit of envy and anger. Had it not been for Hitler and the Nazis, my father likely would have had von Trott–like status as an attorney.

And it was not only that my grandfather had built up thriving businesses before the Nazis stole them; it was also that my father came to America penniless and often worked hard at two jobs to provide professional educations for me and my brother. Gerhard's career was destroyed because he was Jewish. The Nazis forbade him to be a lawyer and to train as a judge. Similarly, my mother had dreamed of becoming a doctor, then was banned from graduating high school because she was Jewish. A cauldron of shame, envy, and anger.

It was intuitively clear to me that my parents were victims of an ancient, insidious, murderous hatred that the Nazis magnified beyond imagination. As my mother's and father's lives in Germany disinte-grated and they—*the lucky ones!*—were forced to leave without any assets, they were made to feel contemptible, and finally, disposable. The psychic injuries imposed on them were passed on to me, a trait as palpable to me as the color of my hair and eyes, a trait that opened

wide the fathomless chasm separating me from this man who purported to be my advocate.

Von Trott was prattling on. "Look, my goals in this case include
clarifying the facts preceding the forced auction, in order to prove that
the Aryanization of 16 Wallstrasse, accomplished through the transfer
of the property to the Aryan firm Heim & Gerken, occurred due to
antisemitic discrimination."

"But how exactly was 16 Wallstrasse Aryanized?"

Von Trott shrugged.

"I don't know exactly. So far, we haven't found any paperwork for
the forced auction. Our case hinges on whatever official documentation can be turned up proving that antisemitic duress imposed on
the Intrator–Berglas owners was a direct cause of the forced auction.
We *have* found some relevant evidence. For example, we've got some
of your grandfather's bank records proving the family paid punitive
taxes to prevent Jewish people's money from leaving Germany. Those
banking records also show that your grandfather was made to pay
the Nazis' general assessment on Jewish wealth, used to finance war
bonds. While this confiscation of considerable assets was a steady
drain on your grandfather's personal financial resources, the banking
records we have so far aren't considered sufficient evidence of racism
when it comes to the forced auction."

Von Trott continued, "You *will* win the first court battle, but
we expect the Heim & Gerken descendants to appeal that decision.
And you *would* most likely win the appeal, but to fight it will mean a
lengthy and costly legal battle. By the time the entire process ends, it's
likely that many members of your family would be dead. So, I advise
you to be practical."

I started to ask what he meant by "practical," but von Trott lifted
his hand to quiet me.

"Practical means joining forces with the descendants of Heim & Gerken and then splitting the money."

I was speechless.

Split, like splitting a dessert? What was he thinking? What an abhorrent strategy! I could feel myself preparing to challenge him with these questions, but Jack looked over at me and held my gaze. He could sense I was getting worked up.

Von Trott looked satisfied with himself, as though his suggested arrangement truly made sense. He never fully made eye contact with me. It was as though he were reading from cue cards, auditioning for the role of a highly evolved German.

Later, as I was mulling over the meeting, I came to understand how deliberately von Trott had chosen these words, "By the time the entire process ends, it's likely that many members of your family would be dead." To talk that way to us in the wake of our father's death was, if not cruel, manipulative—a skillful strategy wielded by a motivated dealmaker, this German lawyer specializing in restitution. Did von Trott rehearse these words? Death was close to us, a possibility. The Nazis' crimes surrounded us. How would we not be influenced by such a remark?

How *dare* von Trott suggest joining with the Heim & Gerken descendants! Then he presented a second, even more outrageous option: "You could sell your interest in 16 Wallstrasse to the Heim & Gerken heirs outright and get your share of the money when the building is sold."

What could possibly be going through his mind? Maybe von Trott thought something along the lines of "So what if the Intrator–Berglas family joins up with Nazi descendants? They're practical people, the money is good, we're allies now, and—haven't you noticed?—Holocaust memorials are springing up in Germany like weeds on a hot summer day. It's all good. Just get over it."

Hoping I was somehow misunderstanding him, I interrupted. "Herr von Trott," I said authoritatively, pausing to be sure I had his attention. I folded my hands and then unfolded them. "Did you *really* mean to suggest we join forces with the *Ariseurs* and divide the proceeds from the sale of the building with *them*?"

He nodded, then added blandly, "Ninety percent of the files pertaining to the history of this building were destroyed by the Gestapo in the last days of the war. By the end of the war, most of center-city Berlin had gone up in flames. Indeed, 16 Wallstrasse was partially bombed in 1944. The building has since been restored, but that's of no help as regards to the documentation we need."

Next, von Trott started reciting a lengthy list of documents required for us to win the case. Sometime during his recitation, I must have stopped paying attention. For the first time that afternoon, I noticed him looking at me as though expecting me to say something.

On a page in front of me on the table, I had been jotting down individual words and phrases taken from von Trott's presentation. *Gestapo. Nazis. Make a deal.* I kept jotting down, then rereading von Trott's words and phrases, buying more time to think.

Gestapo. Nazis. Make a deal.

It struck me that von Trott uttered these words as if he were talking about chairs and tables. Had he conducted so many of these presentations that he lost all sense of the seriousness of what we were discussing? Was his thinking so simplistic that he believed since Jack and I were born in America, the Holocaust's impact on us was trivial?

Much later, I would also consider how casually von Trott tossed off the term *Ariseur* at our meeting; eventually I understood why he was so free with it from the first day we met—he was, quite simply, thoughtless about the power of that word for his Jewish claimant. At the time, I naively interpreted *Ariseur* to mean *Aryan*, simply referring to people who were non-Jewish. I was not ready that afternoon to fully grasp the word's particular association with Nazism, and von Trott, with his casual, insensitive style, was in no hurry to enlighten me. Looking back, I recognize my misunderstanding as defensiveness. Everything von Trott said was very scary, no matter how calmly I tried to present myself.

I would discover—much later—that a lot more than 10 percent of the files pertaining to 16 Wallstrasse survived the war. To say, accurately, that the Gestapo destroyed 90 percent of the 16 Wallstrasse files, von Trott would have had to have specific knowledge of the Gestapo having done that. Did he? Doubtful. Could he have been relying on our emotional reactions to the word "Gestapo" to throw us off the track of learning more about the building's history? Was von Trott counting on us feeling hopeless so that we would believe our only option was to negotiate with Heim & Gerken?

No wonder that afternoon, my father rose, practically from the grave, to challenge me.

With an uncharacteristic edge to my voice, I spoke up. "Seeing as some documents in our case have already been filed, exactly *how* are the legal costs of our claim being paid?"

"There's a man named Joseph Weinfeld, a survivor of the Buchenwald concentration camp, who is now a London-based attorney with an interest in Berlin real estate investments. Weinfeld also owns Sonex, a research company in Switzerland, through which he finances restitution cases like yours. Should you win, or settle the case, Sonex will receive fifteen percent to cover the costs of research and legal services as well as of marketing and selling the property. I'll be sending you a letter of agreement so we can begin the process of obtaining the legal certification that you two are your father's heirs."[5]

Von Trott folded his napkin. "By the way, I'm actually *not* your lawyer." He announced it almost as an afterthought. "I'm the Berglas family's lawyer. A colleague in Berlin, Dorothea von Hülsen, will represent you, to avoid a conflict of interest with the Berglases. And Clemens Lammek, from my law firm, will be working with von Hülsen."

I felt sucker punched. I was flooded with sadness to think that Aryan actions in the 1930s were now forcing me into a potential conflict of interest with the Berglas relatives, whom I so fondly remembered from my childhood.

Reeling, I didn't even ask why von Trott, rather than our attorney, was the presenter here at the Waldorf Astoria. But Jack spoke up. "Why do the Intrators and the Berglases need separate attorneys? Don't we all have the same interests?"

Ignoring Jack's question, von Trott suddenly stood as though to leave, catching me off guard. I wasn't expecting such an abrupt end to our conversation. I pushed myself to stand up, so as not to take this sitting down, so to speak. If internally I felt like Munch's *The Scream*, I nonetheless wanted to leave von Trott with a professional impression of me, in hopes that doing so might function in our favor during his work on the 16 Wallstrasse case.

I said, "This October, after presenting a paper on my medical research in Munich, I'll be in Berlin."

In a second he was gone, muttering some inaudible *auf Wiedersehen*, leaving me feeling ridiculous, and as though I had egg on my face from my ineffectual, if valiantly manufactured, boldness. I looked to Jack for some reassurance, given how profoundly vexing the meeting had been.

"Can you believe this?" I asked.

If Jack had a keen interest in how Nazi crimes affected our family legacy, he did not quite share my consuming obsession with the origins and history of Hitler's depravities. At least one of us kept his feet on the ground. "Joanne," he said, "it was just business. And don't worry. We are *not* going to negotiate with the *Ariseurs* or the Aryans or however you want to put it. Uncle Alex would never agree to do that either. What we have to do now is move forward with getting all the necessary paperwork in on this."

We hugged, and Jack headed back to work. I exited the hotel into intense late afternoon sun on an empty stomach, a recipe for trouble. "What does 'just business' mean in the face of Nazi crimes?" I asked aloud of the architectural palisades of Park Avenue and the passersby between them. I thought about how the use of silence has power. Silence can be used to make the other person feel uncomfortable and awkward—awkward, as von Trott made me feel with his abrupt departure, not addressing my final comment; and uncomfortable, as he made Jack feel when he ignored my brother's question about why there were separate lawyers for the two sides of our family, given our common interests.

On my way into work the next morning, I read over my notes from the day before. Sure, lawyers must be able to talk about crimes with emotional detachment, but crimes of the *Third Reich*, spoken about in such a banal way? Deeply troubling. These words mattered. Fantasies of the Gestapo and Nazis had caused my childhood terrors and were driving my professional research on psychopaths.

My prior emotional and intellectual relationship with the roots and history of Nazism was complex and at times overstimulating, yet I had always been able to find ways to take breathers from the related issues—that is, to put some protective distance between all of it and myself. Now that I was being drawn into the very things that I had so long feared, what was going to become of me?

7 An Ally

A few days after the meeting with von Trott, I drove from Croton-on-Hudson to the house where I grew up.

In 1946, the year of my birth, my parents moved to Forest Hills, a leafy oasis in Queens that also hosted significant events like the Beatles' legendary 1964 concert and the US Open Tennis Championships. Our home was one of twenty-four identical row houses lining both sides of the street, newly built in the mid-1940s. Spacious undeveloped areas of trees and grass braced all four corners of this development. Like my parents, most of the people living around us were refugees from Nazi-occupied Europe. Their voices were accented, and most of the parents were without surviving parents of their own.

This day, I wanted to spend time in my father's study, seeing what I might be able to learn about my family's prewar Berlin life. I was to discover a treasure trove, some of which has already been disclosed in previous chapters, but on this day, just weeks after my father's death, I hadn't yet set foot in his office. I intended to comply with von Trott's advice on assembling documentation for the case, but I was suffering corrosively nagging doubts over whether von Trott would ever prove open to refusing negotiations with the *Ariseurs*.

I descended the steep steps from the kitchen to my father's office. Unlike the rest of the house, stifling from the summer heat, my father's basement study was pleasantly cool. His desk and chair faced a small garden darkened by the six-story apartment buildings that had sprouted up in the early 1950s, dwarfing the houses on our street but providing welcome shade on steamy summer days. Atop a rickety metal stand was my father's black Smith Corona typewriter. I smiled, remembering him declaring, "I am the world's *fastest* two-finger typist!"

Across the room was a whole wall of steel file cabinets, sixteen drawers in total. To the right of my father's desk were enlarged sepia photos of his parents, Jakob and Rosa, taken shortly after their marriage, which occurred in London in 1902 when both were twenty-seven. My paternal grandparents each had large brown eyes, something my father and I shared. First cousins, they mildly resembled each other.

Poster-size photos of me at one year of age—wall decorations for my surprise thirtieth birthday party—still graced the space. My father's desk was organized exactly as I remembered: sharpened pencils in one open box, paper clips and rubber bands in others. There was a neat stack of partially used writing pads. On the middle of his desk, I saw an envelope addressed to me in bold print.

I pulled out the chair and sat down. The envelope looked fresh and new, as though it had been placed there moments before. I balanced it on my hands with greatest concentration, regarding the envelope as something similar to a crystal ball from which, on my fingertips, I might divine a trace of my father, some residue of his living self— energy, perhaps—from what I hoped was his ever-present soul.

The letter must have been one of the last he wrote before going to Florida, where he died. I opened it, careful not to tear the envelope. Inside were three typed pages on heavy white paper with details about insurance policies, bank accounts, and his last will and testament. Attached to the documents there was a note written in large, self-assured print: "Goodbye. Love, Dad."

I looked through the pristine pages to see if there might be a letter from him, maybe with words of wisdom about how to live my life without my parents. But no, there was just the "Goodbye," as if it had been too painful for him to write more. I didn't know whether to laugh or cry. As serious as he was, Gerhard did have a sense of humor. Putting the letter down, I pushed myself away from the desk and then swiveled around to look at the black file cabinets across the room.

The cabinets had been there forever, yet I had never opened a single drawer. After taking a deep breath, I walked over, sat down, and made myself comfortable on the cool tile floor. One by one, I opened every drawer. Each—at least two feet deep—was packed with letter-size files, all labeled in my father's strong, clear print. I found mundane if meticulously kept archives of medical records and house-hold bills, but also my brother's and my report cards, and my father's letters to us at summer camp: for each letter, a carbon copy of his, and ours in response to him. I longed to spend time with these personal documents, so evocative of my childhood, but that emotional luxury was going to have to wait.

Finally, I found the treasure I was hoping for: letters from my grandfather to my father. These files were labeled by year between 1937 and 1943. In each were at least fifty missives, most handwritten. That they were in German was not a problem (I could still get the gist, though I'd stopped speaking the language after my mother's death), but the handwritten ones were in *Sütterlinschrift*, an elaborate, archaic style of cursive impossible for me to read. I made a mental note to hire somebody to read them.

Other files I went through contained typed, formal business let-ters, their sixty-year-old pages giving off a musty odor and crumbling into small flakes at the edges. For a second I panicked, thinking that handling these papers might cause them to disintegrate. I carefully put the file containing the letters ending my father's career in Germany on the daybed, where he used to rest when he was feeling poorly yet had to work at home. Within it was the official Nazi letter informing my father on his birthday that he had to request a leave of absence from his position—an act calculated to see him expelled from his profession.

Imagine how I felt. German courts were demanding I prove that my German Jewish family had been the victim of racism under the Nazis. And here in my hands, in my late father's office in Queens, I was holding detailed proof of the Nazis' destruction of his professional life in Berlin, professional destruction from which he would never fully recover.

I wanted to cry inconsolably for my father, and to scream at the Germans and the *Ariseurs*. There were the letters with black-and-red-ink swastika stamps from German banks, sent between 1936 and 1941. Von Trott had told us that punitive, antisemitic taxes alone would not prove that my family had lost 16 Wallstrasse due to racism. But these files contained more information. I intended to copy the contents of all these files and send them to von Trott. To think that direct documentation of my father getting booted out of his legal career in Germany, only because he was Jewish, could not be counted as any sort of evidence in our 16 Wallstrasse restitution case was outrageous.

Many weeks later, in early August, Jack received a piece of certified mail from Sonex, the Zurich-based firm that would be financing our restitution case. Externally, the envelope had a thoroughly professional appearance. Inside were two property research and management contracts for our signatures. It looked as if these were Sonex's boilerplate agreements, and they were riddled with spelling errors. In the multipage contract, moreover, the paragraphs were misnumbered.

We deliberated, wrote to Sonex about our concern, asked for

more information about the company, and decided to sign the contract anyway in good faith. The deadline was approaching.

As time went on, however, excusing Sonex's laxity began to play on me. Why should I have accepted their sloppiness along with the implied disrespect? I worried that by signing such a carelessly proofed document I had acted impulsively, showing bad judgment and setting myself up to not be taken seriously.

This Berlin lawyer, just out of the starting gate, had too much power over me. It was time to get a second opinion.

But where was I to find one?

My mother had done volunteer work for an organization, Selfhelp, committed to serving as "the last surviving relative to victims of Nazi persecution" by providing Holocaust survivors the services they need to live in comfort and dignity. One of my parents' Selfhelp friends mentioned the name Hans J. Frank as somebody who might be perfect for the second opinion I was seeking.

Hans Frank was a founder of the international law firm Fried Frank and was prominent on the boards of organizations helping Holocaust survivors throughout the world, including Selfhelp. And he was an attorney for the same Claims Conference that had previously been guardian of our 16 Wallstrasse claim. But I had no direct personal connection to him.

I suspected Hans Frank would be too busy ever to talk with me. Still, one day in my office at the Bronx VA Hospital, I gathered up the courage to dial his office phone number. "Please wait a minute," a secretary told me.

The VA Hospital is at the top of a hill with views over the whole Bronx. I let my gaze sweep over the scene, feeling almost certain the secretary would return to the phone and tell me Mr. Frank was unable to take my call.

"Good afternoon," came Hans Frank's voice, surprising me, and also delighting me with a liltingly soft German accent that sounded just like my father's. "How can I help you?" Though we were speaking on the phone, for a second I felt enveloped by an aura. He sounded both elegant in a continental way yet exceptionally kind.

"So, the story is," I began, and then filled him in.

"I understand how upsetting this is for you," he said when I had finished. "I'm sorry it's gone that way so far." Listening to Hans Frank's engaging voice on the phone, with his German accent drawing me into my father's world, I felt a tinge of sadness but, at the same time, nostalgia for the soothing comfort of my Oma Rikka. It was all I could do to hold myself back from speaking German and weeping.

"Jost von Trott actually has an excellent reputation as an attorney. You mentioned you'll be in Berlin in a few months. By coincidence, I'm scheduled to be there during the same period. Why don't we plan on my accompanying you to Herr von Trott's office? We'll see where things stand with your claim."

Back in Croton-on-Hudson after work, I took stock of where things stood in the case. I imagined my father would be pleased with my energy in assembling powerful evidence to prove our rightful inheritance, as well as with my gumption in enlisting Hans Frank in our cause.

I might have been a little lost in thought that night as I prepared our dinner.

8 A Shadowed Childhood

As a child, I managed my preoccupation with Nazis largely by reading as much as I could about the dark side of human nature. When I couldn't sleep, which was most of the time, I would sneak downstairs into the quiet, dark kitchen and grab a handful of chocolate chip cookies. With a flashlight, I read under my covers, the cookies providing solace. Following my extensive, profoundly disturbing reading, I would invent stories involving the swastika-bearing enemy capturing me and my eventual escape.

Repeatedly, I rehearsed what I was certain would be my ultimate fate. At all times, I had a bagful of survival supplies ready to go. I had staked out all the best hiding places in my neighborhood. And, in case our house was invaded, I kept scissors and hair spray under my bed—the hair spray to blind the intruder and the scissors to stab him. By studying the monstrous past and preparing my defenses in advance, the young me magically believed a Holocaust-like period could never happen again.

My nighttime preparedness exercises went unremarked and perhaps even unnoticed by both parents. When my usual rituals proved insufficient and I still could not sleep, I would return downstairs, put on the Tchaikovsky Violin Concerto—a favorite—and dance frenetically in front of our large living room mirror. My reflection looked wild and out of control. My mother's frequently delivered, harsh admonition, "Joanne! Pull yourself together!" would dominate my thoughts as I tried to slow my movements into a more disciplined state. But it was hopeless: I was in too much of a frenzy. I needed the crazed movements because with every frantic leap and turn my spirits lifted, calming me. As I write about this now, I wonder if my body intuitively knew that my dancing served as a release valve, sparing me from having the many pressures I experienced in our household coalesce into some dangerous, stress-related disease. I am sure dance saved me then as it would many times later in my life.

That my parents seemed oblivious to my activities, taking place directly under their bedroom, was beyond me. I suppose, from their point of view, it wasn't problematic. Would my parents have had the wisdom to know I was coping in the only way I knew? At least I wasn't bothering them. I doubt anything would have been different, had they known what I was reading and that I was wildly dancing. Contending with their own misfortunes, they needed to believe Jack and I were free from the societal and governmental oppression that had ruined their young lives.

All that is *not* to say my parents didn't realize I was a distressed child. In fact, considering me an attention-seeking actress, they deprecatingly nicknamed me "Sarah Bernhardt." My mother especially loved using that one.

At one yearly checkup, a pediatrician asked me, "Does anything bother you? Or hurt?"

"Sometimes my stomach really, really hurts me," I responded.

I did not reveal all the nights I was spending asleep on the bathroom floor, fearing I might have to vomit. The doctor, a Jewish émigré from Belgium, turned to my mother. "Why haven't you mentioned this before?" he asked. "It sounds like she's in pain."

After that visit, every day I carried to school a bottle of a prescribed green liquid along with a teaspoon tucked in a pink satin pouch decorated with embroidered pearls. Having that medicine with me made all the difference. I only needed it intermittently and it didn't have an unpleasant taste, but when I did need to take it, it calmed me down quickly, unknotting my gut and relieving the pain. Years later, as a medical student overcome with similar symptoms, I looked up that green medicine in the *Physicians' Desk Reference*, learning it was a stomach tranquilizer for irritable bowel syndrome. The soft-spoken, gentle Belgian doctor had died before I could contact him to express my gratitude. He was the only one ever to tell my mother, "If Joanne says she isn't feeling well, you *must* pay attention."

My mother just did not quite listen to me.

The Nazis continued to dominate my nighttime worries well into adulthood. Whereas in childhood I read about the Nazis and fashioned perverse bedtimes stories based on my reading, in college I studied German history and discussed Nazism on a more scholarly basis. Later, as a doctor, I became imaginatively and intellectually absorbed in my research on psychopaths. In attempting to shield myself from the terror that Nazis engendered in me, I found myself with no accessible emotional feelings about them. Though of course I knew the Nazis had committed unspeakable atrocities, however gruesome the imagery of their violence was, I could stare at it without blinking an eye.

In 1954, my father unexpectedly had a high fever. His kidneys malfunctioned, retaining urine and excreting albumin, a vital protein without which he would die. My mother located a Jewish physician from Berlin, Dr. Kurt Lange, who saved my father's life by putting him on a combination of steroids, the very first treatment protocol for this disease. My father was in and out of hospitals for most of the rest of my childhood. The life-saving steroids had their own harsh effect, serious cardiovascular disease.

By my eighth birthday, I was determined to become a doctor. The nurses who took care of my father tolerated my curiosity and my wish to help care for him, letting me dab 4711 cologne on his forehead and fluff up his pillows. By the time I was a teenager, volunteering as a candy striper in the same hospital where my father frequently was admitted, I knew my way around sick grownups and was comfortable in hospital settings.

For a time my father was unable to work, creating more burdens for my mother, including additional strains on their relationship. Over time, his disease became under control, so that it was no longer life-threatening. He found a good job as a salesman for a family-owned cotton waste manufacturing company headquartered in North Carolina. Kind to him, the owners tolerated his periodic hospitalizations.

When my father was well enough, he worked two salesman jobs, starting before 6:00 a.m. and finishing after we went to sleep. He sometimes traveled two or three days in a row. When he had a relapse, everything fell apart.

My mother, who had taken merchandizing courses before she met my father, went to work as a buyer in New York City's Garment District for her sister Irma's ladies' clothing stores in Philadelphia. With my mother working, Jack and I became latchkey kids. Sometimes my mother would leave me unsupervised. For overnights, my brother was sent to the home of her parents' former maid in Miltenberg. Occasionally I was sent to that house too. I never ventured far from their backyard, except when they took me on Sundays to a Catholic church. Jack was occasionally beaten by boys in that neighborhood, and the woman's husband had recordings of Hitler's speeches. I never told my parents, knowing they would accuse me—as they often did—of exaggerating.

My precocious helpfulness lost its charm as I aged out of the single digits, so I sought to please in other ways, but I found it hard to get just right.

School performance was crucial. It was universally prized, but in our insular world of German Jewish refugees, and in my particular world as circumscribed by my mother, it probably meant more than it should have. There is no doubt, as first-generation Americans from a German Jewish family, we were expected to make up for the loss of status and place destroyed by the Nazis. That I was attractive, too, was useful, as I belonged to a generation for which a well-placed marriage could substitute fine for a profession.

I was never sure which was more important, good grades or good looks. I could never get it right in my mother's eyes. Her face would scrunch up in anger at me and then she would punish me with cruel, callous words that defeated me even more. She would build me up as the smartest, most beautiful girl outside of our home, only to tear me down over some minor weight gain or a less-than-perfect test score.

I may have brightened corners of my elders' lives, I but deeply absorbed their darkness.

Irrational anxiety, oppositional behavior, and paralysis handicapped my social and academic functioning as I progressed through school. In 1964, my senior-year high school French teacher wrote to my parents, "with much disappointment that the cooperative, delightful, eager-to-please girl is now indifferent, uncooperative, most of all rude and almost completely unrecognizable." Between the time I entered high school in 1961 and graduation in 1964, my test scores plummeted. In my senior year, I was barely a C student. It took me decades to find solace in psychotherapy.

Years later, I came to learn that my out-of-kilter childhood was not unlike that of many other children of Holocaust survivors. I could have used somebody telling me that I wasn't alone. I could have benefited from the then-nascent field of child psychology. But my parents, raised in a forbidding, older Prussian culture, viewed therapy with distrust and as a sign of weakness.

They had an unspoken rule: never discuss our troubles beyond the four walls of our house. My father's occasional bad temper was never meant to be a secret, but my mother skillfully hid hers from the outside world. To us, she expressed scorn for our next-door neighbor, who shrieked at her children from their front porch. Repulsed by that woman's public displays of anger, my mother shamelessly attributed the behavior to our neighbor's Eastern European roots. Similarly, my mother would scorn me if I used a Yiddish word picked up in the neighborhood; the derivative language was anathema to her with her prized German education, curtailed as it was by the Nazis. Only much later did I realize that my mother was blind to the fact that her arrogant attitude towards our neighbor was all too close to the Nazis' despicable attitude towards *her*.

Unlike my father, who was nine years older, my mother lacked even the shadow of a professional identity to fall back on. I wonder if that was why she was so determined to rid herself of her accent, angry that her German identity did not protect her? But how is one to explain her failure of empathy for her own children? German child-rearing of her era was notoriously strict and forbidding, but it seemed there was more to it with her.

Whatever the answer to that question, I ultimately married into my obsession with the trauma of the Holocaust and its Nazi perpetrators.

I met my husband, Gregory Lombardo, at St. Vincent's Hospital in Greenwich Village in 1983. At the time, I was chief resident of the psychiatry program. Greg, who had a PhD in English literature from Columbia University, was finishing medical school at Columbia's College of Physicians and Surgeons. He came to us to explore the possibility of serving a psychiatry residency at St. Vincent's, where his father had been a cardiologist.

Greg and I went one day to eat at Elephant & Castle, a Greenwich Village institution. I said to myself, *This is the only man I've ever met who is more intense than I am.* I did not yet realize that Greg and I had tragically parallel family histories. His maternal grandparents were deported to the Theresienstadt concentration camp in Czechoslovakia, his grandmother first from a psychiatric hospital in Germany, his grandfather from their home in Berlin. The Nazis later murdered them both.

Greg's mother, Ruth Benjamin, managed to escape to New York, sponsored by her older sister, a physician who arrived in the United States in 1938. (Our son was named Benjamin to honor Ruth's family, including her ill-fated parents.) Greg was the product of her brief affair with a married Swedish man, a photographer and writer. Ruth did not tell Greg's biological father she was pregnant.

Prone to depression, a vulnerability exacerbated by her parents' terrible deaths, Ruth gave Greg up at birth. That was shocking enough, but worse yet, Greg's remaining family members dithered over who was responsible for the boy while he languished in a Jewish orphanage. After four months, the agency insisted the family either take him or place him for adoption, as they were not a long-term facility. With his relatives still unwilling to take him, or even to make any responsible decision about him, Greg was transferred to the Foundling, a home for abandoned children established in 1869 by the Sisters of Charity of New York. He endured nearly three years until becoming a medical emergency, having developed marasmus, severe malnutrition typical of infants with depression.

Once Greg was officially released for adoption by his biological family, he was adopted by Dr. Carmyn J. Lombardo, a cardiologist, and his wife, Ann, a former nurse. Gregory was raised Catholic. As loving a mother as Ann was, Greg's unfortunate early experiences in a 1940s orphanage left their marks.

In the early years of our relationship, Greg often remarked on how disturbing it was for him to observe me watching documentaries about the Nazis. My face, he noted with concern, would be expressionless, a full-blown neutral stare. He wondered if I felt anything at all as I watched the gruesome films. One was supposed to be distraught, repulsed, sad, or horrified, but I seemingly was not.

What was that about? I asked myself. *My professional training?* Sure, but more importantly, it was the way I had long managed what frightened me most. My brain set emotions aside, allowing me to watch documentaries about Nazis as though I were either a dispassionate clinician about to jot down something relevant or an objective historian preparing a lecture, rather than a flesh-and-blood human being whose family had been torn apart by the Nazi regime.

Thanks to psychological defenses that allowed me to convert disabling emotions, I was able to see, hear, and understand documentaries about the Nazis without experiencing any emotions over the horror the Nazis perpetrated on Jews. Those defenses carried me rather far in life from childhood on, but as the 16 Wallstrasse case evolved, I wondered whether they could shield me against the darkly looming shadows of Nazi ghosts in Berlin.

9 Deutschland

In October 1993, three months after my first meeting with von Trott, I traveled to Germany for a professional triumph: presenting my research on psychopaths. First in Munich, then in Berlin, I was accompanied by a German colleague who graciously ushered me around, greatly helping me to manage my anxiety over traveling in Deutschland. If, on one hand, I was certain of being an accomplished professional and a righteous claimant, on the other, I felt like an out-of-place intruder and a petrified child.

My generalized sense of unease and my fears did not stem exclusively from the Nazi darkness that had overshadowed my inner life since childhood. I was also plagued by fears for, and worry over, the child I had at home.

At age seven, my son, Benjamin, had adjusted to my absence for relatively short professional meetings within the United States, where I was never away for more than three days. Leaving him for a whole week felt more serious, especially so soon after his grandfather Gerhard's death. As the date for my departure to Germany approached, Ben was still calling for me at night and asking about his grandfather. I kept my responses as simple as possible.

"Ben," I said, "a very long time ago, your Opa owned a big building in Berlin, Germany. The bad guys took it away from him. Now I'm leaving on a mission to get that building back."

Giving me a thumbs-up, Ben smiled. Simple worked.

I left on one of those perfect fall days when the sun is its brightest yellow and the sky its most intense azure blue, while the mild air
carries just a hint of chill in an occasional breeze. With their brilliant
reds and luminescent yellows, oak trees lent autumnal splendor to
our property. Until the airport limousine arrived, with our dogs lying
nearby, Ben held my hand tightly in the driveway. Our wonderful,
caring nanny stood a discreet distance behind us. Oh, how I hated
leaving Benjamin!

Hovering in my thoughts was a recollection involving a day
shortly after my father died. I was on a living room couch with Ben,
who said, "Mommy, some day, when both of us are dead, I'm going to
dig through the ground all the way to wherever you are and then we'll
be together forever." I was more than a little surprised by that image,
which gave me a heavy, melancholy feeling.

After we had said our goodbyes and hugged each other, I waved at
Ben from the rear window as the limo drove up our drive. He waved
back until I was out of sight, whereupon I burst into tears. Given my
corrosively scarring childhood, how was I ever to trust that I was
doing the right thing for my beloved son? I slipped into a funk. Greg
knew all about my anxieties over being so far from Ben, and he reassured me he would take extra-extra good care of him. Yet Greg, too,
was working tirelessly, building a psychiatric practice while fulfilling
the demands of additional jobs. He was on call at a hospital besides
being part of an emergency psych team that worked throughout
Westchester County.

What had I done? What was I *doing*?

Nerves can get stretched to a breaking point and then nevertheless stretch even further without breaking; such was my condition
while aboard the plane to Germany. Loudspeaker announcements *auf
Deutsch* helped not a bit.

Several things kept turning over in my mind during the flight, among them my father's vexatious questions: "Are you tough enough yet?" and "Do they know who you are?"

Another thing I could not get out of my mind during this flight was my first, ill-fated trip to Germany in 1967. Together with a girl-friend, I was supposed to be going for a grand tour of Europe. My father wanted me to do a family favor during my trip.

"Joanne," Gerhard said, "as you know"—and I did know already, for he had talked to me about this favor more than once—"Karl Schulz was the porter in our Berlin apartment building at 185 Kurfürstendamm. He was not Jewish. But he bent over backwards to help your Oma and Opa when they were most in danger from Hitler and the Nazis. Even when it was no longer safe for them to go outside, Herr Schulz helped them, bringing them mail—including my letters, no doubt—and, when he could, food. I am deeply indebted to him. It would be so meaningful for me if you went and saw him when you're in Berlin. Please do this for me."

"I promise, I will," I had said.

Once I was in Berlin, though, the prospect of calling on Herr Schulz, the porter, at that time proved more than I could bear emotionally, for reasons I did not then in the least understand.

The girlfriend with whom I had planned to tour Europe ditched me for some guy in Madrid, leaving me to travel alone for ten weeks. Once I got to West Berlin, after traveling throughout Europe, I found it as vibrant as New York City, with a crucial difference: I was walking among many Germans who, during the Holocaust, were either enthusiastic Nazis or had looked the other way.

I stayed in a modest little place that, in 1967, was one of the few Jewish-owned hotels in Berlin. It was mere blocks from where my grandparents had lived, but that short distance loomed large for me. I was as terrified of the typical German walking the streets as if it were 1937 instead of 1967. I was tormented by and felt physically ill from my dreaded obligation to visit Herr Schulz. I would set out to walk those few blocks and then, unable to make it, sit down at a Kurfürstendamm café, wrenched with stomach pains. Then I'd return to the hotel in a state of gloomy malaise, intending to try again the following morning. I suffered through the nights as well.

I felt deeply, irredeemably ashamed. I was failing to keep a solemn promise I'd made to my father. Without feeling any inner sense of determination but hoping to head off the shame, I made one final attempt—only to find myself unable to move, one block from the building. Instead, I stared unseeing into the front window display of a women's clothing store.

I called my father that night and struggled to explain what was happening. I might have sobbed. I perceived broad and deep disappointment in his voice: I had let him down. I felt like a pathetic, ignominious loser. I was also letting my mother down, for she expected me to travel from Berlin to her hometown of Miltenberg to visit people she knew there. The typical American youth traveling through Europe is there for culture, fun, and adventure, but I was not the typical American youth; I was the daughter of Jewish refugees from Nazi Germany.

"Come home," my father said.

We never spoke about my leaving Germany so precipitously. Indeed, we never even discussed my trip to Berlin at all.

In James Joyce's *Ulysses*, Stephen Dedalus says, "History is a nightmare from which I am trying to awake."[1] In something like that spirit, then, I stepped off the plane in Munich decades after my first trip to Germany. My taxi ride to a Munich hotel, with a background score of sinister-sounding train whistles and police sirens along the way, brought Nazi-era newsreel images to my mind.

I was able to achieve some measure of calm once I met up with the nuclear physicist Peter Stritzke. Peter was my first-ever non-Jewish German friend. We affectionately called ourselves "The Nineteen Forty-Sixers," as we were both born one year after the end of World War II. I cultivated the notion that those of us born in '46 were conceived with some degree of optimism that the world could become a better place.

Peter was the scientist who designed the imaging process for the research on psychopaths that I was presenting in Munich. We first met in connection with our work; in the United States on sabbatical from his German university, he had helped set up the brain imaging division of the department of nuclear medicine at Mount Sinai Hospital in New York. There, my chairman had recently appointed me administrator of the then-new Single Photon Emission Computed Tomography (SPECT) machine to be placed in the VA. I had to ensure this extremely sophisticated equipment was properly uncrated and subsequently shepherded through various hospital committees— shown, demonstrated, and taught to them—which was no small task for a non-physicist. As I had established a reputation for strong administrative skills, I was teamed up with Peter to accomplish those goals.

Professionally as well as personally, Peter had been a daily part of my life for three years, though we drifted apart after he left New York. Peter had long enjoyed being a sly, quick-witted collaborator in my obsessions with the Nazis. Now here we were, walking arm in arm in Munich, outdoors in the early morning following a raucous, no-holds-barred Oktoberfest. In good German fashion, the cobble-stone streets had already been immaculately tidied after the event.

"Look over there," he said, tipping his head towards a corner diagonally across from us. "See that old man with a severe frown? He was definitely, positively, absolutely an early, fully willing Nazi Party member. Spotting them isn't that hard, you know."

Before I could respond, Peter was directing my attention in another direction. "Over there," he said, "is the former site of the *Bürgerbräukeller*, where Adolf Hitler mounted his attempted putsch in 1923." I well knew the history of Hitler's obnoxious Beer Hall Putsch, just as I knew that after Hitler was convicted of high treason for that failed coup d'état, he was sentenced to five years in the most comfortable sort of German prison. Then, despite having dictated *Mein Kampf* to his fellow prisoners Emil Maurice and Rudolph Hess, the future *Führer* was released after only nine months for "good behavior."

The relative contemporary mundanity of these city blocks in Munich—which were not without their charms, to be sure—only made it that much more surreal to me that this was where Hitler's fame and political fortunes took a quantum leap forward.

A chill went down my spine. Did I have what it was going to take to speak up and be heard in this country?

For the time being, I spoke up to Peter. "I am preoccupied by two challenging questions my father directed at me from his deathbed," I explained. "And additionally, I'm plagued by recollections of my emotionally catastrophic first trip to Berlin. Let me tell you a little about it."

Peter, always a wonderful listener, gave me an encouraging pat on the shoulder.

"Joanne," he said, once I was done, "what you've told me just now is of course very interesting, and poignant, but you are no longer a panicked twenty-one-year-old college student. You are an accomplished psychiatrist, three years into seminal research, the importance of which is being recognized around the world!"

We then walked onto the campus of the Ludwig Maximilian University of Munich. Before my presentation, we planned to have lunch. My brain was playing tricks on me, though. A long, narrow staircase descended into an underground cafeteria; my mind's eye saw it as a place where Jews would be marched into gas chambers. I did not reveal that to Peter, whose lunchtime company was delightful, even if the German lunch meats—the *Bierschinken wurst* and all the rest of it, which I have never especially loved—were not.

Next, my nerves on a razor's edge, I stood in front of a sternly concentrating audience of German professors and graduate students. Quickly, I found my voice. I was well enough prepared that my presentation went smoothly, like a sled ride down a long, gently sloping hill.

When I finished, my German audience started heavily thumping, rapping, and banging on their desktops with their knuckles. I was alarmed; this was not applause. It was a bizarre display and, to me, emotionally discombobulating. What had I done, and what was going on? Did they know my interest in psychopaths was rooted in German history?

Sensitive to my confusion, Peter eased me out of the university auditorium. I was so mired in my mental space that I couldn't recall whether anybody had made comments or thanked me for the presentation. The next thing I *do* remember, Peter and I were fueling ourselves with coffee and cake before setting out for Berlin.

"Joanne," he said, "that knuckle rapping on desktops—that *Schlagen und Klopfen*—is an old German university tradition. They were showing their appreciation."

Peter laughed along with me. But then my trepidation grew again as we drove in his BMW along a roadway originally built on Hitler's command as a *Reichsautobahn*. The autobahn was roughly paved, amplifying the whooshing, roaring sounds of massive trucks thundering all around us.[2] White-knuckled, I shrank into my bucket seat as Peter blithely passed towering truck after towering truck. It was nightmarish for me to be riding in a car on a Hitler highway; I was overwhelmed by thoughts of Hitler's merciless industrial effort to prepare for war, tanks rolling into position and trucks transporting fearsome, murderous weaponry.

I pressed my eyes shut. The speed at which we were moving made me dizzy. Holding my breath, I gripped the seat as tightly as I could. Feeling suddenly panicked that Ben would lose both his Opa and me in the same year, I whispered, "I am afraid I will die in Germany."

Reaching over, Peter covered my hand. "We'll be all right," he said, comfortingly. That was Peter: a real mensch. And I loved him for it.

Berlin is about 366 miles from Munich. Not until the wee hours of the morning did Peter drop me off at the Hotel Kempinski on Kurfürstendamm, just four blocks from my father's and grandparents' former home.[3] The Kempinski's side entrance faced the site of the Fasanenstrasse Synagogue, where my family had been members. Only a remnant of the temple, a stone doorframe, remained standing after Kristallnacht. A more modern, utilitarian-looking structure behind that remnant was now used as a Hebrew school.

After resting several hours in my hotel room, I went out walking amidst the bustle of people going to work on this bright Berlin morning. On my way to 185 Kurfürstendamm, where my family used to live, I thought about the ditty "Berliner Luft"—"In Praise of Berlin Air"—from Paul Lincke's operetta *Frau Luna*. How curious that despite everything, many *Yekkes*, or German-speaking Jews, commonly sang, and still sing, this song as though there were no better place for them in the world than Berlin.

Across from 185 Kurfürstendamm was a high-end boutique, while the street level of my family's former apartment building housed a similar shop. When I looked up at the fourth-floor balcony to the apartment where my grandparents and father had lived, though, what I saw in my mind's eye was the monstrous past. I knew that from this balcony, my grandparents and my father had watched Hitler's motorcade en route to the 1936 Olympics. I pictured the streets lined dozens deep with Aryans barking, "*Sieg heil!*" while making the *Hitlergruss*, clicking their heels and thrusting an arm up at an angle. I imagined young Nazi women crying hysterically out of demented Führer worship, Nazi flags and banners on all sides.

There was something else I knew had happened, and this day could as good as envision. During Hitler's Berlin Olympics, for international public relations purposes, the Nazis had removed the most vicious of their antisemitic posters for the duration of the games. The International Olympic Committee had awarded the 1936 games to Berlin in 1931, before the Nazis took power. The United States considered a boycott but ultimately decided to participate.

I wondered how my grandparents had interpreted the Olympic-period break in the gathering storm of antisemitic terror. Did they use the period to argue with my father that things were not going to get as bad as he was predicting?

Only one year earlier, in the summer of 1935, there were anti-Jewish riots throughout Germany, including some on this very street, Kurfürstendamm.[4] Hitler used those disturbances as a springboard to the Nuremberg Laws, stripping all German Jews of citizenship. Those laws rendered my family members stateless overnight. They became refugees in what had been their own country and found themselves without citizenship in any country. For a time their relative wealth shielded them, but their isolation continually increased. In 1938, my grandparents wrote to my father: "One feels the urge to go outside, but the possibilities for this are very limited."[5]

I walked to von Trott's office feeling apprehensive. Our meeting at the Waldorf Astoria had not exactly left me optimistic. The woman who had met with him there had been vulnerable to the dichotomy of appearance and reality; I had badly wanted von Trott to be what he purported to be—a lawyer who would help our family, not someone indifferent to our case. I worried it was distinguished-looking German men with pedigrees, unctuous politeness, and agile use of words who had seduced vulnerable Jews like my grandfather, a successful businessman, into thinking they had a life remaining in Germany once Hitler took over. During that first meeting in New York, with the death of my father so recent and raw—at a time of great emotion for me—my wishes and fears as a second-generation Holocaust survivor had obscured my understanding of the obstacles I was facing. I had been unable to articulate my dismay, much less confront von Trott about matters I questioned or outright opposed.

Now, fortunately, I arrived at von Trott's Berlin office at precisely the same moment as Hans Frank, the attorney who had previously offered to accompany me to this meeting. Born in Magdeburg only one year before my father, Hans managed to escape Hitler's Germany in 1934 for the United States, where he earned an American law degree from New York University. At the time, even in the United States, prejudice against Jews was prevalent in certain quarters, yet Hans became a co-founder of the highly regarded law firm Fried Frank.

When he greeted me, Hans projected so dignified and kindly an aura that my anxieties over von Trott receded significantly. Through the New York City grapevine, I knew that Hans had recently suffered the loss of his daughter Evelyn, who was my age. Thus, in the same period that Hans lost his daughter, I lost my father. Entertaining the notion that we could be emotional support for each other, I was struck with an overpowering desire to hug him, but before I could embarrass myself, von Trott's younger associate attorney, Clemens Lammek, appeared.

Although von Trott previously told us that von Hülsen had been designated as the Intrator family's attorney, she was unable to attend. I had yet to accept that the Intrator and Berglas families needed separate attorneys for the case, so I was relieved not to be meeting her.

Next, von Trott arrived, greeting me not as "Frau Doktor Intrator" but plainly as "Frau Intrator." Because Germans customarily articulate an individual's professional title, von Trott addressing me as "Mrs." and not as "Doctor" offended me; the dropped honorific seemed purposeful. Or had he not really paid much attention?

Von Trott ushered us into a conference room where, before I even took my seat, he asked, "Will it be all right if we speak German?" Not yet having fully processed the "Frau" business, I nodded, failing to grasp the consequences of my overhasty acquiescence. In mere minutes I had neutered myself, relinquishing my hard-earned professional status as a physician by not insisting he call me Doctor Intrator, and simultaneously surrendering my ability to fully comprehend our conversation. What was the impulse—to fit in? And at what cost? I was being imprudently submissive, reminding me of how our beloved dogs sometimes lolled around in front of us on their backs, their legs in the air. I asked myself why I should trust this man to have my best interests at heart. Von Trott almost surely did not care whether I understood his German.

The fact that I put myself at such a disadvantage then disturbs me still today. I felt deeply shamed over pretending to be somebody I was not, fully competent in German, as well as for being so accommodating, against my own best interests. I did glean enough from his German to comprehend that von Trott was repeating the same advice he had given at the Waldorf Astoria, namely that we should come to an agreement with the *Ariseurs*.

For this first meeting with von Trott in Berlin, neither my rational mind nor my level of German was up to challenging him. It was just easier for me to fall into line. What if the stakes were higher, such as during the Nazi era? What a pushover I would have been! Would I have been one of those Jews coerced by the Nazis to find other Jews who were hiding? I hope I would have killed myself before it came to that. (Yes, dear reader, Joanne's thoughts take her to those gruesome scenarios.)

Afterwards, Hans Frank took me aside for a little chat.

"I don't agree with von Trott's advice to negotiate with the *Ariseurs*. What's more, the recent changes to the restitution laws should be making it less difficult to achieve restitution for properties that, like 16 Wallstrasse, were lost through forced auctions. Let us plan to speak again about your case in a relatively near future."

Hans Frank's benevolent attitude having calmed me somewhat, it now was time for me finally to visit 16 Wallstrasse. By good fortune, I had another German friend, Kerstin Brichtswein, who was eager to show me around various sights of the German capital, 16 Wallstrasse included.

Originally, Peter Stritzke introduced me to Kerstin, a medical student who ended up living with us for several months in New York while she gathered data for her PhD. Kerstin's thesis involved the methodology of brain imaging used for my research. When she lived with us, I was extremely preoccupied with my father's medical deterioration, so I was unable to spend as much time with her as I would have liked. I, therefore, regarded Kerstin's generosity in being willing to guide me around Berlin as an incomparable gift.

Berlin was Kerstin's hometown. Walking around there together, we spoke a mix of German and English. While her English was superior to my German, she liked to hear me trying out my *Deutsch*, and was kind and patient about it.

First, we enjoyed a relaxing stroll through the Tiergarten, a large park in the center of Berlin. Founded as a private game reserve in the sixteenth century, the park comprises lovely trails through wooded areas with lakes, streams, and a zoo. Outside the more hectic parts of the German capital, Kerstin and I were, I think, privately happy to be in each other's company in this setting, though we did not say a lot to each other. The Tiergarten's abundant greenery and fresh air had a calming effect on me.

We walked out of the Tiergarten through the Brandenburg Gate onto Unter den Linden, the tree-lined street that was to be incorporated into Albert Speer's East-West Axis for Hitler's maniacal dream city, Welthauptstadt Germania, or World Capital Germania. He wasn't even going to call it Berlin anymore. Before we turned south onto Wilhelmstrasse, I looked back, awestruck, at the Brandenburg Gate. It occurred to me that it was the most emotionally significant landmark I had ever seen. No monument in the United States, not even the Lincoln Memorial, had moved me so powerfully.

I realized I should be pulling myself away. I did not want to have to explain my intense and troubling emotions to Kerstin. Had she noticed that I was transfixed? Or did she think I hesitated to get moving because the street we were about to walk down—once home to the Reich Chancellery—was at the time still full of leftover rubble and potholes from the war?

I turned away from the Brandenburg Gate, only to have it return to my mind's eye as it appeared in newsreel images of a bombed and broken Berlin. The skin on my arms prickled. I was already overcome with images of violence, yet we were only at the beginning of our walk along the road that once was the capital of hell on earth.

We arrived at Prinz-Albrecht-Strasse, where the Gestapo had been headquartered. After the war, the street was renamed Nieder-kirchnerstrasse for the East German heroine Käthe Niederkirchner, shot dead in 1944 at the Ravensbrück concentration camp for resisting Hitler. The East Germans had destroyed most of the Gestapo headquarters but left their dreaded torture chambers intact. The surrounding areas were established as an educational and memorial site called the Topography of Terror. In 1993 it looked like a lunar landscape, save for the mound of earth dug up to lay bare the former underground torture chambers.

Leaving the sunshine behind, Kerstin and I descended a wooden stairway into the Gestapo's excavated torture cellar. We walked along the makeshift corridor. Each cell bore an explanatory plaque with the names of individual Nazi-era Germans who had been hunted down, arrested, and then executed for resisting the Nazis.

Among them, I recognized the image of Adam von Trott zu Solz, the relative of our attorney.[6] It was grimly fascinating. After a time, Kerstin decided we had both had enough. Gently, she took my hand before walking me up the wooden stairs back into the daylight where we could breathe deeply that fresh *Berliner Luft*.

Outside, my eye caught a concrete block, a remnant of the Berlin Wall propped against the cornerstone of the former Gestapo prison. The two dull gray ruins, angled side to side, looked like tombstones for repressive German regimes. For a moment, I was stilled, grief-stricken over the catastrophically blackened decades. Then my empathy evaporated as I recalled a diary entry I made during my 1967 trip: "I was moved until I realized the Germans brought this on themselves. They are still getting away rather easily." I had concerns about the new generations of Germans. Given the scale of what had happened, and of the crimes committed, was a determination to do and be better sufficiently widespread? Throughout the 16 Wallstrasse case, I was to ponder such questions.

Wallstrasse was now just a few blocks away. The street took its name from a rampart built in the mid-1600s, but it had since turned into a commercial center. As I first saw it, I could have sworn it was a charming nineteenth-century street, though in reality, nearly all of the buildings had suffered some damage during the war and subsequently gone through meticulous reconstruction.

My family's commercial building at 16 Wallstrasse was built in 1908 on the former site of a Baroque-era fortress. Many people had told me that 16 Wallstrasse was an imposing structure, so at first blush, I was disappointed by the modest-sized facade.

Kerstin, though, said, "Come over here and look. The front is only one short side of the whole structure. See? The building is a very, very long rectangle." When I looked, I saw Kerstin was correct. The building, almost as deep as a New York City block, had real grandeur.

"I'm not sure if you realize this," Kerstin continued, "but for us East Germans, Wallstrasse is notorious. Right next door to your building, with the address 17–22, was the headquarters of the East German secret police, the Stasi's Division of Foreign Trade."[7]

My family's former building had recently been placed under the management of the unified German government. We discovered it was locked and stood waiting, hoping somebody would come out and allow us inside. A young man carrying cardboard boxes appeared in the vestibule. We caught the door he opened before it closed, and he then remained with us in the confined space. Speaking German, Kerstin introduced me.

"This is Dr. Joanne Intrator from New York. She's a descendant of the family that owned this building before the Nazis." I imagined the young man must have been wondering what the phrase "owned this building before the Nazis" meant. Kerstin's German words made a surreal impression on me, as though she were talking about somebody else, a stranger. I was not quite fully processing that she was talking about *my* family being victims of the Nazis. I imagined the young German man figuring out that I was Jewish. Surely, he had some understanding that with German unification, it had become possible for victims of the Nazis and/or the Communists to claim properties in former East Germany.

The moment briefly shared in this cramped space felt suffocating. I guessed the man was in his late twenties, and obviously had no direct connection to Nazi crimes committed fifty years before. His face looked unperturbed, but I wondered if he might be resentful. This fleeting encounter gave me pause. I was becoming wary of the potential impact of restitution on the lives of ordinary, contemporary Germans who felt unconnected to the Nazi Reich. I imagined thousands of similar scenarios playing themselves out in various locales throughout former East Germany. What magnitude of hatred of Jews might resurface because of the vast sums involved in these property restitution lawsuits? Would that happen to me?

Kerstin and I, now inside the building, took some time to explore. In total, the property included four interconnected structures separated by three interior courtyards.

At intervals, my mind returned to the young German man in the vestibule. He became an archetype for me, and I feared that his type was going to wind up with intense future resentment of Jews. Kerstin interrupted my anxious projections, though, by saying things such as, "Look at those high ceilings and huge windows!" If the facade had first tricked me into thinking the building was smaller than it really was, the interior dimensions were now powerfully bringing home to me what an imposing edifice my grandfather and his nephew had once owned.

"Do we dare have a look in the basement?" Kerstin asked.

Downstairs we found no ghosts, no hidden document troves, just a faint musty smell and a faucet dripping in a corner. We had a little laugh. Back outside, Kerstin suggested, "Let's walk over to the Lindenoper. I want to show you one of my favorite places in the whole city, the Opern-Café."

We had a pleasant, leisurely twenty-minute walk back to Unter den Linden and the Berlin State Opera. Kerstin was giddy, leading me into the café, situated in a stunning Baroque palace. She slowed down and made sure I got a good look at what was, by far, the most sumptuous arrangement of colorful cakes, tortes, and petit fours I have ever seen. There was a luscious-looking Hungarian Dobos torte, a seductive Linzer torte, gorgeous formal German cakes, almond sponge cakes layered with chocolate creams, and elegant, powder-sugar-dusted berry fruit tarts.

As luck had it, it was still plum cake season. The heady, familiar combination of fragrances of the rich, baked, concentrated fruits and of the heavenly buttered crust carried me back forty years, to when my Oma Rikka rescued me from a threatening dog and consoled me with plum cake afterwards. I thought of how my father must have eaten in places like this, perhaps after classes at the Kaiser Wilhelm University across the street, or with his parents after a Sunday afternoon stroll down the "Ku'damm."

Seated on a posh velvet settee, surrounded by potted palms,

Kerstin and I noted the finer points of the interior decoration, including the crystal chandeliers and the decorative wallpaper. At one point Kerstin announced, to my delight, that she might return to New York to finish her dissertation. As we were walking out through the Opern-Café's front door, she pointed and said, "Look over there."

Kerstin seemed to be directing my gaze to something close by, but I did not immediately understand what I was supposed to be looking at. "Come with me," she said.

Just steps away, we were standing over the Israeli sculptor Micha Ullman's underground work, *The Empty Library*. The artwork serves as a reminder of the evil of the Nazis' book burnings, some of which took place at this spot on Bebelplatz.[8] The memorial's subterranean portions, seen through a square glass plate in the ground, consist of starkly empty white bookshelves. Two brass plaques above ground include lines from Heinrich Heine's tragedy *Almansor*: "Where they burn books, in the end they also burn people."

This, then, was the city of Berlin—an emotional chiaroscuro of comfort and terror. I stopped by 185 Kurfürstendamm one more time to say goodbye to the building. I was disappointed that I couldn't enter it, but some construction prevented me. I could vividly picture my family's former apartment there, having gazed at family photos of it over the years.

Before I could return home to life with Greg and Benjamin, and to my hospital work, I had one last meeting, with Joseph Weinfeld, who was financing the case.

Our benefactor was a short, rotund, dapper older man who met me for drinks in the Kempinski's bar lounge, a cozy space off the main lobby. Weinfeld awaited me in a club chair at a round, highly polished, ebony-black table for two. He stood up as I approached, and we shook hands. Off to the right was a huge vase filled with an arrangement of brilliantly colored birds-of-paradise.

At first, we made lighthearted conversation about the new Berlin. Eventually, I asked him what I most wanted to learn. "Why are you financing our case?"

"Well, you know, not every survivor or descendant has been as lucky as I've been, and I want to help people who lost so much and now need assistance. I'm able to front their costs, and happy to do it."

He winked at me, then continued. "It also happens to make good business sense. Berlin is booming. The German government will be moving the capital from Bonn to Berlin before the end of the twentieth century. Center-city Berlin properties acquired now are going to be selling at a premium in just a short time. And I must say, I'm exceedingly optimistic about your case."

He took a sip of cognac before saying something that left me stunned. With the casualness of a long-established co-conspirator, he said, "Once 16 Wallstrasse is sold, I can help you move your share of the money to Switzerland. It hasn't yet been determined if money acquired from restitution cases in the former East Germany will be taxed as income in the United States."

As Weinfeld went on describing the advantages of having money in Switzerland, I fancied I was whispering with Peter Lorre or Orson Welles in a 1940s film noir, complete with an overhead fan, a piano bar, and potted palms. I listened with rapt attention bordering on disbelief while burning with curiosity about how he had survived Buchenwald and climbed out of so much loss and hardship to become so successful. But I was not comfortable enough with him to ask so personal a question.

My return flight to New York was uneventful. Satisfied over

having survived, I deemed my trip a success. Kerstin sent me with gummy bears for Benjamin, which I presented to him. And I had to smile warmly, because after I had worried so much, for so long, there was no end to the stories Ben told me about the exciting adventures he and Greg shared while I was away.

The more I described my trip and Berlin to Greg and various friends, the more I emphasized the exhilarating, glamorous aspects of the German capital and the less I focused on Nazis, book burnings, Gestapo torture chambers, and the Topography of Terror. Many friends were aghast over my enthusiasm for the city, while Greg was profoundly skeptical of it.

Eventually, I realized I was way too exuberant. With the benefit of hindsight, I understood what was going on. Temporarily, I had entered a counterphobic state in order to protect myself, block out fears, and thus be able to function effectively. One could say I was too afraid to be afraid.

Classic Joanne.

10 Eggs and Kafka

The clarity I was able to bring to my autumn 1993 Berlin trip helped me overcome the bewilderment and shame of my previous journey to that city in 1967, but once back in New York, I went through a heartbreaking health-care-related calamity.

I had been working at VA hospitals for seven years, committed to improving the quality of our veterans' care. For drug-dependent spinal cord patients in the Bronx VA, I created a substance-abuse treatment unit that was locked to prevent illicit drug use. The Bronx VA has its own police force, and I worked closely with the chief to keep banned drugs out of our facility. There were, nevertheless, rumors of drugs being sold.

A middle-of-the-night phone call in early 1994 ripped me out of my sleep. I heard the hushed voice of a co-worker calling from the hospital. A young man under my care, a heroin addict, had died. After many weeks in our hospital, he had been getting better and was close to discharge. But the security of our unit had been breached, and the patient was able to get his hands on this fearsome poison. He had injected a dose that his body could formerly, but no longer, tolerate, and it killed him.

Horrified, I obsessed, faulting myself, unable to understand how our security had been breached. Deeply saddened by this death of a US veteran, I wondered how much longer I would be able to work at the hospital. Though the veteran's death was not my fault, I blamed myself for it, feeling, however irrationally, I had not done enough.

Meanwhile, I unexpectedly received a letter about an additional Intrator family legal matter pending in Germany. Attorney Karl-Heinz Hintz of Celle, a German city south of Hamburg, having learned of my father's recent death, wrote to me to introduce himself.

Though I had vague recollections of a pending Nazi-era business claim, I learned from Hintz's letter that he represented my father's and Alex's interests in Intrator-Schimmel, an egg import-export company that my grandfather had co-owned but was stripped from him by the Nazis.

It occurred to me that whatever proof I could turn up of Nazi antisemitism in this matter could potentially be used to help prove antisemitism in the Nazi theft of 16 Wallstrasse. So I returned to my late father's home in Queens to search in the file cabinets for relevant documentation.

I found an "Intrator & Schimmel" dossier crammed with correspondence between my father and Hintz's law firm. The material had more than a whiff of *Waiting for Godot* about it, as my father and Uncle Alex had filed their compensation claim back in the mid-1950s, but the case had yet to be resolved.

The earliest document was a 1954 affidavit sworn in Geneva, Switzerland, by Intrator-Schimmel's former bookkeeper and office supervisor, Selig Riegelhaupt, who worked for my grandfather from 1919 through the 1930s. In his affidavit, Riegelhaupt attested that before the Nazis destroyed it, the Intrator-Schimmel egg business was turning a profit of about $300,000 annually. Adjusted for inflation, that would be about $4.7 million in 2020 dollars.

Yearly, the company had been importing between fifteen hundred and two thousand train wagons of eggs from Galicia, Poland, to Germany. Beginning April 1, 1933, Nazi boycotts of Jewish businesses damaged the company's earnings. In 1935, Intrator-Schimmel was forced out of business altogether when the Nazi government denied import-export licenses to Jews.

That my grandfather was a financial victim of Nazi antisemitism when the Nazis stripped him of his import-export license—only because he was Jewish—could not have been any more straightforward. I sent the Intrator-Schimmel documentation to Dorothea von Hülsen, our assigned attorney in the 16 Wallstrasse case. I had yet to meet her in person but understood that she supported von Trott's repugnant notion of playing "Let's make a deal!"

Von Hülsen's response was Kafkaesque. Jack and I had, one year ago, already sent her all the documentation needed to prove we were our grandfather's and father's legal heirs, yet in this reply, she asked for our inheritance certificates from the "eggs lawyer," Hintz. Her response made no mention of any progress in our 16 Wallstrasse case. Von Hülsen's failure to use the evidence I sent—or, at least, to explain why she would not be using it—was annoying.

Over time, the Intrator-Schimmel case wound up opening a window for me onto a little-known, ugly corner of Nazi history. What I learned was that the Nazis had a targeted abhorrence of "Jewish eggs." My grandfather fit into this dark history, as it was his success in the egg business in Galicia that had enabled him to move his young family to Berlin. Once the Nazis succeeded in driving all Jews out of commerce in eggs, Berlin's Nazi paper, *Der Angriff*, declared that specific business sector to be *Judenrein*—cleaned out of Jews.[1] One 1936 advertisement boasted, "Now you can have Aryan eggs again for Easter!"

Meanwhile, in June 1994, the German Ministry of Justice issued an encouraging "Commentary." Properties like 16 Wallstrasse, lost through forced auctions, were now going to be included in the restitution law. It certainly sounded as though a barrier to our achieving restitution had fallen.

My secret father figure, Hans Frank, then wrote to von Trott, suggesting the time was ripe to present our case to the LAROV. In English translation, LAROV stands for "The State Office for the Settlement of Unresolved Property Issues." I had heard that the LAROV was inundated with filings from around the world. Hans asked von Trott how, in light of these recent developments, his strategy in our 16 Wallstrasse case would change. Von Trott did not reply.

Likewise, our inquiries to Joseph Weinfeld about the status of the 16 Wallstrasse case went unanswered. What to do?

Hans Frank was a far more *gemütlich*-seeming attorney than von Trott. If I had had the funds, I would have wanted him to be the Intrator family's sole attorney for the 16 Wallstrasse case. As a compromise, I asked if Hans would serve as a paid consultant and advisor for us. He accepted, saying during a subsequent meeting, "Well, Joanne, I believe doing something that will more strongly draw von Trott's attention to your family members' plights could prove helpful. I'm going to be drafting a legal brief for this case. To that brief, I'd like to attach a summary of your grandparents' life in Berlin from 1933 through 1941. Do you think you'll be able to put such a summary together?"

"Of course," I responded.

I hurled myself into the assignment. Through the research for it, I learned a great deal more about how my paternal grandparents struggled under the Nazis.

"Something else I recommend," Hans said, "is for you to plan another trip to Berlin. Let them know you're alive and kicking."

Not long after that meeting, he sent a brief titled "The Persecution of Mr. Jakob Intrator" to von Trott as well as to von Trott's colleagues Lammek and von Hülsen.

To his brief, Hans attached compelling documentation, including a Nazi government agency's "Security Order," sent to my grandfather, demanding all of his foreign assets in payment of the "Reich's Flight Tax," a confiscatory emigration tax then being imposed on Jews. Hans also attached documentation of the Aryanization of an additional four properties that the Nazis stole from my grandfather in Berlin. (After the war, those four properties fell within West Berlin. My father received compensation for them in the 1960s, though he got only a fraction of their worth.)

Hans Frank's brief concluded, "The totality of these repressive measures demonstrates that at the time of the forced auction of 16 Wallstrasse, the Nazi regime had financially stripped Mr. Intrator of his ability to defend himself against a forced auction."

Von Hülsen acknowledged receipt of Hans Frank's brief. But instead of addressing its contents or actually *doing* something with them, she announced that the 16 Wallstrasse case was being put on a back burner. Von Trott and Lammek—representing the Berglases—had made a decision: they were going to concentrate on going after restitution for the major center-city Berlin building at 1 Hausvogteiplatz, which the Nazis had stolen from the Berglases. There were no Aryan counterclaims.

That meant the case would be easier for the attorneys to pursue and conclude.

At some intellectual remove, I could understand why von Trott decided to pursue that strategy. However, he had told us that our attorney would be von Hülsen. So why couldn't *she* do something with the documentation I had sent to her? How long was it going to take to achieve some measure of justice in this 16 Wallstrasse case, anyway? Aldous Huxley once said, "Every ambition is doomed to frustration at the hands of a skeleton." I understood what he meant.

I was nursing hard feelings against "our" attorneys. They seemed to be playing a three wise monkeys game of "see no evil, hear no evil, speak no evil." They were refusing to adequately consider the factual details proving that the Nazis stripped my grandfather of 16 Wallstrasse through antisemitic Aryanization schemes. The fact that my Heim & Gerken adversaries in the case were the *Ariseurs* was itself a significant clue. The meaning of the word *Ariseur* had finally seeped into my brain.

Piecing together what was going on with these Berlin attorneys, I wondered how insignificant they considered the Intrator claim to be in comparison to restitution claims filed by our Berglas relatives. The Berglases, while part owners of 16 Wallstrasse, had owned other properties for which it appeared it would be much easier to achieve restitution. Jack and I, meanwhile, each only held a 3.15 percent share in 16 Wallstrasse.

The Intrator-Schimmel egg matter apparently was of no consequence to the Berlin lawyer. I felt left out of the deliberations.

At this stage, my enthusiasm for returning to Berlin had waned. But Hans Frank had given me inspiring food for thought when he said, "My hope is that you going to Berlin again will help stir things up. And there's a legal point that's crucial for you to understand, Joanne. You are adamantly opposed to settling with the Aryan claimants. And as you know, I support you, and don't blame you for that. So please realize that your shares in the property give you and your brother veto power over any move to negotiate with the *Ariseurs*. You hold the cards. I am urging you to return to Berlin."

~

It would be about six months before I actually returned to Germany. In the meantime, Jack and I attended to the emotionally fraught preparations for selling our parents' home. In the weeks leading up to New Year's Eve 1995, I frequently returned to Forest Hills. Fifty years were rushing to an end. I set aside generous chunks of time for myself, wanting to be able to spend unhurried moments in each room, opening every drawer and closet, looking at the remaining items, signifiers of our parents' lives.

From the bedrooms to the basement spaces, I visually memorized everything—every item, no matter how small—so that later on, I would be able to walk in my imagination through our parents' house, the home where Jack and I grew up. To this day, I can construct every inch in my mind's eye.

Shutting the front door of that humble dwelling for the last time was almost as painful as watching each of our parents' coffins being lowered into their graves.

11 Deceptions and Cruelty

On January 25, 1995, I returned to Berlin. When I arrived and throughout my time there, which fell during the fiftieth anniversary of the liberation of Auschwitz, the weather was bone-chillingly cold as well as unrelentingly drab and gray.

How appropriate, I thought as the plane landed. Obviously, I had conflicting feelings about this trip.

Ben was now nine. "I'm going on a mission" was typical of the excuses I gave him for my upcoming absence. Even to my ears, though, these excuses fell flat. "It'll only be four days," I would add lamely. Kissing him goodbye, it felt as though I were going to be gone an eternity.

Am I worrying too much? I worried to myself.

Upon arriving in Berlin, I went to the Savoy, right off the Kurfürstendamm on Fasanenstrasse. The Savoy Hotel, built in 1929, survived the war and was occupied by the British as their headquarters in the divided city. Among the Savoy's other guests through history were Greta Garbo, Henry Miller, and Thomas Mann. I enjoyed speaking a little German with the taxi driver on the way to the hotel. And heading into Berlin's Charlottenburg neighborhood, I found myself feeling like I knew my way around.

But I was haunted by thoughts of my family attending the synagogue on this same street before the Nazis ordered it shut down and then, on Kristallnacht, demolished. What exactly were these legendary, comfortable hotel surroundings, to me, for this trip?

I needed conditions that would help me, psychologically, to do battle with my attorneys. My 1993 Berlin trip had featured exceptionally mild, sunny weather; Kerstin's friendly company; and the fatherly counsel of my advisor, Hans Frank. All of that, and much more—including unforgettable Berlin Philharmonic concerts, scrumptious tortes, and the cosmopolitan energy—had muted my association of Berlin with the colossal personal fiasco that was my 1967 trip. But I was on guard against feeling too comfortable here now. I needed to keep in mind that this was the city Hitler, Himmler, Goebbels, Eichmann, and Mengele viewed as their Jew-free Aryan capital. To achieve that they would stop at nothing, as history sadly proved. Accordingly, I discovered a good purpose for this dank, frigid, gloomy weather of January 1995: it helped me focus my thoughts and emotions on Berlin's dark side, empowering me to retain my determination to stand up for myself and my family.

My meeting with von Trott was scheduled for several hours after my arrival at the Savoy Hotel. While luxuriating in a nice warm bath, I reviewed some of the details of our 16 Wallstrasse case. *I'm here to get updated on the status of our case*, I reminded myself. *And as Hans Frank advised me, one goal should be to get von Trott and his colleagues to pay more meaningful attention to my family's Nazi-era history. But there are business blocks to that. What is at the core of these blocks?*

I gathered my thoughts, then formulated the answer for myself: *The Intrator and Berglas families might have different goals. Sure, the Berglases, too, are parties to the 16 Wallstrasse case. They signed the same Sonex agreement we did. And yes, their relatives, too, suffered during the war.* But overall, I imagined the Berglases had prepared to escape from the Nazis far better than my grandfather Jakob Intrator. On the

Berglas side, they knew to get some of their assets out of Germany early. When the time came for them to escape, they had something to escape *with*, and somewhere to escape *to*. By contrast, my grandfather had waited until after the last minute, lost every *pfennig* to the Nazis, saw his health plunge, and then, essentially, didn't survive his escape, dying the day after his arrival in New York.

Still, I thought, *don't the Berglases want to know that history as much as I do?*

Another voice inside my head countered, *Of course, but they, too, are aging like Alex and want matters resolved.*

I recognized that the 16 Wallstrasse case was far more complex than the Hausvogtei property, due to the *Ariseurs'* counterclaim on the building. In sum, 16 Wallstrasse was everything to us, while to the Berglases, it was only one case among several. Nevertheless, my mind would not stop posing questions. *What does it mean to go from being well-to-do to being completely desperate as a result of cold-blooded persecution?* I wondered. I was developing a habit of trying to *feel* my way into the shoes of my Holocaust-era Jewish relatives.

As I was imagining their feelings and their point of view, and as my bath was coming to an end, I vowed to dig my heels in. *You are going to insist on uncovering as many details as possible of the forced auction of 16 Wallstrasse.*

Before leaving the Savoy for my meeting with von Trott, I enjoyed an *echt* German breakfast like the ones I remembered from my childhood: crusty rolls with soft-boiled eggs and *Milchkaffee*—coffee with warmed milk.

Guess who I finally met when I entered von Trott's offices that day?

Dorothea von Hülsen, my attorney. She was pleasant looking enough. But she offered me the most tepid of uninspiring handshakes, which did nothing to assuage my sense of uneasiness. She was supposed to be providing independent representation for us in the Intrator claim to 16 Wallstrasse. But then something popped out at me as I perused von Trott's letterhead while waiting for our meeting to begin.

Von Hülsen had her own private practice specializing in restitution claims. But listed on von Trott's letterhead as a partner in this firm was the name Dr. Karl-Christoph von Hülsen— Dorothea's husband. What exactly was the relationship between the big von Trott firm and Dorothea's smaller practice? Had they just thrown her a bit of business?

Whatever the answer to *that* question, Dorothea von Hülsen had thus far invariably toed the bigger law firm's line that Jack and I should agree to negotiate with the *Ariseurs*. Somewhere between the pit of my stomach, my heart, and my brain was an increasing awareness that this woman might not, nor would be able to, stand up to the Berglases' attorneys, Lammek and von Trott, on behalf of the Intrator family.

In the conference room, von Hülsen and I joined Lammek and von Trott.

"May I suggest we speak English?" I asked, not wanting to wait for von Trott to assume that speaking German would be OK.

Von Trott then began. "Some pertinent background," he said. "The LAROV has a backlog of one hundred eighty thousand restitution claims to process. In the wake of the reunification of Berlin, a glut of vacant buildings has come on the market, with a result that 16 Wallstrasse is worth only sixty percent of what one could have gotten for it two years ago. And the German government, which is paying to maintain that property while managing it ahead of the case being resolved, is pressing for the building to be sold to private owners."

These numbers and circumstances meant nothing to me. What I

wanted to know was, exactly *how* did the *Ariseurs* steal this building from my family?

Von Trott continued. "Going to court to challenge Heim & Gerken would take a great deal of money. To get them to drop their claim to 16 Wallstrasse would cost between thirty and fifty percent of the sale price."

In a monotone, von Trott elaborated on those thoughts, and details about those thoughts, and then more and more details until— maybe it was jet lag—I caught myself nodding forward before jerking my head back so I would stay awake. Von Trott did not blink, just droned right on.

Out of the corner of my eye, out the window over Kurfürstendamm, I saw it had started snowing, which naturally made the mother in me think of how Ben would soon be setting off with Greg to the Killington ski resort in Vermont. Rapidly enough, I brought my mind from the Green Mountain State back to this Berlin attorney's conference room, where von Trott was saying, "The wisest, most practical thing to do with 16 Wallstrasse is to reach a quick settlement in the case. The best way forward would be to not even contest the Heim & Gerken heirs' claim. Get the building sold, and then split the money between your family members and the Heim & Gerken heirs. Agreeing to *that* process will move the 16 Wallstrasse case to the top of the LAROV's pile."

Von Trott plainly was unaware of how callous he sounded. How could he imagine that I would agree to split the money from the sale of 16 Wallstrasse with members of the Aryan family who had stolen the building from my Jewish grandfather?

The next thing von Trott said, though delivered in his droning monotone, hit my ears like a thunderclap. "There's a rumor that inside 16 Wallstrasse, Nazi flags were produced."

I was completely floored. "Do you mean to tell me that the Nazi flag was manufactured inside—and I repeat for emphasis—*inside* the building that the Nazis stole from my family?"

He nodded.

How could this information only now be emerging? Von Trott had spent the lion's share of the time allotted for this meeting aggressively pushing for us to settle with the *Ariseurs*, Heim & Gerken, but he was only *now* dropping this bomb as if blandly noting that it had started to snow outside.

I gasped, "Nazi flags! With swastikas. My God!"

Von Trott was silent.

Had von Trott's shock revelation been a sort of Freudian slip? Did he mean to tell me this? What was going on? Until now, I thought his motivations were straightforward and bottom-line driven. Might he be feeling culpable for pressuring the Intrator heirs to negotiate with the *Ariseurs* while keeping concealed from us the dirty secret that enthusiastic Nazi Party members—true believers, swastika flag-makers—had taken part in stealing the building from our family, Aryanizing it through a forced auction?

How did this bombshell not change everything in the case? Why were these attorneys not seeing that it did? Why was von Trott not excited to use this information to our advantage?

Another question: Did I *really* believe that looking across the conference room table towards Clemens Lammek and Dorothea von Hülsen for support, as I did, would really have any good effect? Both had their heads lowered, reading documents. Obedient German children!

I took a breath, then said flatly, "No one but a Nazi could have been mass-producing Nazi flags."

The trio of attorneys seemed uninterested. Von Trott responded nonchalantly, "We have no way of getting Nazi Party member information. And if we *could* determine that the *Ariseurs* of 16 Wallstrasse were Nazi Party members, it wouldn't make any difference in this case, because at the time of the forced auction, so many people were members of the Nazi Party."

What did he mean by that? That just any old person could have gotten an order for the mass production of Nazi flags? Was there not some sort of hierarchy among those who opted into the Nazi Party? Was there no difference between your average Aryan in the street with a lapel pin and somebody who established an entire flag-making company to boost a brutal dictatorship?

I could barely contain myself. It simply *had* to matter to our 16 Wallstrasse case that after Aryans stole our industrial building through a forced auction, the Nazi flag was produced inside. Think of the high-level Nazi Party connections Aryans must have needed in late 1938 to be able to steal a center-city Berlin property from Jewish owners and then get awarded a contract to produce Nazi flags.

"The *Ariseurs* of 16 Wallstrasse, these Heim & Gerken people, who *were* they, exactly?" I asked. Strangely, until this meeting with von Trott, it had not occurred to me to try to find out independently who the Heim and Gerken clans were. Why had I not looked? They were our adversaries in this case, but I had not yet requested any paperwork attesting to what they had done before, during, and after the Holocaust. I must have been stunned, without any agency, waiting for the grownups to do something. I was still under the sway of their authority, and vestiges of the anguish I felt during my lonely 1967 trip to Berlin were still, however subconsciously, stopping me from seeing things as clearly as I should.

With evident impatience, von Trott shook his head and gave a quick flick of his hand, brushing my question away as though he were swatting a fly. I glared at him. I was stunned at his apparent disregard for its impact on me and, more importantly, on the case.

What was his mindset that enabled von Trott to be so blasé about the likelihood that Heim and Gerken had been Nazi Party members? Was this issue not at the core of the work he was supposed to be doing? Yes, during the Third Reich, obedience to the Führer was required and enforced, yet only about 10 percent of the population were actual Nazi Party members.

Von Trott was attempting what I liked to call a "dilution effect," minimizing the importance to my case of the Nazi Party membership of the *Ariseurs* of 16 Wallstrasse. To my face, this lawyer was incorrectly alleging that because "so many people" had been Nazi Party members, the issue could not possibly be of any importance.

From von Trott's junior colleagues, not a peep—as though my desire to learn the truth were out of line. What was I supposed to do? Forget that once *Ariseurs* stole 16 Wallstrasse from my family, they used our building to mass-produce Nazi flags?

Von Trott, I suspected, was using a slippery, disingenuous tactic with me. Not by mere Freudian slip had he come out with this information about the Nazi flag having been produced at 16 Wallstrasse. Rather, he must have thought I likely would find out about it one way or another, so he wanted to protect himself against eventual accusations that he had been derelict in his contractual duty by neglecting to supply me with crucial intelligence about our stolen, Aryanized property. In short, he was covering himself, revealing to me the production of the Nazi flag, then immediately distorting the fact by alleging it to be of no importance.

If my presumption about von Trott's motives was correct, he was straddling a moral fault line. His responsibility to do relevant research was written into our contract, and he was competent to carry out the needed research. And surely before now, he had known about the production of the Nazi flag at 16 Wallstrasse. However, he was *not* mentioning the production of the Nazi flag at 16 Wallstrasse in order to strengthen my position against the *Ariseurs*; he was only mentioning it in order never to be accused of having *not* mentioned it.

Exasperating! I was experiencing a full-on, all-out agonizing simmer. But if I had laid into these attorneys, which they richly deserved, what good would it have done me? At one point, having a moment alone with von Hülsen, I asked, "Did *you* know that the *Ariseurs* used 16 Wallstrasse as a Nazi flag factory?"

"Well, yes, but I hasten to point out that this fact does not prove your grandfather lost the building on account of antisemitism."

That was her alibi for never having told me the Nazi flag was made in our building.

I was livid.

What in von Hülsen's nature, or her circumstances, had kept her from informing me about this momentous crack in the case? Did she feel she knew best? Or, with von Trott and Lammek having more leverage, did she feel she lacked the authority to discuss the subject with me? Given that Jack and I had veto power over decisions in the 16 Wallstrasse case, my expectation that my own assigned attorney would tell me so important a fact as this one was entirely reasonable.

But these attorneys had the goal of selling the building and wrapping the case up as quickly as they could, whereas my goal of stopping the *Ariseurs* from profiting off the situation was becoming ever more significant for me. How dare these German attorneys have kept this Nazi-shielding secret from me!

I now was more worried than ever. Von Hülsen's husband worked with von Trott's firm. Was von Hülsen, therefore, falling into line behind von Trott and not thinking independently, or was she in conflict with the historical role of women in Germany, described as *Kinder, Küche, Kirche*—children, kitchen, and church? That couldn't be, not in the late twentieth century. It had to be about the appearance that the Intrators were being represented independently from the Berglases. But what better way than bringing me into the discussion?

I certainly was in no position to fire her, as I simply did not have the financial resources to sign full-time with Hans Frank or some other attorney. I felt compromised and stuck, dependent on professionals I could not trust.

Just then, von Hülsen surprised me and led me in another direction.

"Why don't you try to find out if any of the tenants at 16 Wallstrasse were Jewish?"

"Why?" I asked.

"The Nazis' antisemitic laws often destroyed Jewish-owned businesses. If Jewish tenants at 16 Wallstrasse lost their businesses through Nazi antisemitism, and so were not able to pay rent to your grandfather, how could he afford the ongoing expenses of the building? This would, possibly, be an explanation of how Nazi antisemitism caused your grandfather to lose the property in a forced auction."

A light bulb went off in my head. Once again, an attorney was giving unintended emphasis to a detail crucial to my case. "Were there Nazi tenants in the building too?" I asked. "If so, is it not correct that under Nazi law, they would have been under no obligation to pay rent to my Jewish grandfather?"

There was a pained silence before I pressed the matter by asking, "Who exactly were they? Before the forced auction, who were the tenants at 16 Wallstrasse?"

Von Hülsen shook her head. "I don't know," she confessed.

Was this feigned ignorance? Was it really so hard to grasp the importance of the answers to these questions? Suddenly, von Hülsen said, "There is a man still living in Berlin who, for forty years, was the *Hausmeister,* the superintendent at 16 Wallstrasse."

"Do you know how I can get in touch with him?"

"No."

I was now really annoyed, not to mention suspicious. Why were these key details being offered in such a slow drip? Who was research-ing this case? Anybody? Was von Hülsen giving me some sort of fake-out charade of being forthcoming? Had she known about this 16 Wallstrasse *Hausmeister* before? If so, might I have had a chance to contact him?

How eager I felt, now, to find this superintendent, in order to learn whether he knew anything about the Nazi flag production issue. But I could see that *this* day, I was not going to learn more from any of these attorneys. At a time when I needed to stay sharp, they were wearing me down with their personality styles, rattling off so-called facts devoid of useful detail. Vexed and frazzled, I yearned to escape from their crazy-making, guileful insincerity.

I returned to my hotel, retreating under the bed's comforting down covers, much as I used to do to escape from my parents and their innumerable challenges. The lawyers' information tease had me slip-ping into a revolving state of confusion, rage, and defeat. I was too exhausted to sort it all out. Of course, I was somewhat foggy from jet lag, but on top of that, the innuendos about the Nazi flag and the *Hausmeister* and the tenants at 16 Wallstrasse were starting to make me feel lost and ungrounded, the way I felt when I was supposed to meet the porter in 1967.

Hoping to distract myself, I turned on the television. Every available station was broadcasting programming about Auschwitz, in observation of the fiftieth anniversary of the liberation of the remaining prisoners there.

There was no way I could escape the topic, so I decided on a more personal confrontation with it. Throwing off the warm quilt, I called the front desk to hire a car and driver. What I was about to do was travel twenty-two miles north of Berlin, to the site of the former concentration camp in the Sachsenhausen district of the town of Oranienburg, minutes away from Berlin.

At the time, I had not discovered the letters that revealed my relative Max Karp had been taken to Sachsenhausen. Unable to read through all of the letters in my father's files before his house was sold, I brought them to my office with the hopes of photocopying them. At first, I searched for any information about Wallstrasse and evidence of direct antisemitism for the legal case; eventually, I would delve into the personal letters, including those pertaining to the fates of my family members.

Had I but known about Max—how much more terrible and poignant my visit would have been! As it was, though, I felt powerfully compelled to make this trip.

Do what you're most afraid of, Joanne. Just do it. Get dressed and go. It's not the first camp you've been to. Remember how angry you were in 1967 when you realized Dachau was only ten miles outside Munich, so they all had to have known what was happening? Go get angry.

I also wanted to pay my respects to the murdered Jews. Given the overwhelming enormity of the crimes committed against them at the camp, paying respects was a small gesture. Nonetheless, I was going to do so. Instead of retreating to my bed, dominated by my anxieties, I felt impelled to do the opposite.

I arrived at the gate with its sadistic taunt: *Arbeit macht frei.*

"Work sets you free." In a cold rain, I waded through slush and mud, walking from barrack to barrack.

In 1936, the Nazis used Jewish slaves to build this camp, this *Konzentrationslager*. Heinrich Himmler—the "Reichsführer of the Schutzstaffel"—conceived of Sachsenhausen as a prototype and testing ground for all other concentration camps. As the Reich was metastasizing, Himmler in 1938 moved the central administration for all concentration camps from Berlin to Oranienburg.

My driver had come onto the grounds but kept an appropriate distance behind me. I did not see other people at Sachsenhausen this day. Entering a drab building, I found myself in a damp room that stank of mold. Here, I learned, Nazi doctors tortured Jews in the name of scientific inquiry. The white-tiled room had antiquated medical equipment hung on its walls, as well as an examination table for experiments and "medical autopsy." From many years of poring over photos, articles, and books about rooms like this, I was not unfamiliar with the setup.[1] I had forced myself out of a warm, cozy hotel room into the world of my nightmares. And now this Sachsenhausen torture chamber seemed perfectly designed to overwhelm my well-honed counterphobic strategies. It was giving me considerable pause, but I managed to push myself forward through this disquieting concentration camp footslog.

The central question remained: How could so many Germans, men and women both—including doctors, lawyers, teachers, tradesmen, bakers, shopkeepers, restaurant owners, and waiters—have set aside their everyday ethics, education, and understanding of society to become murderers of Jews? That question was at the heart of my enduring interest in studying cold, ruthless people who lack all empathy. It is what led me to conduct a study on psychopaths' processing of emotional language.

Were Nazi physicians similar to the psychopaths I studied? Or had they only morally devolved under the specialized conditions created by Adolf Hitler? What were these Nazi doctors like before 1933? These torture chambers, these killing rooms, required a pervasive absence of empathy or some hardwired theory that dehumanized Jews and others. Once the Nazis came to power, did previously normal-seeming German doctors believe that the faux-medical barbarities they perpetrated on Jews, Slavs, Roma, and homosexuals were justified by those "others" medically contaminating the Nordic ideal? For many individuals who find themselves in a Nazi-like social environment, rationalization often is safer than saying no to barbarity. Rationalization was facilitated by particular psychodynamics relevant to Germans.

The apparent paradox of intelligence and culture on the one hand and murderous, sadistic behavior on the other is present not just within German society before and during World War II but also within other nationalities subject to authoritarian regimes. The power wielded by such regimes warps the natural interaction of conscious and unconscious thoughts, manifesting in primitive behaviors no longer kept in check by whatever conscience a person had.

In early development, a child faced with an authoritarian parent (one who requires strict obedience) perceives that approval will come only if their parents' expectations are complied with; resistance will not be tolerated. Such children learn to perceive their parents' wishes more clearly than their own. We all know that unlike other mammals, humans are more helpless and dependent, requiring more time in the care of their parents, leaving the child little choice but to conform. Longings and rebellions do not disappear but are subordinated and suppressed. In time their persistence is regarded as a threat to the child's compliant facade, even seen as immoral or perverse. As development unfolds, the child's ability to perceive not only their own feelings but those of others fades. Consequently, during late adolescence, the task of formulating an authentic identity is beyond reach.

Feelings are at the foundation of identity. Within the suppressed atmosphere of an authoritarian upbringing, young people hunger for an ideology that offers a defined, glamorous, or powerful identity. At the same time, beneath the impeccable facade develops—perhaps is even cultivated—a remote distance, often perceived as an air of superiority. On occasion, however, long-suppressed fundamental wishes, now suffused with rage, emerge in a characteristic viciousness and taste for perversion—a characteristic of Nazi Germany, especially among its leaders, and certainly among those who presided over the concentration camps. Perversion here means taking pleasure out of inflicting pain.

At least since the chancellorship of Otto von Bismarck in the late nineteenth century, authoritarian rule permeated much of the German culture down to the individual family. Authority was to be followed; resistance was unthinkable. At every level, compliance became almost automatic. The rage generated by such compliance as it emerged could be directed towards the noncompliant or at an imagined foreign power. Such a force empowered both the unification of Germany in 1871 and its subsequent imperialism. German dominance was sanctioned by the highest authority, and German aggression ignited the Great War and its savage conclusion in the Versailles Treaty in 1919, meant to disarm and punish a still-threatening Germany. After the country's humiliating defeat in World War I, the authoritarian soil from which Germany's Nazi Party grew was highly fertile ground. The defeat was manipulated into a striving for superiority, Hitler using the myth of a German master race. His chosen people, Aryans, would psychically merge with him and, subliminally, create a force outside the limits of life and death to become the thousand-year Reich.

To consolidate his following, Hitler needed an outside enemy. The long history of German antisemitism made Jews the ideal perpetrators. "It is them, not us": this well-honed, centuries-old strategy binds groups of like-minded people who feel victimized, offering their psyche some stability, if only temporarily. Through an unconscious psychological dynamic, what is intolerable inside a person in the group, such as a sense of failure or weakness, gets projected on the designated "other," and then the "other" is attacked. A bully does it in the playground; Hitler did it in places like Sachsenhausen. The doctors saw their role as ridding the German people of the contaminants corrupting the German ideal.

Trudging on through the sodden muck of Sachsenhausen, and deeply feeling the weight of this place where Nazis perfected their use of gas chambers, I suffered through waves of dread. While I was out there in the marrow-chilling cold among the desolate barracks, vaguely formed thoughts and their accompanying negative emotions free-floated through me. Doubts about the importance of my case. Flickering impressions that, perhaps, the attorneys, the Berglases, or both were right to want to get the case settled quickly, even if that meant negotiating with the *Ariseurs.*

Yet I found myself obsessing again over the *Ariseurs* of 16 Wallstrasse. After they stole our building, what exactly had they done on Kristallnacht? What were the Heim & Gerken *Ariseurs* who stole my Jewish family's building doing, thinking, and feeling when the Nazis imprisoned six thousand Jews *here*, in Sachsenhausen, in the wake of Kristallnacht?

But there was more than the question of what the *Ariseurs* were doing on Kristallnacht. Another element in my swirling thoughts was the vague notion that 16 Wallstrasse was *just a building*. Nobody died as a direct result of it being stolen from Jewish owners.

Then, too, there were my feelings about the Nazi flag having been mass-produced at 16 Wallstrasse. As I was thinking about it at Sachsenhausen, the information regarding the Nazi flag seemed like some paltry crumb I could follow (or not) towards more crumbs, Hansel-and-Gretel style, not knowing whether the crumbs would lead me out of the forest or into an oven.

Nonetheless, despite doubts that troubled me at various times, now resurfacing at Sachsenhausen, I had always wound up determined to fight on. And it was there at Sachsenhausen that I finally understood why I persisted. While working on "The Persecution of Mr. Jakob Intrator," I learned about the four additional prime center-city Berlin properties stolen from my grandfather, in payment of punitive, confiscatory taxes that the Nazis were levying only on Jews. Those Nazi acts were targeted at Jews to make them feel worthless and hopeless. And there had been umpteen similar additional cases of Nazi persecution of Jews. It was not the *buildings* that were persecuted when they were stolen; it was the *Jewish owners* who were persecuted. Therefore, the thought that 16 Wallstrasse was "just a building" was not an accurate framework for thinking about my case.

In that instant of realization, I felt free from the waves of noxious, miasmic thoughts.

For many people, the connection—the through line between the milder forms of Nazi persecution, like forcing Jews out of their jobs and stripping them of their citizenship and assets, and the Final Solution—might seem obvious. But to me in 1995, it had not been obvious until that day at Sachsenhausen. Then it all came together and

I saw it like some perverse, sickening rainbow of evil: the forced auction of 16 Wallstrasse and similar crimes committed against so many
other Jews formed an arc of injustice that bent towards concentration
camps like Sachsenhausen and the attempted so-called Final Solution.
In the frigid wind and rain, I tried to fathom the depths of
depravity that led the Nazis to the crimes committed here. There were
ritualized humiliations, such as forced singing. At the end of a long
day's slave labor, Sachsenhausen prisoners would be herded into the
prison yard. There, standing at length in the cold—exhausted and
deliberately undernourished—the prisoners would be commanded to
sing songs that mocked their condition, for example, "*Fröhlich sein*,"
which means "Be happy." They had to sing the song over and over
again, depleted and humiliated, until the Nazis gave them permission
to stop.[2]

And then there were the killings. In the early stages of perfecting
their techniques, the Nazis would tell individual prisoners they were
being placed in a small room to have their height and weight mea-
surements taken. Often, music would be playing in the room. A Nazi
would then open a small panel in the room's rear wall and shoot the
prisoner in the neck.

The matter was settled in my mind. There was to be no discussion.
There would be no negotiating with the *Ariseurs*.

Before I left the German capital, I stopped again at my father's former
home at 185 Kurfürstendamm, which I had first visited during my
1993 trip. Seeing that the building's directory listed commercial tenants, I realized it would likely be easy to just walk right inside, unlike
last time, when some construction had been in progress. So I did. I
went directly up to my grandparents' floor. I had never been inside

the building, let alone in their former apartment. What I found on their floor was not a hallway with apartments but instead a modern law office. The space faced north onto Kurfürstendamm. My eyes went to the oversized windows and the balcony familiar to me from family photos.

"Feel free to look around," the office manager said, after I told him my family had lived there.

I went immediately to the balcony. I knew my Jewish family had stood in the very same spot where I was now as they watched Hitler in his limousine, the sidewalks thick with bystanders. Though the law firm was sleek and shiny in its chrome and pale grays, with sparse if elegant office furnishings, family photos had given me a sense of how the apartment looked in the 1930s. There had been high ceilings bordered with gracious, intricate moldings. It did not take much effort to imagine inlaid wooden floors covered with Persian rugs, an enormous dining table set for twelve, brocaded dining chairs, velvet couches, and a grand piano.

I had college girlfriends who had grown up in New York City apartments not unlike my father's apartment in Berlin. Every time I stepped into their homes, I was in awe of the quiet wealth and the ease with which these friends led their lives. They were accustomed to maids and to shopping on Fifth Avenue. Their families vacationed together in Switzerland and the South of France. I was envious of the casual affluence they'd enjoyed throughout their childhoods. Now in my grandparents' formerly grand home, I could taste that once-upon-a-time life in Berlin, knowing the misery and destruction that ultimately befell my family. I was flooded with heartache and sadness, thinking of my father, so often desperately sick in our tiny row house in Queens.

On the flight back to the United States, I brooded over the Berlin lawyers' thought processes: their sophomoric mix of so-called facts and innuendos, their double-talk and repetitions. My brooding led me to a question: Was I going to have the stamina to see this struggle through? And beyond the isolated question of stamina, would I be able to balance the time requirements of the 16 Wallstrasse case with my work and family life?

I sighed and gazed out the window, seeing nothing.

12 Movement

The New Year in 1996 began with a blizzard paralyzing the East Coast, shutting down cities from New York to Washington. Huge snowdrifts walled us inside our new home in Katonah, New York. Ben was ecstatic over having us all together—Greg, me, and the beloved dogs. He needed the break from school in ways not yet clear to us. We were stuck, totally unable to go anywhere. We two parents were prepared for natural emergencies, so there was plenty of food, firewood, lanterns, and bathtubs and pots filled with water. On our woodburning stove, we made thick, hearty soups and sopped them up with warm bread. Coffee and cocoa, too, we did very well. Since both of us were second-generation Holocaust survivors, perhaps there was something more to our extreme preparedness. If Ben could have willed it, the storm and its shut-in conditions would have lasted forever. For me, it was an enforced slowdown, one I truly needed.

My research was finally close to wrapping up. The resulting paper, "A Brain Imaging Study of Semantic and Affective Processing in Psychopaths," was going to be published the following year in the *Journal of Biological Psychiatry*.[1] Psychopaths became an academic interest of mine rather than just a nightmare terror. This transition occurred following my residency at St. Vincent's Hospital in Greenwich Village when I began a fellowship in psychiatry and law at the Albert Einstein School of Medicine. To explain it simply, my last assignment was to become the acting chief of the Bronx Criminal

Court Clinic. There, I assessed perpetrators for concurrent psychiatric pathology that could impact sentencing. The clinic was known for its outpatient sex offender treatment program. During my time in the clinic in the mid-1980s, several employees of child day-care centers came to us for evaluation for suspected child abuse. These well-dressed, well-spoken men with no obvious psychiatric disorders were accused of behaviors demonstrating total disregard for the safety of children while appearing sympathetic throughout the interviews. But given the mental status exam commonly used for initial psychiatric evaluations, how could I possibly delve into the personalities of these men or contribute anything to establish their guilt or innocence? How could the determination of antisocial personality disorder (ASPD), a common diagnosis in a court clinic, be of any help to me? In the 1980s, the ASPD description was an unhelpful hodgepodge of behaviors.

Later, I found some help in the writings of Dr. Robert Hare, who assessed the personalities of prisoners in the Canadian justice system. He used the word "psychopath"—not "sociopath," a dated term—to identify a subset of prisoners found through a semi-structured, intensive questionnaire.[2] That information, along with criminal records, enabled Hare to predict recidivism. He maintained that the core clinical feature of psychopaths is their emotional detachment from and indifference to the feelings and welfare of others. Hare was influenced by the work of psychiatrist Hervey Cleckley, whose abundant clinical experience suggested that psychopaths have mechanically correct language, which disguises a deep-seated and profound disconnect between the dictionary definition of the words and their emotional connotation. Cleckley referred to this as the psychopath's "mask of sanity."[3] It is often said that psychopaths know the dictionary definition of a word but not the music behind the word. Hare studied the subjects' idiosyncratic use of language, which he described as superficially captivating through their glib and facile use of words, yet hollowed out from their emotional meaning. Through his research, Hare demonstrated the cold, ruthless nature of these subjects, with their ability to feign involvement and interest in the unsuspecting.

A professor of Greg's, the eminent psychoanalyst and scholar Dr. Otto Kernberg, knew of my interest in the psychopathology of Nazis and my research with Hare. Kernberg suggested I read *Licensed Mass Murder* by the British psychoanalyst Henry Dicks, who had assessed eight imprisoned members of Hitler's notorious SS.[4]

One of his conclusions was that the men he evaluated were not psychotic by medical standards or insane by legal ones; nor were all of them full-blown psychopaths assessed by characteristics similar to those firmly established by Hare years later. Outside of research study parameters, we do not think of human beings as falling into dichotomic, yes-or-no categories, even Nazis. Individuals are far more complex. At Sachsenhausen, I thought of the Nazi doctors as possibly on a spectrum—that under the specialized conditions of Nazi Germany, their behavior was psychopathic.

What aspects of personality styles lend themselves to being vulnerable to psychopathic-like behavior? Certainly, malignant narcissism; but people with other personality traits can succumb to psychopathic behaviors. For instance, someone who impulsively cannot tolerate the careful processing of emotions and does not have the patience required to assess the pros and cons of various behavioral choices. A person who is passive has not developed their own way of thinking and is easily swayed—goes along with the group. These qualities are often found among psychopaths.

I met Dr. Hare in 1990 just after I was appointed assistant chief of psychiatry at the Bronx VA, part of the Mount Sinai School of Medicine. I quickly joined a group of like-minded researchers interested in ASPD. By then I was using motion pictures to illustrate the heterogeneity of ASPD. That same year, I taught a course at the New School for Social Research called "The Psychopath in Fact and Film." My long-standing love of movies served me well in illustrating concepts like psychopathy. My favorite example is *The Third Man* starring Orson Welles.

Within days of Peter arriving at the VA with the SPECT machine, I was presenting a much-abbreviated version of my New School course on psychopaths at the American Academy of Psychiatry and Law annual meeting in San Diego, where Hare was also speaking. After introductions, we decided to combine resources: he would visit Mount Sinai and the VA and train a group of scientists I had been working with, and I would provide the SPECT.

We would determine which subjects were psychopaths through a semi-structured interview called the Psychopathy Checklist (PCL) that Hare created, consisting of twenty questions that probed affective and interpersonal aspects of the subject as well as antisocial behaviors. Results for each question were 0, not present; 1, present to a partial degree; and 2, fully present. In criminal populations, a psychopath scores 30 and above; in clinical populations such as mine, 25 was the cutoff.

Though Hare's work began in the Canadian prison system, we thought that the inpatient substance abuse unit at the Bronx VA Hospital, where I worked, would provide a ready source of subjects. By excluding substance abuse as a causal factor for psychopathic behavior, we had two groups of patients—psychopathic substance abusers who scored above the clinical cutoff of 25 and non-psychopathic substance abusers who scored below. Our psychopaths' mean score was 29.9 and our non-psychopaths' was 9.1. We also recruited normal controls through advertisements.

Both groups were carefully assessed; none of them had major

psychiatric disorders. All had been off medication for a minimum of two weeks, and all were right-handed, with English as their first language. Such exclusionary criteria had not been present in previous brain-imaging studies of psychopaths.

Next, we challenged our subjects using a Lexical Decision Task (LDT), which presented groups of letters on a computer screen and asked, "Is it or is it not a word?" Prior research done by Hare's group found that psychopaths doing an LDT had more difficulty than normal people in processing emotional words as compared to neutral words in that they processed both identically. Normal subjects processed emotional words faster and registered larger brain waves during prior studies on a modified EEG (electroencephalogram) because emotional language carries more information than neutral language. For the psychopath, appreciation of the emotional connotation was simply absent.

Before carrying out that task, the study subjects were injected with a nuclear isotope that traveled to their brains. When viewed with SPECT, the isotope colorfully lit the region of the brain where a subject processed each word. We looked at regions that included the cortex's frontal, temporal, and parietal lobes and the adjacent subcortical regions, areas known to be language-processing regions both cognitively and emotionally.

My team found that when processing emotional words—like "maggot," "torture," and "coffin"—the psychopaths' brains showed brighter color or more activation (indicative of cerebral blood flow) than the brains of normal people and non-psychopathic substance abusers. What did this mean? At first it seemed counterintuitive, but we postulated that for psychopaths, emotional words were something like a foreign, or second, language requiring extra brain resources to process. For "normals," it was as if emotional language was hardwired.

My collaboration with Robert Hare was the first research to use nuclear brain imaging to examine this difference. Now our research was complete, and I was excited about the article's upcoming publication. At the same time, I was ready for a change.

The disturbing overdose death of my patient the previous year had led me to reassess my professional priorities. With my research completed and my clinical projects drawing to a close, I decided to reduce my hours at the hospital and start a private practice in Manhattan. Sadly, the VA had become a more difficult place for me to work, and what it meant to be a physician was changing. Throughout the United States, managed care struck a blow at medical doctors. Where I once provided full care, medical and psychotherapeutic, these two crucial, interwoven aspects of psychiatric treatment were bifurcating. Doctors were to do the medication, and psychologists and social workers, the therapy. In private practice, I could do both. Still, bureaucratic though it was, the VA had been my community for ten years. Now I would be heading out on my own, with all the isolation and unpredictable income that was likely to entail.

The 16 Wallstrasse case, meanwhile, was on hold.

My attempts at researching the mass production of Nazi flags inside the property had, thus far, not turned up additional substantive facts. My attorneys were dismayingly apathetic about the moral weight of the Nazi flag. I lacked the strength and time to push against their bullheadedness, especially as I lived so far away and the Internet was barely in its infancy. Those attorneys' reverence for German law, the LAROV's requirement of proof of antisemitism, was freighted with its own irony. Not that law invariably serves justice anywhere in the world, but in Germany, much of the postwar judiciary was peopled with former Nazis.[5]

I passed through a period when I started suspecting that the whole history of 16 Wallstrasse was more than I could, or even wanted to, take on. My home life was again moving to center stage, and I was finding it fulfilling. Ben was making new friends and doing well in school. My life was becoming delightfully ordinary.

But one day, my relaxed attitude towards the 16 Wallstrasse case suddenly changed with a phone call from my uncle Alex.

"Joanne, I have a very sad thing to report about Bella," he said, referring to his wife.

"What is it, Uncle Alex?"

"She misplaces things. Her thinking can be confused."

"Oh? What's an example of that?"

"For instance, the other day at the bank, she had a terrible time making herself clear."

I wondered if these could be early signs of dementia and worried about my elderly aunt. What if she were to die? I worried about my uncle Alex too. Because Alex was a claimant in the 16 Wallstrasse case, my concern now was that if I failed to move towards a resolution of the matter, which was advancing at a glacial pace, Alex might eventually die alone and penniless. If I was fully justified in wanting to hold out in order to learn the full Holocaust-era history of 16 Wallstrasse, it nonetheless would have felt criminal of me to interfere with my uncle Alex receiving money he likely needed to live on.

I booked another trip to Berlin. *You'll only be away a short time,* I told myself, worried about leaving Ben, as always. The thought that Kerstin would be there for this visit was comforting.

On January 23, 1996, I returned once again to the city of my father's birth.

In a narrow sense, I did not depart from my custom of arriving at my hotel early in the morning, taking a bath, then enjoying room service before heading over for my meeting with von Trott. This time, though, I was more daring. Instead of staying in the familiar area of Charlottenburg, blocks from my family's former home, I stayed at the Grand Hotel on Friedrichstrasse in the eastern part of the city.

This Grand Hotel was built in 1987 on the former site of the Kaisergalerie, demolished in an air raid during the war. Truly grand in scale and design, with its light-filled atrium and extra-wide central staircase, it was intended to evoke the eponymous 1932 film with Greta Garbo. Parts of the 2004 film *The Bourne Supremacy* were filmed on the premises.

Most of Friedrichstrasse had been severely damaged in the war and was only now getting rebuilt. Marketers were exuberantly referring to this area as "the new Berlin." But I had to question whether Friedrichstrasse was truly getting restored to its prewar glory, given the stench of sewage in the dug-up, puddle-filled street. Other roadways in the immediate area were vast and desolate, almost looking as though the war had only ended the month before.

In keeping with the theme of desolation, the meeting at the attorneys' office commenced with von Trott saying, "As you will remember, the Federal Republic of Germany took over the management of 16 Wallstrasse after the dissolution of East Germany. The building sits empty and unused. Its upkeep is very expensive—the equivalent of about two hundred thousand US dollars per year."

In correspondence, von Hülsen had indeed already impressed that on me. Von Trott continued, "I want to underline that as I've said before, if you would agree to negotiate with the *Ariseurs*, your case would go to the front of the line at the LAROV. I, therefore, continue to urge you to make every effort to settle this case promptly. The more so that in our work, we are facing significant new legal complications."

"Oh?" I asked, my neutral tone not matching my internal reaction to his distressing statement. *Stay calm*, I said to myself. *Was everything he said a tactic to get me to give in?*

"Yes," von Trott continued. "There's a new, legally mandated process to be carried out in connection with a law that in German is called *das Investitionsvorranggesetz*. The new, legally required process is *das Investitionsvorrangverfahren*."

I knew that the *Gesetz* part of the first compound German noun meant "law." I probably grasped that *Investitions* had to do with investment. However, hearing these two compound German words for the first time in this context was a disorienting experience. Even if I only paused three or four seconds to think about what the compound German words might mean in total, those were three or four seconds during which von Trott continued talking. Did fleeting bewilderment cause me to miss some of the substance of what he was saying? I could not afford to blow him off completely. Embedded in his drone-like speech might be another breadcrumb like the Nazi flag.

"A further difficulty," von Trott continued, "is seen where the German government has placed a minimum sales price of 7.6 million German marks on the property. I'm sure you understand that price is just one-third"—he broke off to arch an eyebrow—"one-third of what I told you the property was worth three years ago. And, without doubt, it is now an egregious undervaluing of the land and the structure. But unless we find a qualified buyer for 16 Wallstrasse, the government could locate a buyer, and its choice of a buyer could undermine the restitution case."

What?

To say I did not completely follow von Trott would be an understatement. The problem did not come entirely from the language barrier either. The waves of new information were complex and hard to follow. I am not certain whether von Trott cared about making sure I was clear on the purpose of this *Gesetz* and its newly mandated processes. Moreover, for whatever reasons—perhaps jet lag on top of lack of sleep—that day, I lacked the energy to insist on a thorough understanding of this new law he was describing and its effects on our 16 Wallstrasse case.

After von Trott finished his tsunami of *Investitionsvorranggesetz*, von Hülsen started speaking about the LAROV. "As we have said, your case is languishing at the bottom of a pile of thirty thousand claims for six thousand properties formerly owned by Jews. The LAROV can only work through and resolve about five hundred of those restitution cases annually."[6]

Why did I sit there that day passively listening to this recitation of facts about the LAROV? I could do the math. Given the laborious pace of case resolutions, many older claimants—among them, my uncle Alex—could well be dead before seeing justice done. So why did I not speak up, asking something like, "Well? Why is the German government letting these cases languish at the bottom of huge piles? Is this snail's pace deliberate? Couldn't the government hire more personnel for the LAROV? You know, so the restitution cases would be processed fairly and promptly for all of the victims?"

Instead of speaking up, though, I heard von Hülsen and then von Trott ending the meeting with the refrain, "The best strategy is to negotiate with the *Ariseurs*." I ignored them.

I left the meeting dispirited, temporarily staggered. What did *das Investitionsvorranggesetz* have to do with my helping Uncle Alex? I had come to Berlin hoping to be able to move things forward to help him, but now I was doubting my own resolve. Where was the energy to engage in this labyrinthine fight supposed to come from? I indulged in a fantasy of returning to a less wrenching life in New York immediately, but that fantasy was interrupted by a recollection of my father's deathbed challenge to me.

My exceptionally comforting hotel room was close enough. I could easily have retreated under warm bed covers, fallen asleep, and temporarily forgotten my dilemma. Instead, I pulled myself together, vowed I would not succumb to that temptation, and hailed a taxi to the Brandenburg Gate.

From the Brandenburg Gate, I walked down Unter den Linden to Friedrichstrasse and then north across the Spree in the direction of the old Jewish section. A powerful but welcomed Siberian-like wind pushed me along. On Oranienburger Strasse, I saw the New Synagogue, heartening with its gold-ribbed domes and polychrome brickwork—though I noted with shivers of apprehension that it had a heavy police guard. German police protecting a synagogue reminded me that I could not afford to allow defeated resignation to encroach on my thoughts. So I tried to sort through what von Trott and von Hülsen had told me about Germany's new *Gesetz* or *Verfahren* or whatever it was. Who exactly had come up with this process that was making my attorneys lean into pressuring me to settle with the *Ariseurs*? And why? The reason was that a law would interfere with our having any say in its sale price. Reasonable, yes, but not enough to make me settle with the *Ariseurs*. Even Alex wouldn't want that, and I was beginning to have an idea in my mind that I would rather give him money than settle if it came to that.

Despite those and similar questions, though, when Kerstin and I met for a cognac, I took great joy in her company. We talked at length about the final preparations for bringing my research paper to publication.

The next morning, I flew back to JFK Airport, then took a car service to Katonah. The pristine, sunlit snow cover and fresh, bracing cold seemed a universe away from the sooty remnants of snowbanks and freezing drizzle in the eastern sections of Berlin. Ben and the dogs came running up the driveway to greet me.

I was where I belonged, home.

Being back with Greg and Ben was so satisfying, it lessened my will to fight attorneys in Germany. Still, my father's challenge haunted me, if not nearly as persistently and potently as in the first two years following his death.

At intervals I would reflect on the 16 Wallstrasse case without reaching a solid decision about how to proceed. Just when I had talked myself out of its importance, relative to my home life with my husband and son, I would realize that I must *not*, under any circumstances, slough it off. Somehow, I was going to have to get the money from the case—mainly for Uncle Alex—without giving in to the *Ariseurs*.

Benjamin was now ten. I did not want to burden him with details of this case, but he picked up on casual remarks I made about 16 Wallstrasse at odd moments to Greg. My son gave signs of understanding that I felt fatigued and lacked confidence in the face of it all.

One day, Ben startled me by asking with a spectral flatness, "Do I have to go to Berlin when you die?" I felt ill. I had underestimated the impact of the case on him, and how I was weaving him into the family's dark legacy. I knew then that somehow I would face down the lawyers and their insufferable obstacles and get to the bottom of the theft of Wallstrasse. For Ben to have this as a burden already now in his young life was unacceptable.

"Sweetheart, I'm going to solve the whole matter. You don't have to worry at all about going to Berlin."

I had always aimed to give Ben a sense that in America, we were safe. In telling him about our family background, and Nazi history, I was careful to make the information appropriate for his age. If one is being honest, though, there is of course no way to avoid telling a child that their surviving family members were hounded out of Germany because they were Jews.

As a boy, Ben knew little about my research on the brain imaging of psychopaths. I do not believe he experienced my work life as disturbing. So it would be profoundly unsettling to me if the stress of my Berlin trips was seeping too deeply into him.

One night soon after my return from Berlin, I had a nightmare that I was walking on Wilhelmstrasse through bitterly cold Siberian winds. Kerstin had led me along this route three years ago when accompanying me to 16 Wallstrasse via the area of the Nazis' former headquarters. This time, though, I was alone in an abandoned landscape.

My hands held a map of the Topography of Terror scrawled on hotel stationery with, decisively marked, the location of the ruins of Gestapo torture chambers. Stumbling over shattered sidewalks, and facing the harsh wind, I was simultaneously terrified of tripping forward and of falling backward. The full moon occasionally showed from behind dense, ragged clouds, only to disappear behind them again.

In a panic, I called out, "Dad! Dad! Where are you?" Suddenly my father appeared, but not as the sickly man I had known. Instead, he was young, strong, and robustly healthy, as he must have looked in 1937 when escaping Germany for America aboard the SS *Normandie*. His handsome face appeared to me from the bow of a great ship, his expression determined.

"Keep moving, Joanne! You can do it. Go on! *Mach schnell!* You *must* keep going!" he shouted with a pleading, heartfelt urgency. Gestapo police cars, their sirens ear-piercing, raced towards me. I searched for a place to hide between the towering, darkly shadowed stone buildings. My legs felt heavy. It was hard to move, as though I were attempting to walk along a deeply mucked river bottom. I tried lifting one leg, then the other, but their dead weight kept me immobile while my arms flailed all around me.

In soul-arresting unison, the Gestapo's sirens went silent. I heard Nazis ferociously barking German while their police dogs snarled. Booted footfalls were coming closer. My mouth opened wide in a soundless scream. My eyes darted about the cold, stone-gray monuments of death on both sides of the street, which offered not a sliver of space to hide. The buildings were closing in. The dogs' yelping, along with more guttural shouting, paralyzed me.

I looked for my father, but he was on the other side—too far away to help—beckoning me to run towards him. When my father saw I was unable to move, he weakly smiled at me. One last time, he waved before receding into blackness.

I woke up in a cold sweat.

I was unworthy of my father's deathbed challenge.

I struggled to understand the full effects and purposes of the Investment Priority Procedure. The legal procedure was specific to Germany; American publications were not reporting on it. It seemed connected with making sure buildings in central Berlin would be used either for creating new jobs or for affordable housing. One thing I knew for sure, though, from being copied on correspondence, was that this legal mandate had spurred von Trott and von Hülsen into a lot of activity attempting to demonstrate the market value of 16 Wallstrasse.

Then, in August 1996, came a surprise development. Von Hülsen and Lammek suggested I return to Berlin. As von Hülsen put it, "The LAROV assigned a clerk to review your case. This clerk then decided the 16 Wallstrasse case does not warrant assigned judges. If the LAROV hears you are coming to Berlin, though, that could very well change."

And it did change. Once the LAROV was told I would be coming, two higher-level administrators were assigned to the case.

Movement!

I had succeeded in getting somebody to pay attention. The problem was, I did not want to go. The judges were, by all reports, indifferent to the matter. I also heard they did not speak English. What would be the point of taking time away from my new private practice, and of leaving my family, to challenge the contempt of LAROV bureaucrats?

My heart and mind were strongly leaning towards remaining at home and not returning to Berlin. Then one day, Ben came to me.

"Mom, I'm going to do a class project on the Holocaust. I want to learn more about my Opa," my son said. "The stuff that happened in Germany. And why he came to the United States."

I wondered what was motivating Ben. Sure, it was natural to want to know more about his grandfather. But was he similar to his mother, having to confront and master what he most feared?

I thought about how part of being Gerhard's daughter was becoming Ben's mother. And Ben's mother decided she must go to Berlin and fight for 16 Wallstrasse, so that her son would not one day have to continue that battle.

It was time for me to brush up on my German.

13 Snapped to Attention

Strange to say, though German was my first language, it is not my mother tongue. With me, my cherished Oma Rikka spoke exclusively in German, and so I retain many fond associations with the language. But she died when I was seven, and my parents mainly spoke English to me, so by the time I went to school, there could be no doubt my native tongue was English. Thus, though German has always sounded entirely familiar to me, it became a foreign language after my early childhood. When the 16 Wallstrasse case began, I could, given time, understand German correspondence regarding the matter, but I was not yet up to contending with *die Sprache* in meetings or in court.

The prospect of appearing in person at the LAROV motivated me to elevate my command of German. I was going to show those LAROV officials! I was not going to depend on interpreters or my attorneys when it came to language. And why *should* I permit a language barrier to stymie my understanding of the case, when in my childhood, German was spoken all around me?

As an undergraduate, overall, I did all right academically but fell off a cliff when it came to a course in German thought. I managed to finish reading Thomas Mann's novel *Buddenbrooks*, but then something clicked in me—the wrong way—and I could not continue processing German thought as a dutiful student. The professor's drone bored into me until all I heard was her German accent. The class moved on to *The Magic Mountain*, but I most certainly did not.

I wound up with a failing grade, a disgraceful anti-achievement for Gerhard and Lotte's daughter. A girlfriend later said to me, "You were something else. You were *really* provocative. You were determined to make that professor hate you."

My next experience with German came when I was in my third year of medical school. Many Washington Heights neighborhoods at the time—1979—were still heavily populated by Jewish refugees from Hitler's Europe.

I was in rotation on a neurology floor. An elderly man, recovering from a stroke, suddenly became agitated, crying and muttering in German while attempting to swing his legs to the ground. Unable to make his limbs go where he wanted, he felt pained and frustrated. An orderly caught the man before he fell. I was compelled to approach the patient. Taking his hand, I spoke to him in German. I am not sure who was more surprised: me, over my fluency, or the man, over being understood.

"You are in the hospital," I explained. "You are being well taken care of."

Lifting my hand to his lips, he kissed it. After a moment, I gently separated his hand from mine and left.

A few months later, as my mother lay dying at New York's Lenox Hill Hospital, I postponed my surgery rotation to be by her side. I fell into speaking German with her as though it were the most natural thing in the world. We conversed in soothing whispers, completely unlike the harsh sounds I associated with her anger and all her disparagement of me.

Though I had stopped speaking German after my mother died, I realized that I needed the language again now, to help me navigate my way through the restitution case and its German lawyers. In preparation for my meeting with LAROV officials, I enrolled in a total immersion German program at Berlitz. Three instructors rotated in and out of a small classroom where I was ceaselessly bombarded with this language at once so familiar and so alien. For the last hour each day, two instructors joined me for in-depth discussions, *auf Deutsch*, about history, politics, and film. Not only did I enjoy the learning experience, but it left me feeling more confident about taking on the case.

Still—even though the plan was for Ben to be away, having fun skiing—it was not easy for me to leave my son, or my new psychiatric practice, to go challenge the LAROV's contemptuous processing of our 16 Wallstrasse restitution case.

My plane landed in Berlin on January 29, 1997. My meeting with LAROV officials was scheduled for the next morning.

I had decided to stay in Charlottenburg rather than Mitte. On the way from my hotel to von Trott's office, I walked into the garden of the Käthe Kollwitz Museum on Fasanenstrasse. I have always felt a deep affinity for Kollwitz's art, which to me conveys the heart-wrenching experience of separation and loss that—against my good sense—coincidentally was binding me to Berlin, the Berlin of my father. Outside the museum stood a bronze sculpture of a mother tightly holding her children, expressing the transcendence of motherhood. I connected the emotions that this Kollwitz sculpture awoke within me to my relationship with Ben. Was I hugging him tightly enough? Or, by trying to make up to him what I had lacked and most yearned for in my own childhood, was I suffocating him?

Though undecided about the supernatural, as I was leaving the Kollwitz Museum garden, I suddenly felt my grandfather Jakob's presence. His warm, enveloping aura benevolently accompanied me down

Berlin streets. The feelings this gave me were diametrically opposed to the ones I experienced during my terrifying nightmare of being trapped on Wilhelmstrasse, paralyzed with fear, alone, and outside my father's reach. Opa Jakob's conjured presence powerfully reassured me.

Was it Jakob's gentle being that nudged me inside a camera store close to von Trott's office? *Something* made me enter the camera store and purchase an Olympus camera. The shopkeeper was good enough to load the camera with film at my request, and, on autopilot, I then placed it in my leather purse.

After I joined the lawyers, von Hülsen and Lammek, we entered the Zoo Station of Berlin's S-Bahn train and rode east to the LAROV's offices. No conversation. I do not remember the stop where we got off, or the building housing the LAROV. My vista coming up out of the subway into the eastern part of Berlin was filled with block-gray concrete, visuals associated with the Communist era, as well as some newer construction.

Something I do remember is feeling a frisson of anticipation—excitement commingled with fear—as I hoped we would finally be able to make some progress in the case. Arriving on time—*pünktlich*—we entered a lackluster room lit by bright fluorescent overheads. The three LAROV judges awaiting us would ultimately decide the ownership of 16 Wallstrasse. They consisted of a middle-aged woman and two dour-looking men. I recall the woman as plain-featured, colorless, unadorned, and seated behind a desk, with her male colleagues off to one side, also seated.

After introductory words were exchanged in German, one of the men said, "This case is very, very difficult. There's a paucity of documentation for the period prior to the forced auction. And to be frank with you, we at the LAROV are inundated with cases much easier to deal with than yours."

The second man jumped in. "We have questions about the *Grundbuch*," he said. The *Grundbuch*, like a registry of deeds, would show the ownership history of the property. "It looks to us like in 1933, your grandfather took out a second mortgage on 16 Wallstrasse."

I was shocked to have this German judge speaking to me this way, because 1933 was the year the Nazis seized power and started cracking down on Jews. The man paused before giving into himself. Seething with hostility, he muttered something to the effect of "Your grandfather bled this building dry."

Though infuriated, I held it together. I calculated that my best move was to listen more and not interrupt. It would be almost impossible to convey in mere words how disgusted I was by what seemed to be a complete lack of empathy. I was there because my family's world had been destroyed. But if I stopped this LAROV bureaucrat midstream, I might not learn the full measure of his animosity, of his resentment at having to deal repeatedly with stories about Nazis stealing properties from Jews. I wanted to see how far he would go with his rancor, to learn the truth about him and possibly his indirect expressions of antisemitism.

He looked away from me, out at some larger imagined audience. Then, he lashed out rhetorically: "How could this have been persecution? Your grandfather took money out from the building—and he *had* money." He took a breath, as though he were warming up. "Perhaps," he continued, "by the time of the forced auction, your grandfather had already bled the property dry for his own purposes. And so, while the auction was forced, that may have occurred more due to all his careless spending than to Nazi persecution."

My God! Was this really happening? Was I *really* in an arbitration room in Berlin, having to suffer the egregious insult of this non-Jewish German specimen of my generation leaning in on his perverted conjecture that my grandfather's downfall—the destruction of his property and his life—which occurred at a height of Nazi legislation aimed at stripping rights and assets from Jews—was due solely to my grandfather being a bad businessman?

It was so very easy for this gentile German bureaucrat. What was the real cause of the forced auction? Let us see! Was it the Nazis' antisemitism? No! *Surely*, it must have been that my grandfather was a shoddy businessman!

The woman, who thus far had remained silent, now appeared almost morbidly infected by her associate. She could not hold herself back. Excited, almost ecstatic, released from her role as a faceless judge, she chimed right in. "He must have exploited the mortgage to drain the building dry financially, leading to the forced auction."

Looking at her rapturous face, I wondered whether she was any different from those women I could see in my mind's eye, screaming for their Führer down in the street outside my grandfather's apartment building in 1936. At that point, could there be the least hope of this meeting changing anything for the better in my 16 Wallstrasse case? As though what the woman had said were not already chilling enough, she continued, "They all die when they get their property back."

Dumbstruck, I could hear her words reverberating in my head. I struggled to find my voice, then shouted, "My father is already dead!" Tears were now streaming down my cheeks.

This woman was the very face of the institution allegedly entrusted with righting a historic wrong, but she now appeared to me like a direct descendant of one of Kafka's most intimidatingly detestable characters. In a bizarre, unguarded moment, she confessed that German officialdom was dragging restitution out for such interminable stretches that its intended beneficiaries most often died before German officialdom permitted them access to its benefits.

The situation was precisely as von Trott had said at the Waldorf Astoria. If we did not negotiate with the *Ariseurs*, we would win a first decision, but the case would then get dragged out endlessly in an appeals court. Therefore, before seeing any justice done in the case, most of us would die. I looked around at my lawyers and the two LAROV men, wanting to see if their faces at all registered the obscenity of the woman's words, but all of them were expressionless.

I grabbed my purse off the floor, whipped out my camera, and photographed the LAROV woman. For a suspended second, the flash on my camera filled the room with a stunning light. I broke the silence. "I am going to show my family in the United States what you look like!" I shouted.

My action was, in some ways, childlike. What could it possibly matter to her that I would show my family how she looked? Yet I felt like Sally Field as Norma Rae. With small satisfaction, I thought, *No more hiding behind twisted interpretations of restitution law for you!*

The flash had been a catalyst for silence, but the ensuing motionless quiet crackled with tension. Suddenly, a cacophony of German voices erupted. Totally still and all but ignored, I stood among these strangers, weeping. The woman scrambled to give me, of all damned things, vitamin C candies. I wept for how difficult my father's life had been, and for how pathetic this official was, staring at the candies in my palm as though willing them into my mouth so they might magically shut me up.

Von Hülsen motioned for me to sit down, which only irritated me more. I shook her off. My eyes traveled from the woman to the two men on the panel. No one would so much as meet my gaze. It was as though the entire German state's skill at remaining unaccountable was simply outpacing me.

Then there was a shift. Looking chastened, the woman mumbled, "I'll look very closely at the case and make it a priority." When I did not respond, she said, more loudly, "I will make this case a priority."

Robotically, the men stood up. Lammek and von Hülsen thanked her. She offered me an outstretched, limp hand while her eyes looked past me as though I had already left. Just before we closed the door behind us, I turned and asked this LAROV judge, "Do you know for certain that the Nazi flag was mass-produced in 16 Wallstrasse?"

"Yes," she said simply.

So, it was not, as von Trott suggested, a "rumor." Was von Trott's suggestion of a rumor as insincere as it now seemed? "We weren't sure," our lawyers had insisted.

Rumors! How convenient. What an easy way out of knowing a fact, of slipping out of inherent responsibility through feigned uncertainty. Rumors! Like rumors of deportations east to explain the disappearance of Jewish neighbors and friends. Uncertainty and doubt—they made a horrific reality easier to ignore. Rumors! Saying that something is "only a rumor" can provide a means for human beings to shun responsibility, whether one is living under an authoritarian regime or not. To live by facts means to take responsibility, to make reasoned and careful choices. To use rumors as an excuse to avoid thoughtful actions suggests either lying about the truth or accepting a passive, uninformed stance to avoid the consequences of knowing the facts. And in the context of that so-called rumor that von Trott mentioned ever so casually, I very much wanted to know what the facts *were*—the truth, the whole truth, and nothing but the truth—regarding the Nazi flag having been mass-produced inside 16 Wallstrasse.

Outside, I was prepared for Lammek to lambaste me for

photographing the LAROV judge. Instead, he beamed. "You were brilliant!" he exclaimed. "You have single-handedly turned the case around."

Had Lammek not fully considered the *meaning* of these officials' viciousness against my grandfather? Was he emotionlessly accepting it as a bullying legal strategy, just some routine business tactic to be used against Holocaust victims and their descendants? I replied, "What they were saying about my grandfather—given the *gesamt* (total) known circumstances of Nazi antisemitism—was and is completely abhorrent."

Waving his hand as though dismissing my expressed concern, he said, "I'm telling you! What you did was a stroke of genius." He talked as though my behavior in snapping the photo had been a premeditated strategy rather than a spontaneous reaction. Would we always be at such cross-purposes?

It was liberating to be out of the stifling LAROV confines, in the crisp Berlin air with pale winter sunlight pushing through the clouds.

"May we take you back to your hotel?" Lammek asked, with von Hülsen seconding the motion.

"Thank you very much, but I don't think so," I responded, needing to walk alone in order to settle down.

Walking meant crossing Potsdamer Platz, bombed to rubble at the end of the war—and, in the 1990s, still an enormous construction site. I was going to have to navigate it carefully. Just three months before, Maestro Daniel Barenboim here conducted nineteen "dancing" construction cranes to the tune of Beethoven's *Ode to Joy*, marking the completion of a new Daimler-Benz high-rise designed by the Italian architect Renzo Piano. My goal was to traverse the enormous construction pit and wind up at the champagne bar in KaDeWe, the Berlin equivalent of Harrods.

Once at the bar, I ordered a flute of champagne, then silently toasted myself. I was just *aching* to tell somebody what happened at the LAROV, but it was too early to call New York. And Kerstin was in class, so I took out a notebook, then wrote down every word I could remember from the meeting.

Still wishing there were somebody with whom to share the news of my victory, I looked around for a friendly American face, but the only other patrons at the champagne bar, several seats away, were two elderly German women, fur coats casually draped around their shoulders. When they saw me noticing them, they leaned in towards each other, their eyes still on me, and laughed.

Instantly, I hated them.

I did not need my friend Peter Stritzke to tell me these women yearned for the good old days. I moved my chair out of their view so I would not have to see their smug faces. The effects of another glass of champagne hardly helped my tiredness and did not ease the women's nerve-jangling, lingering laughter in my ears. I summoned my grandfather Jakob to make them go away. I thanked him for his presence that morning, my unseen guardian angel, directing me to the camera store. A wave of melancholy passed through me. There were no apparitions to soothe me. My grandfather and my father were both dead.

Hours later, Kerstin helped me understand the impact of what I had done at the LAROV. We met at my hotel, where carefully and quietly, she told me, "One doesn't behave that way in Germany. You can think what you want about German officials, but you don't openly protest like that."

Kerstin grew up in Communist East Germany, where decades of authoritarianism made the people wary of all government officials. They had perfected the art of keeping their thoughts to themselves—especially comments critical of authority. That had long been Kerstin's reality. It was a mandatory strategy for anybody living with the ever-present Stasi secret police. Growing up in 1960s America, I had the opposite experience. We questioned everything and everyone. Would I have been able to speak out about similar injustices were I born and raised in Germany? I fear I would not have been so brave.

We called Peter to tell him what had happened. The three of us agreed to reunite soon for a champagne toast.

Lammek and von Hülsen's decision that I should appear before the LAROV officials had been good, but it took snapping that photo to galvanize those LAROV judges' attention. When I reached Greg on the phone, he reassured me. "Your instincts are correct, Joanne," he said. "Taking the official's picture embarrassed them all."

I could not wait to get home and discuss what happened at the LAROV in more detail with my husband. When I returned via JFK to Katonah, Ben and the dogs came running out to greet me, while inside our home, Greg had a gorgeous flower arrangement waiting along with a celebratory bottle of champagne. "I am *so* proud of you!" he enthused.

Later, we talked about what had gone on in Berlin. "There's one reason, and one reason only," I said, "that this judge decided to put our 16 Wallstrasse case at the top of the pile."

"Damage control!" Greg exclaimed.

"Exactly. I mean, if it had been a matter of principle, why did her previously expressed moral outrage over Opa Jakob's alleged refinancing of the building precipitously vanish with a camera flash? With one photograph—poof! I blew a hole in any legal concerns she had."

Because of his family's Holocaust-era history, Greg was keenly interested in anything that involved obtaining some smidgen of justice for the victims. "Again, I'm so proud of you for what you did, Joanne," he said. "You ripped the veil off her bureaucratic cover, exposing as null whichever principles she thought she was abiding by."

My photograph had captured an indelible moment—the woman's malignity was visible and memorialized. She could no longer be part of a completely faceless LAROV, and she was no longer impervious to accountability as a human being. One photograph put an end to all the LAROV judges' bullying, at the very moment one of those judges casually confessed that the restitution process was so slow that by the time Jews got their property back, they would be dead or nearly so.

Any doubt that that analysis was wrong soon evaporated.

The LAROV woman called von Hülsen to "confirm" she would decide in our favor, but she wanted the negative of my photograph. Von Hülsen suggested I turn it over. "We should not irritate her," my attorney advised. "It would be best if you cut out the negative and sent it to me."

As a psychiatrist, I understood the LAROV judge's motivations. The power of my photograph was its potential to expose her behavior and make her feel ashamed. Here it is essential to understand the crucial distinction that exists between the emotions of shame and guilt. Shame is characterized by fear of the consequences of being seen. Shame is general and impersonal: it is not a fear of being seen by a specific person or specific people; it is the fear of the consequences of being seen *at all*.

Guilt, by contrast, occurs within a relationship. One person feels guilty in front of another person or entity. A person who really *feels* guilty—and wants to restore the relationship they have damaged—wishes to be seen as distressed by their guilt. That desire to be *seen* as feeling guilty, within the context of the guilty party's desire to restore a relationship, constitutes remorse.

True reparation can follow only from remorse. Whereas a person who feels guilty might be motivated to restore a relationship, a person who feels shame is only motivated to save face. The LAROV judge I photographed was motivated to save face. What if she had felt no shame at all? Clearly many Nazi murderers, and all psychopaths, had no shame. The judge acted out of shame after being photographed and decided she would prioritize the case. What if she were unfazed? I never even considered that.

At any rate, I had no intention of parting with my LAROV judge photo or the negative.

Sadly, by this point, von Hülsen's suggestion that I take my leverage with the LAROV judge and throw it away could hardly surprise me. Because the Nazis' progression from Aryanization to industrialized mass murder was so overwhelming in its relentlessly savage inhumanity, I previously had—quite misguidedly—assumed that *Wiedergutmachung,* or "making good again," might entail erring on the side of the Jewish victims. Yet all too often, there were stark differences between German officials' publicly declared purposes in restitution and what they felt, viscerally, when nobody was watching.

My memory of arresting the judge's attention by surprise-snapping her photo had me riding an emotional high for weeks, but then a letter from von Hülsen brought me crashing right back down to earth. There it was again, in von Hülsen's letter: settle with Heim & Gerken, the *Ariseurs.* And von Hülsen urged us to settle with them *before* the LAROV decided in our favor.

Maddening! Despite having snapped the LAROV judges to attention, I had not (yet) at all moved them on the fundamental issue of justice here, namely that Aryans should *not* profit off of having stolen a building from my Jewish family. What von Hülsen was now urging me to do was the same thing von Trott had wanted when I first met with him in the Waldorf Astoria.

Much more, though, was afoot in this German legal labyrinth. Von Trott and Lammek decreed that Lammek would compose a sample LAROV decision for the LAROV to consider. That draft would let the LAROV know our position and give Lammek an "in" for closer communications with them.

Towards the end of October, von Hülsen told me we should expect the LAROV soon to issue an "intended decision." What was meant by that term? I soon found out that the "intended decision" meant that LAROV would not decide in our favor unless we first negotiated with the *Ariseurs*, Heim & Gerken. Von Hülsen added that I should return to Berlin "to engage in the matter as we discussed during your last visit."

Did she mean that in Berlin, I should look up the 16 Wallstrasse superintendent, research the building's tenants, or research the production of Nazi flags there? Or did she mean I should do all three things?

I stepped back a moment for some perspective. Why was any of this on *me*? Were lawyers not supposed to work for their clients? Why was I having to work for my attorney? And why was my attorney still pushing me to let the *Ariseurs* profit off this case? In my mind, letting the *Ariseurs* take money from 16 Wallstrasse would be tantamount to another robbery. Did the Germans working on restitution feel no remorse for the way my grandfather was abused by the Nazis? And did they feel no remorse whatsoever over attacking his memory for having refinanced a building he had *owned*?

It was now clear to me that minus my showing up in Berlin to serve as a living, breathing memorial, the paper-thin reckoning I was achieving would disintegrate completely. And so, reluctantly, I decided that in the upcoming year I would return to Berlin.

14 Stalled

Winter. My Berlin time of year.

And high time to go be a thorn in the flesh of certain Berlin bureaucrats, as doing so seemed the only leverage I had. I returned to Berlin on January 29, 1998, rewarding myself for the stress of the trip by staying at the Adlon Hotel. Recently rebuilt on Unter den Linden, overlooking Pariser Platz, the Adlon is evocative of a golden age in Berlin. It was, for example, the model for the film *Grand Hotel*. And in the film *Cabaret*, Liza Minnelli's character says that she went to "the Adlon."

Through 1940, the American writer and journalist William L. Shirer reported from this hotel about the rise of the Nazi Party. He escaped after learning that the Gestapo were building an espionage case against him. He risked receiving the death penalty. A compilation of his Nazi-era reports from Germany, *Berlin Diary*, was influential in my thinking, as was his later book, *The Rise and Fall of the Third Reich*.[1]

Upon arrival, I received a pleasant surprise. Because the newly reopened Adlon was not full, I was upgraded to an ultra-luxurious room overlooking the Brandenburg Gate. Such history here! When President John F. Kennedy visited the German capital in 1963, the Soviets hung red banners over the Brandenburg Gate so he would not be able to see into East Berlin. And it was in front of the Brandenburg

Gate in 1987 that President Ronald Reagan declared, "Mr. Gorbachev, open this gate! Tear down this wall!"

Now another American, Dr. Joanne Intrator, was looking out her Adlon Hotel room window at the monumental Brandenburg Gate. Mesmerized by the spectacle and the metaphysical weight of history, I found myself marveling over how I—granddaughter of Jakob, daughter of Gerhard—managed to get into this position. But what *was* my position, exactly? In my own small way, was I going to have a "Tear down this wall!" experience? Or was I following a trail of breadcrumbs only to wind up more deeply lost in the forest?

My meeting with the attorneys was exasperating. Von Trott said, "Once again, Frau Intrator, we urge you, your brother, and your uncle to agree to settle with the *Ariseurs*."

There exists a spectrum of fallacious reasoning involving endless repetition that ranges from *argumentum ad infinitum* to outright brainwashing. The Nazis brainwashed Germans against Jews with endless repetition of bigoted falsehoods, including "The Jews are our misfortune."

The repetitive fallacy von Trott was deploying against me is exquisitely known as *argumentum ad nauseam*. His tactic was not convincing me that his position was fair, just, or well reasoned, but it *was* making me feel deeply nauseated. In connection with the history of 16 Wallstrasse, both brainwashing and *ad nauseam* fallacies had been used to inflict injustices on Jewish individuals.

I drew my lips in and narrowed my eyes, but then relaxed my expression back into a studious blank. Looking down at my interlaced fingers atop the conference room table, I quietly said, "No. We are not going to do that."

Von Trott tensed and paused. The other attorneys shifted around uncomfortably. Then von Trott raised the stakes by adding, "The

LAROV will not finalize any decision in your favor until you have solved the Heim & Gerken side of the equation."

While he was getting to that point, a voice in my head spun a counterpoint: *Joanne, if you can just manage somehow to unearth documentation linking Heim & Gerken to the mass production of Nazi flags in 16 Wallstrasse, the LAROV won't dare continue insisting you pay those Nazis off.* I had no clout apart from my power of refusal. No hallucinatory apparition of my Opa Jakob. No surprise flash photo. Lammek, however, had an unpleasant surprise for me. "We've recently found a document from 1928. The upshot of it is that whereas we previously presumed that the Intrator branch of the family held a 15 percent share in 16 Wallstrasse, the real percentage is only 12.5 percent."

My father would have expected me to demand a full accounting. What were the circumstances in 1928? Was Lammek correctly reporting to me what the documentation shows?

But I just let it go. It seemed like quibbling over distractions. Lammek was still going on, but I was *not* allowing myself to forget what I wanted to know, namely, exactly how these *Ariseurs*—Heim & Gerken—took possession of 16 Wallstrasse, and what they did with our property afterwards. I felt moral outrage. The Sonex contract under which these attorneys were working for me was supposed to include *research*. My own attorneys were using their research energies *against* me, alleging we held a smaller percentage than originally thought, but continuing to ignore what the Nazis did with our property after they stole it.

I left the meeting feeling deeply disheartened. What else could I do to help our cause? On a prior trip, I had distracted myself from the legal morass by visiting Sachsenhausen. This time, I hired a car and driver, then headed out in the winter drizzle for the imposing, opulent

House of the Wannsee Conference. There, on January 20, 1942, the Nazi regime planned to fully operationalize the extermination of the European Jews.

The Wannsee are twin lakes southwest of Berlin. Stately, magnificent villas grace the waterfront. Art world eminences who owned villas at Wannsee included the painter Max Liebermann. And, as I knew from my father, the Berglas branch of my family had owned a Wannsee villa too. It was one he had loved to visit with his family.

After the Nazis came to power in 1933, they stole Jewish-owned villas at Wannsee using many of the same underhanded tactics they used to expropriate 16 Wallstrasse from my family. The villa at 56–58 Grossen Wannsee, the eventual Wannsee Conference House, which I was visiting this afternoon, had long been owned by the Nazi Friedrich Minoux, who can be seen in photos wearing a Hitler-style mustache. Minoux had helped to plan Hitler's failed Beer Hall Putsch in 1923. He wound up prosecuted by the Nazis for financial fraud, after which the villa fell under the control of a lead architect of the Holocaust, SS-Obergruppenführer Reinhard Heydrich.

By the time of the Wannsee Conference, Hitler had already decided upon his goal of murdering all Jews. Along with fourteen other high-level Nazi officials at Wannsee, Heydrich formalized the plans. Towards the end of the war, the Nazis tried to cover their tracks by destroying copies of the Wannsee Conference meeting minutes. In 1947, a US prosecutor, German-born Robert Kempner, a Jew, turned up a copy that had belonged to the Nazi bureaucrat Martin Luther.[2] (Not to be confused with the sixteenth-century theologian and antisemite Martin Luther, who wrote *On the Jews and Their Lies*, a screed that proposed burning all Jewish synagogues and schools, and murdering all Jews.)

It was through the twentieth-century Martin Luther's copy of the

Wannsee Conference meeting minutes that the Allies became aware of the conference and its purpose. Starting in the 1960s, Jewish groups lobbied for the Wannsee villa to be turned into a memorial, but the West German government refused their requests. Only in 1992 was the House of the Wannsee Conference finally made into a museum.

On this forbidding January 1998 day in Berlin, then, under unyielding legal pressure to reward *Ariseurs* for having stolen 16 Wallstrasse from my Jewish family, I walked into the House of the Wannsee Conference. I was somewhat prepared, having recently seen a German television reenactment of the eighty-five-minute conference.[3] In the actual villa dining room was a large table with Nazi officials' names laid out atop it, as though they were dinner party place cards. I recalled that towards the end of their planning for the Final Solution here, Nazi officials had toasted each other with cognac.

Back in the car, I told my driver, "Next stop, Grunewald."

I knew the address where Greg's grandparents and mother had once lived on Winkler Strasse near the Dianasee lake.

I found their beautiful, wood-framed white stucco home nestled among fir trees. It had been divided into fourteen different residences!

I also knew that Greg's family had illustrious neighbors, the Bonhoeffers. Karl Bonhoeffer was a prominent neurologist and psychiatrist who had treated Greg's grandmother. Karl's son Dietrich Bonhoeffer was the celebrated co-founder of the Confessing Church, an anti-Nazi group that actively resisted Hitler's efforts to subsume all German Protestant churches into an envisioned Protestant Reich Church. The Nazis murdered Dietrich Bonhoeffer just twenty-one days before Hitler committed suicide.

In the car on the way back to the Adlon, I reflected on the different types of Germans I had either met or thought about that day. The decent Bonhoeffers. The monstrous Heydrichs and Martin Luthers. And my attorneys, pressuring me to reward *Ariseurs* for having stolen 16 Wallstrasse from us.

Throughout the remainder of 1998, I was put through a Kafkaesque hell of developments in the 16 Wallstrasse case.

In May, I received a letter from von Hülsen, who seemed to be calculating ways to exasperate me. She was asking for my uncle Alex's date of birth. The LAROV's documents were incomplete, she reported, adding: "I very much regret this further bureaucratic delay."

Five years into the case, none of the people responsible for processing our 16 Wallstrasse restitution claim were sure of my uncle Alex's date of birth. With sarcastic feeling but a neutral front, I sent von Hülsen my uncle Alex's birthdate: May 28, 1905.

Back in 1993, we had sent all the basic paperwork—of course including documented proof of Uncle Alex's date of birth. Suppose it were true that the LAROV was uncertain of Uncle Alex's birthdate. My German attorneys should have been prepared with documentation of the correct date.

Like so much pertaining to restitution, this was a maddening error that simply could not be challenged. It intensified my sense of being ground down by indifferent Germans through endless bureaucratic obstacles. Under Bismarck in Germany, bureaucracy was painstakingly refined towards the goal of maximum achievable efficiency.[4] German professional culture became widely admired for prioritizing attention to detail. In the legal field, that meant crossing every *t* and dotting every *i*. Given that context, what should I have concluded about my attorneys? That they acted out against me by alleging they had not retained Uncle Alex's birthdate in their records? No. I was not paranoid, but I knew as a psychiatrist that obsessive traits demanded in professional settings require a hyper focus that can inadvertently leave vital information out of view. Birthdates were the key person identifier in German bureaucracy. It wasn't trivial.

To make matters worse, Lammek sent me a supremely irritating fax. He was writing because a Berlin probate court had determined that our certificate of inheritance was incomplete. The court wanted to know whether German or American law had been applied in determining who my grandfather's heirs were. According to Lammek, all we needed to do to see a valid certificate of inheritance issued promptly was to submit a document proving my grandfather Jakob's nationality as of April 23, 1943, the day he died.

With shocking oblivion, Lammek further wrote, "We believe that Jakob Intrator was a citizen of the United States and ask you to forward us a notarized copy of the certificate of naturalization or any other document proving his American citizenship."

Lammek! *Gott im Himmel!* My grandfather died of heart failure just *one day* after reaching New York! How could Lammek think he was an American citizen? How did Lammek (and von Trott, and von Hülsen) not know that because of Hitler and the Nazis, my grandfather was a stateless refugee?

The fact of my grandfather's statelessness was the heart of the whole story. When the fax arrived, I was awaiting a patient running late. In my mind's eye, I pictured myself dialing Lammek's number, and then, when he answered, exclaiming, "I am crushed, *crushed*, that you know so little about our family. Why, why, *why* were you not able to answer this question about Jakob's citizenship yourself?"

But I did not do that.

Offended. Resentful.

And there are other words I could use to describe how I was feeling.

Indignant, for example.

That my attorneys had lost track of my uncle Alex's date of birth, I might *just* have been persuaded not to make such a big deal of—perhaps even been willing to chalk it up to a mindless bureaucratic oversight. But this gaffe—communicating with me as though my paternal grandfather had been a US citizen—spoke to much deeper problems. These attorneys had repeatedly been entrusted with proof of the details of my grandparents' desperate struggles under the Nazi regime. I certainly would not expect them to remember, off the top of their heads, the exact dates that my grandfather was made to pay punitive taxes that the Nazis imposed only on Jews, or the exact amounts he was forced to pay. But the fact that the Nazis stripped my Jewish grandfather of his German citizenship, leaving him stateless for the rest of his life: that my attorneys did not have this internalized, many years into the case, shows an indifference that ran much deeper than mere bureaucratic error.

My own Berlin attorneys, collaborating as a group, *still* did not have in their working memories the fact that my grandfather died stateless, proving their failure to grasp the historical and emotional context of this case. Whatever I had been holding on to, thinking these lawyers might eventually do the right thing, was irrevocably shattered. That it was possible for them to think and state their belief that my grandfather Jakob Intrator had been an American citizen at the time of his death was, to me, an utter abomination.

When I had sufficiently calmed down, I sent a return fax stating, "I am disgusted by this situation."

Another blow came in September 1998. The LAROV had, I was told, issued a decision in our favor. We—meaning the Berglases and the Intrators—were the rightful owners of 16 Wallstrasse. This German government agency had determined that my family was the victim of Nazi antisemitism and, therefore, deserved restitution. Yet the LAROV's decision came with Nazi-era strings attached. As the laws and rules were being applied to our case, the LAROV's decision in our favor could only be enforced if we first paid off the heirs of the Aryans who took 16 Wallstrasse from our Jewish relatives. At this stage, you could think of it facetiously as Schrödinger's restitution decision.[5] One could not truly be sure whether the LAROV was delivering justice for the persecuted Jewish family, because to achieve justice through the LAROV's decision, the Jewish family in question first had to reward an Aryan family for having stripped the Jewish family of their property—and for having then used the premises for the mass production of Nazi flags.

I kept casting my thoughts to everything I knew about what the Nazis had done to my grandparents and other family members. My poor, self-deluded paternal grandparents—especially Oma Rosa! She had been among those German Jews who, against all evidence, hoped or believed that everything would turn out well. My own ardent wish for everything to turn out well in my current home and family life was dovetailing with the hopelessness I felt over the 16 Wallstrasse case. No place felt secure.

Greg seemed more distracted than usual, more than just the absent-minded professor behavior we sometimes teased him about. This is what happened. Greg went out for a long run with our dogs Virginia and Athena. They ran on the Bedford horseback riding trails—one hundred miles of groomed pathways right off our property.

Greg returned from the run with Athena, but without Virginia. By ordinance, dogs were required to be leashed on the trails at all times, so as not to spook horses. Heedless, Greg frequently let them run free. I could not count how often I cautioned him, but this time he did not just silently dismiss my concerns; he flashed me a contemptuous look for calling him out. He was hampered by an anthropomorphic delusion involving our dogs' ability to stay close by, and so not run into trouble. Virginia was something of an alpha-huntress, easily distracted by squirrels, foxes, and wild turkeys. Sooner or later, through Greg's looking in some other direction or daydreaming, it was bound to end badly.

I laced up my hiking boots. It was the end of the day, and the sunlight was waning. Through the darkening woods we searched.

"Virginia! Virginia!" I called out in distressed tones. And then I despaired: "This is awful. She's lost."

Greg yelled at me: "She *will* come back!"

There was no sign of her.

"I'm returning to the house," I said. "Do you want me to come back with a flashlight so you can keep looking?"

Though Greg continued the search for Virginia, he refused my offer to bring him a flashlight, ratcheting up my worry. Athena lay lengthwise along the sliding kitchen door facing the woods, her breathing making little fog circles on the glass. Her dinner was uneaten. I felt heartsick for us all. Telling Ben Virginia was missing was beyond tough. Yes, we found her with the help of the neighboring town police four days later. The household settled down, but Greg and I did not. It was one thing to forget his keys or lose his wallet. It was another to lose track of one of our dogs.

At length, I made efforts to ponder the deeper meanings of both German law and my Berlin attorneys treating my family's Holocaust-era history as though it were almost incidental and trivial. The 16

Wallstrasse case was indeed complex, but to my attorneys, it appeared to be "just a case." I reminded myself that after the wall came down, East Berlin might have been the largest real estate parcel in the Western world. Money was to be made. Restitution cases were abundant. As earnest as the lawyers might have been about restitution, a contingency payment arrangement, such as ours, must have put the lawyers under a great deal of pressure to settle the case quickly. It makes arithmetical but not ethical sense. How does one balance doing what is right in the name of restitution for crimes against Jews with the impetus to settle quickly? I would think one counts on a deal made early on—when the value of the building is high and the time expenditure low.

One manifest fact was undeniable: for whatever combination of reasons, the German law, and my attorneys, were treating my family's Holocaust-era history as though it were almost incidental to our 16 Wallstrasse case. And that fact compelled me to think back to my visit to Sachsenhausen when I began thinking differently about restitution. Hardening my position, I would refuse to view 16 Wallstrasse as "just a building." That meant finally speaking up and not living so much in my head because I was afraid of standing up to Germans.

I had seen the remnants of Nazi torture chambers at the site of the former Sachsenhausen concentration camp. I had been subjected to German judges voicing false allegations against my Jewish grandfather. I had toured the site where the industrial-scale mass murder of Jews was plotted at Wannsee. Thinking about restitution as merely a question of "This building is mine, not yours," and conceiving of restitution only in terms of material gain was a trap—a distraction from the building's history and from acknowledgment of my family members' suffering.

~

By now, the *Ariseurs* Heim & Gerken were on the warpath over the 16 Wallstrasse case. The battle tactic they chose was to sue the state of Berlin. Yes: they sued the Berlin government because it had declared us, the Intrator–Berglas claimants, to be the rightful owners of 16 Wallstrasse. And if the *Ariseurs'* company was Heim & Gerken, then David Heim's daughter Johanna Weber was the party doing the suing. There was a wrinkle, in that *at least one* of the heirs withdrew from the lawsuit. I never learned why. Whatever the answer, Johanna Weber was determined to stick it to us. Her legal argument to a German court was that Nazi antisemitism had not been the cause of my Jewish grandfather losing 16 Wallstrasse. That the Nazi destruction of Jewish businesses—which began April 1, 1933, five years before her father became an owner of Wallstrasse—had no influence on her thinking confirms that greed and antisemitism are powerful opponents of truth. So she smeared my family's reputation and wanted 30 percent to drop her lawsuit.

Von Hülsen advised us to pay Johanna Weber off. And our Berglas relatives wanted to settle the case. But I knew that Weber's father had stolen my Jewish grandfather's building and that Nazi flags were then mass-produced inside it. I was *not* going to reward Johanna Weber. To von Hülsen and anybody else who asked me to settle the case— and ask they did—I firmly said, "No." I was awakening step by step to the necessity of my becoming a heroine in, or perhaps of, my family's story.

Johanna v. Joanne.

Part 3

Resolution

15 Discoveries and Duplicities

What the detective story is about is not murder but the restoration of order.

—P. D. James

In a step towards shining bright light on what was *really* involved with the Nazi theft of 16 Wallstrasse—that is to say, questions about which Aryans had the necessary Nazi Party connections to trigger the forced auction, what those Aryans did with the building after stealing it, and so on—I hired a detective.

Here is how that happened.

In January 1999, one of my regular seatmates on the commuter train into Manhattan was a young attorney with international clients. He often asked for updates on the 16 Wallstrasse case. I told him about Johanna Weber's lawsuit against the State of Berlin. And I told him all about my repeated attempts to prod my attorneys into investigating Heim & Gerken.

"I have a friend at Kroll, an international investigations firm," he said. "You could try contacting her and see where it goes. I really can't recommend this company's services highly enough."

I loved the idea of hiring an international detective agency! While the Sonex contract with my attorneys stipulated that research would be a significant part of their earning 15 percent of the sale of our building, I had come to the dismal realization that they were never going to do what needed to be done.

Shortly after, on February 2, 1999, von Hülsen sent me a startling fax. She wrote, "I shall do my best to discover how the property came to be used for the production of Nazi flags. It might be a good idea for you to hire a detective agency because merely proving that 16 Wallstrasse was used to produce Nazi flags is not sufficient for our legal purposes. We must prove that the flag-producing company had influence over the forced auction. I doubt we will succeed in that, however."

In that fax, von Hülsen was confessing to me that a path to legally quashing the *Ariseurs'* restitution claim existed in German law. Therefore, it was *not* the German government trying to force me to pay the *Ariseurs* off no matter what. It was my own attorneys who, instead of providing me with the most zealous possible representation, just wanted the case over and done with.

Von Hülsen never reported back to me about any effort she made to learn details of the mass production of Nazi flags inside 16 Wallstrasse. Perhaps when she said she would do "her best" to discover the relevant information about the Nazi flag with its swastika, her best was limited by her position with two other attorneys or her own inhibitions to take a leadership position. In any event, having decided to act on my commuter friend's recommendation of Kroll for their investigative expertise, I made an early March appointment with one of the firm's managing directors, Elaine Wood.

Previously, Elaine had earned a JD from Columbia Law School and then worked six years as an assistant United States attorney. Learning of her no-nonsense background gave me confidence. At the meeting with Elaine, I went over the salient reasons I had wound up seeking help from Kroll. "This is an interesting matter," she said. "And we have somebody ideally positioned to assist you."

"Who?" I asked.

"The American-born director of Kroll Germany, Louis Wonderly. Before joining Kroll, Louis was a top-notch investigative reporter. He worked in Europe for international news organizations. Nazi-era history is among his specialties."

Elaine, Louis, and I subsequently participated in a three-way call to discuss the objectives of an eventual investigation. On that call, both Elaine and Louis sounded enthusiastic and thoroughly professional. What an uplifting, energizing change it was for me to feel truly *heard*.

Louis Wonderly summed things up on the call by saying, "Among our initial objectives for this investigation will be: Number one: collecting the completest possible relevant background information on David Heim, Klaus Gerken, and Johanna Weber. Number two: investigating whether David Heim and Klaus Gerken were Nazi Party members. Number three: discovering if they had connections to Nazi higher-ups who facilitated their acquiring 16 Wallstrasse in 1938. And number four: unearthing as much information as possible about how the Nazi flag came to be mass-produced in the building. How does that sound, Joanne?"

I felt ready to sign on the dotted line but held off until discussing the prospect with Greg. "Interesting," my husband remarked. "How much would this cost?"

"They require a $10,000 retainer. And they say costs could run a minimum of $20,000."

Steadily and calmly, Greg looked me in the eyes. "Nothing ventured, nothing gained," he said. Then he added, "There's one thing you should keep in mind, though. Yes, it's true that with uncertain motives, von Hülsen made a half-hearted suggestion for you to hire an investigator. But actually going ahead and doing it will drive another wedge between you and your attorneys. It'll be like directly telling them you lack faith in their work."

"When I send them that message, may I tie a shiny blue ribbon around it?"

Greg raised an eyebrow. "You'd be tying a shiny blue ribbon on it, in effect, by seeking answers to questions the attorneys—for reasons not fully understood—don't especially want to see answered. Heim & Gerken's Holocaust-era conduct, for example, could be at least shameful and perhaps even criminal. Not to mention your attorneys' failure to work in the Intrator family's best interests."

"Sounds great to me!" I exclaimed, feeling relieved that the tension between us had died down. Thinking back, I imagine that my Berlin experience touched him in ways that were very painful given his fragile beginnings.

I wrote to von Hülsen that I had granted power of attorney to Louis Wonderly, allowing him to talk about the case with them on my behalf. I sent copies to von Trott and Lammek. "Please do not inform Frau Weber or her attorneys of this fact," I said as part of my message.

None of the three attorneys acknowledged my message.

"You know, Joanne," Louis said to me one day, "there are rumors that some people have had success posing as *Ariseurs*, or heirs to *Ariseurs*, to file fraudulent restitution claims. Because German government agencies and courts are so overworked, the fraudsters can wind up chasing off legitimate claimants, or getting legitimate claimants to pay them off. Just rumors, as I said. In any event, though, I would like to review the details of Johanna Weber's lawsuit to assess the merits of her claim."

Von Hülsen, Lammek, and von Trott all told Louis they had no information about David Heim, Klaus Gerken, Johanna Weber, or their company. If they were being truthful with Louis, they were as good as confirming to me that they had done no research towards fending off legal attacks against me and my family from the *Ariseurs*. I really had to wonder why the LAROV had so much information about us when our own attorneys apparently had nothing on our opponents. The lawyers must have been very sure of themselves. Did they assume we would be grateful to get whatever moneys they negotiated, never imagining any claimants would be interested in the story behind the theft? This failure of imagination is not unfamiliar. When people are too focused on a goal, they fail to see any impediment to their approach. In my mind, it is a form of stupidity, a defect in reasoning. We were not on the same playing field. All they saw was the building's financial value, and all I was interested in was its history. That is not to say financial restitution wouldn't have been welcomed. And Kroll costs and my Berlin expenses could have instead gone into Ben's college fund.

If my attorneys did not have the needed information, Louis nevertheless had ideas for going about finding it. Whereas my attorneys' conduct in this case had conditioned me to agonizing, prolonged involvement in a Sisyphean slog, Louis's hard-nosed, indefatigable pursuit of relevant facts proved a heady experience. Louis often contacted me on the phone with major findings. He sent emails with regular updates, and those emails at times were coming in every few days. In one early communication, he wrote, "I have found relevant business registries for Birkenwerder, a northern Berlin suburb where David Heim and Klaus Gerken established their furniture factory in 1919. A number of various Heims and Gerkens are listed as co-owners. Among the co-owners, for example, are David Heim's daughter, Johanna Weber (née Heim), and her husband, Helmut Weber. Helmut Weber was active in the company starting in the 1930s."

I already felt some satisfaction that Louis was starting to find out who these people were. I now knew, beyond all doubt, that Johanna Weber personally had—at the very least—*access* to information about what went on inside 16 Wallstrasse during the Nazi era.

"Johanna Weber's husband, Helmut Weber," Louis continued, "went on to assume the leadership of Heim & Gerken after Johanna's father, David Heim, died in 1945. However, in the Berlin trade registries there are Heim & Gerken files for 1923 and 1938, but then nothing for the company between 1938 and 1955."

How convenient for my *Ariseur* adversaries in the 16 Wallstrasse case that some government records of their business activities from 1938 through the end of the war were missing. I recalled how von Trott had told me that 90 percent of the files pertaining to the history of this building were destroyed by the Gestapo. That the Gestapo or someone tried to cover up what Nazis did inside 16 Wallstrasse by destroying records related to the property was another big fat clue in itself: nefarious activities had been carried out there! But meanwhile, where were the surviving 10 percent of the documents, and what story might they help to tell?

Louis told me that in May 1945, the Nazis sent mountains of Nazi-era documentation to a paper mill in a town in Germany, Schwabing-Freimann, to be turned into pulp. US intelligence agents, though, were able to rescue the trove, which wound up archived in the Berlin Document Center.

"I'm going to see what I can turn up for each of the Heims and Gerkens in that Berlin Document Center," he explained. "And there's an additional angle to my research of these families. Heim & Gerken operated through 1972, when it began to be overseen by the Communist government. This means that records from the former East German government, including the Stasi, may turn up something of interest for us.

"And there's one more thing," Louis said. "I'm going to have my team go through Berlin address books from the 1930s and 1940s to figure out which businesses were located at 16 Wallstrasse when Heim & Gerken took over the building in 1938."

It was all I could do to refrain from shouting, "Yes!"

A short while later, I had another update from Louis. His team had located and interviewed a man named Erwin Ibert, who was the director of a furniture company, Hillerau, which leased space in 16 Wallstrasse from Heim & Gerken. "He was born in 1926, so he would've only been twelve or so when the building was taken from your family, and not the *Hausmeister* we hoped for," said Louis. "But we learned something from him that might eventually prove useful: though Ibert claims to know nothing about the production of Nazi flags, he does know that Johanna Weber is now divorced from Helmut Weber, who at one time was a property manager for 16 Wallstrasse."

The wait to see where these different paths Louis was investigating were going to lead kept me in eager suspense.

Shortly after Ben celebrated becoming bar mitzvah in June 1999, the phone rang.

"Joanne? Louis Wonderly here. I have important news about the investigation."

Louis and his team had combed through Berlin address directories, starting with the year 1930 and working forward until the mid-1940s. They had discovered that Heim & Gerken became commercial tenants in 16 Wallstrasse in 1931.

"They remained listed at the property each year through the mid-1940s. You understand what that means, right?" said Louis. "Once Hitler came to power in 1933, Aryan tenants no longer had to pay rent to Jewish property owners and landlords. Regardless of when a specific antisemitic decree may have been issued, the German courts in any event had completely stopped protecting Jews. So, Heim & Gerken had front-row seats to, and were direct beneficiaries of, Hitler and his henchmen stealing property and other assets from your family." Louis went on to explain, moreover, that in connection with a Nazi decree on expropriation of Jewish-owned property, Göring in 1938 specified that property taken from Jews belonged to the Reich. In other words, unless Heim & Gerken were willing Nazi collaborators, they would not have been allowed to own and manage 16 Wallstrasse after the forced auction.

Our agreement with Sonex stated that these Sonex agents—von Trott, Lammek, and von Hülsen—were to "locate" our property. The contract was boilerplate, but, if Heim & Gerken had Aryanized the property from my family, then Sonex agents had a duty to locate the *whole* of 16 Wallstrasse for us—and discover the story of the *Ariseurs* Heim & Gerken as well.

My attorneys shamefully miscalculated in thinking all members of the Berglas–Intrator families would blindly agree to negotiate with the *Ariseurs*. Once I had made clear we would *not* do so, though, did von Trott not do his own research for the 16 Wallstrasse case? If he had, did he tell himself that the information about Heim & Gerken would never surface? I vaguely felt that might be the case, but if it that were true, it would be so morally repulsive that I could not bring myself, at the time, to seriously contemplate it.

Where did this leave me now? I finally had relevant facts in hand, so I should have felt relieved, but instead I was angry. Angry at myself. Why had I been so pathetically passive during the past six years? Why had I not summoned the courage to demand that the attorneys do the work described in our agreement? Of course, the answer was that I was still too much affected by my own German upbringing to stand up to those whom I considered to be authority figures. And I was an ocean away and then some, working full-time as a psychiatrist while being a wife and mother. And there was no usable Internet to do my own research.

A few days later, Louis called again, sounding exuberant. "I have some really exciting news for you, Joanne! This stuff is fireworks."

"What is it, Louis?" I asked, catching his excitement.

"Doing research in the Berlin Document Center, I found David Heim's and Klaus Gerken's Nazi Party membership papers."

"You're amazing, Louis. But how could those German attorneys look me in the eyes with their damned poker faces and allege there was no way of finding out if Heim and Gerken were Nazis? You'll understand, in this moment, I'm excited but also very, very upset!"

"Oh, I do understand. And speaking of complex emotions, I really did have to check myself coming out of that document center today. On the one hand, I had an overpowering feeling of 'Bingo!' But the reality is, with matters of the Third Reich, there is no overjoyed 'Bingo!' moment, just recognition of the ghastly truth."

"To have it confirmed is kind of satisfying but also very upsetting for me too. The cold harsh reality of what my family was put through."

"Anyway," Louis went on, "to be specific, Klaus Gerken joined the Nazi Party in May of 1933, and David Heim in July of 1937. Given that they began renting at 16 Wallstrasse in 1931, two years before Hitler took power, they were able to see, daily, what the Nazis' antisemitic decrees were doing to your family. You know? Financially bleeding the Berglas and Intrator owners of the property dry. That gave them an advantage in knowing when to exploit the situation and ambush the Jewish owners."

"Like vultures!" I cried. "Inside 16 Wallstrasse, David Heim and

Klaus Gerken waited like vultures to swoop down on the property carcass of my formerly prosperous, happy family."

"*Dem Geier gleich*," mused Louis.

"What?" I asked, puzzled.

"It's Goethe. A poem that starts with an evocation of a vulture."[1]

"I don't know my Goethe, but I do know vultures."

"I'm going to be sending you a chart," Louis went on, "showing the companies occupying 16 Wallstrasse between 1933 and 1945. I'll give you an idea, now, of what it shows. In 1933, besides your family's company, Realitas, and the Heim & Gerken renters, 16 Wallstrasse had another eighteen tenants. Four companies—all with Jewish-sounding names—had left by 1938."

"By 1938," I said, "the year of Kristallnacht."

"Indeed. By 1939, eight more companies, including Realitas, were gone. But I want to make special mention of a concern known as Geitel and Company. Geitel was already there in the early thirties and left in 1935, but returned to 16 Wallstrasse in 1938, occupying four thousand square meters of the building."

"Who were these Geitel people?" I asked.

"I'm going to be researching that very question. For now, though, I can tell you that by 1943, five companies remained in 16 Wallstrasse, among them Geitel as well as Heim & Gerken."

It took Louis some time to do his research on Geitel and Company, but then one day, my phone rang.

"Are you sitting down?" Louis asked.

"What did you find now, Louis?"

"OK, so, first off, Geitel is the company that mass-produced Nazi flags inside 16 Wallstrasse. And I must mention that in the German Federal Archives, I found documentation of Nazi Party membership for Gustav Geitel and his business partner, Max Gerke. When Geitel and Company returned to 16 Wallstrasse in 1938, they rented the lion's share of it. I found audit reports proving that the company made Nazi swastika flags—they called it "the national flag"— for the Wehrmacht, as well as for the Kriegsmarine—that was the Nazi Navy—and the Luftwaffe."

"It is horrible, Louis."

"There's more," said Louis.

"Go on." I took a breath and grabbed a pillow to hold.

"On January 9, 1943, the Reich Ministry of Finance sent a memorandum to the commands of the Wehrmacht and the Nazi Navy, saying that because Geitel and Company was making such huge profits from these two branches of the armed forces, the Nazi government wanted, and I quote, 'a reasonable reduction in prices' for future contracts."

"All that, after this building was stolen from my Jewish family," I said.

"And there's more."

"Do go on."

"Geitel also sold, in bulk, the stigmatizing badges Nazis imposed on Polish slave laborers. Geitel was a one-stop shop for physical markers of Nazi totalitarianism? And Heim and Gerken were making money by renting 16 Wallstrasse space to them."

"And," I said half-heartedly.

"That's not the end of it," Louis continued. "At the Brandenburg State Archives in Potsdam, I went into the special inventory—in German it's called the *Sonderinventar*—and discovered records for twenty Russian slave laborers exploited by Geitel and Company inside 16 Wallstrasse."

"Slaves forced to work inside my family's former building!"

"Yes," said Louis.

This was monstrous. I knew the Nazis used slaves from the

Reich's occupied territories in Eastern Europe for industry as well as in agriculture. But to learn it happened inside 16 Wallstrasse, and to learn it from Louis rather than from my attorneys, was just beyond the pale.

"Those weren't the only slaves forced to labor inside 16 Wallstrasse, or for the companies involved with managing the property," Louis explained. "For example, Heim & Gerken requested additional slave labor for a hefty project—and now, hold on just a minute—I'm going to read exactly what the documents say regarding Heim & Gerken at that juncture: 'The company is in the process of retooling. Currently, facilities are being optimized for the production of anti-aircraft devices.'"

"So, the *Ariseurs* of my family's property exploited slave labor to make Nazi weapons of war?"

"Yes. It seems probable to me that most of that production was done in their preexisting factory."

"Near Sachsenhausen, right?'

"What a coincidence you should mention Sachsenhausen."

"Why?"

"About thirty miles to the northeast of Berlin, there's a town called Eberswalde. And in Eberswalde, there's a government agency for occupational safety and health that retains Nazi-era archives. On May 15, 1944, the Nazi-controlled agency did a review of Heim & Gerken. Documentation from that review shows that Heim and Gerken were then using sixteen female prisoners of war from Eastern Europe as slaves. Further notations show that Heim and Gerken were not providing food for the slaves. Moreover, the agency specified that the slaves had to be housed at a concentration camp. I am betting the slaves were trucked in from Sachsenhausen."

I felt overwhelmed by all this atrocious history and upset by recollections of von Trott's firm assurances that all the documentation Louis was turning up would be downright impossible to find and, therefore, there could be no point in looking for it.

It had been six years since I first met with von Trott in the Waldorf Astoria.

That night, I suffered a nightmare about 16 Wallstrasse after it was stolen from my family. In my nightmare, the figures of Heim, Gerken, and Geitel were all very cozy inside offices on the building's top floor, while sweating slaves labored painfully in the cavernous main floor area, with its towering unfinished ceilings, concrete floors, and broken windows letting frigid air rush in over them. In a heap in a corner, slaves who had starved or frozen to death were discarded like so much rubbish. The dream, which woke me in a full sweat with its gruesome visions of slave labor, pounded into me the realization that my lawyers had utterly failed me.

A while later, Louis called again.

"I've turned up some crucial information about Erwin Ibert."

"The longtime super at 16 Wallstrasse?"

"Well, that's what he said he was. But records I've found show that for twenty-eight years, he was Heim & Gerken's foreman."

"How convenient that when you interviewed him, he forgot to mention that fact," I replied.

"Yeah, well, given the span of Ibert's employment as a Heim & Gerken foreman in the building, he obviously knew that Geitel was mass-producing the Nazi flag there. I'm not exactly surprised he denied it to my face, though."

"Where do you see this all going?"

"I think we now have enough information to share with the attorneys. We can send them a packet that includes a research report and supportive documentation."

"Sounds good. I want to include a cover note to Lammek."

"What do you intend to tell him?" Louis asked.

"I want to tell him that he had best inform Johanna Weber's attorneys about the exploitation of slave labor inside 16 Wallstrasse. Particularly given everything that's come out recently—by means of the Swiss banking crisis—concerning slave labor in the Nazi era."

"Timely! I do know that Chancellor Schröder has set up a slave labor compensation fund."

"Exactly."

My attorneys' reactions to Louis's research dismayed me. Lammek said, "I'm afraid that if we forward this material to Johanna Weber's attorney, potential buyers of 16 Wallstrasse will get wind of a major restitution battle brewing and shy away from making offers."

Von Hülsen sided with Lammek.

I called Hans Frank and brought him up to date on everything. "Joanne," he said, "I understand why you're upset about Lammek currently refusing to forward Louis's findings to Weber's attorneys. But I'm reasonably certain that he *will* use this material when negotiating with the *Ariseurs*."

"Why do you say that?"

"Because in the end, if Johanna Weber gets less money out of this, the attorneys will wind up with more."

"Hmm," I replied. "And what about this repugnant practice of avoiding prolonged litigation by paying off the *Ariseurs*? Is it ever reported by the media?"

"I can't say that I've seen any reporting on the topic outside of highly specialized legal trade publications."

"That this isn't being reported to the general public is reprehensible.

This is the dirty underbelly of restitution. And you know how Germans are about any appearance of schmutz."

"Yes, yes," Hans replied.

"May I ask, what is the standard amount for *Ariseurs* to receive? Johanna Weber was originally demanding fifty percent. I think now, she's down to thirty."

"My experience," Hans replied, "is ten percent."

In late September, Quadriga, a real estate development company, made an offer to buy 16 Wallstrasse. Quadriga had offered enough money that Lammek agreed to withhold showing the property to competitors for two months while the company did a feasibility assessment.

Louis soon called me. "I was communicating with von Hülsen, who told me they're planning a meeting with Weber's attorneys in October."

"They are?"

"Yes. I asked her if you would be invited to that meeting. She said, 'I don't think inviting Joanne would be the right thing to do. It might awaken false hopes for her.'"

I was incensed. "Why shouldn't I be able to face these beneficiaries of Nazi crimes that were committed against my family?" I said. "Look what happened with the LAROV judges and my flash camera! I think it's imperative for me to look Johanna Weber in her *Ariseur* eyes."

I tried appealing to my Berglas relatives for support. In letters to several of them, including Fred Berglas in London, I detailed Louis's findings: "The *Ariseur* Johanna Weber is demanding 30 percent of the eventual sale price of 16 Wallstrasse in exchange for dropping her lawsuit claiming the whole property. I certainly appreciate that we'd all like to see this case behind us. But in light of everything we now know about the *Ariseurs*, we can't possibly cave to their outrageous blackmail."

On October 13, Lammek sent me a fax. It included this: "Using the Kroll material entails a certain risk for the community of heirs." Lammek was my Berglas relatives' attorney. I deduced from his fax that the Berglases had read my letters but remained unmoved.

Von Hülsen told me that the Berglases wanted to sell 16 Wallstrasse at the earliest possible opportunity. "And you know, stirring up a full-blown restitution battle could have a negative impact on the final sale price of the building," she said. "Markets are so complex here. Moreover, Johanna Weber has a say in accepting a purchase offer. Her approval of any sale is mandatory."

I did not fly off the handle, though I might have. Instead, I asked, "What gives her that right?" I never received a satisfactory answer to that question.

On October 23, I wrote to Lammek, "Louis and I have a contact at *Der Spiegel*. We are ready for the German public to know the whole story behind the Aryanization of 16 Wallstrasse. However, so as not to interfere with your negotiations with Johanna Weber, and/or with the sale of the building, I will hold off on contacting that journalist."

On November 13, I wrote again to Fred Berglas:

My attorney, Dorothea von Hülsen, informs me that you want to sell 16 Wallstrasse as soon as possible, but I wanted to hear that directly from you, to be certain it is true. I also would appreciate hearing from you as to your understanding of how it is that the Ariseur Johanna Weber has the right to disapprove of a potential sale of our property. Perhaps you don't know that years ago, when I

met with the attorneys in Berlin, I asked them to investigate Heim
& Gerken's Nazi-era history. They never did so, but through relent-
less perseverance, I've secured documented proof that owners Heim
and Gerken were Nazi Party members, and that after taking the
building from our Jewish relatives, the building was used for the
mass manufacture of Nazi flags and other such things, with slave
labor doing the work.

Fred Berglas did not reply. But on November 19, Lammek copied
me on a letter he sent to the Berglas family. "At the proper time," he
wrote, "I will be using the information found by the Kroll detectives."

At the proper time? I said to myself. The proper time to discover
what the *Ariseurs* did with 16 Wallstrasse, and to use that history for
our case, was seven years ago!

I responded to Lammek the next day:

We of the Intrator family will agree to sell the property for the
best price as soon as possible. But I want you to know how abso-
lutely appalling it is that Heim & Gerken's sordid Nazi history only
saw daylight as a result of my hiring Kroll. Not having this evidence
in a timely fashion forced us into this negotiation with the Ariseur.
If early on you had all this same documentation and evidence, I
question whether the LAROV would have given us such a hard time
these last seven years.

On December 29, Lammek sent a communication to all Intrator
and Berglas claimants that Quadriga had offered 7.3 million deutsche
marks for the purchase of 16 Wallstrasse. The offer was notarized,
meaning that they were bound by it until the end of the year. "However,
there are two additional offers for purchase of the property," Lammek

wrote. "If you all approve, I will move ahead by informing the three bidders that they must present their final offers by noon on January 17, 2000."

The next day, December 30, 1999, the *Berliner Morgenpost* published an article about the *Ariseur* David Heim's other daughter, Gerda Heim (sister of Johanna Weber). In the article, she alleged "absolute ignorance of Nazi policies against Jews. No one ever wants to believe me, but it is true. We were clueless."[2]

Who would be ignorant or gullible enough to believe that?

Then Gerda Heim turned the knife in my family's Nazi-created wound by saying that when Hitler came to power, members of the Heim family were under scrutiny from the Gestapo and the SS.

The Heims, *victims* of the Nazis? I knew better than that. But the journalist didn't ask Gerda Heim any challenging questions. I wondered if the timing of this duplicitous article was mere coincidence— or perhaps the *Ariseurs* anticipated our going public with Louis's findings, and so had begun their own media campaign.

I was reeling.

As time went on, I could accept the psychic utility of not believing the horrendous history that postwar Germans faced. Self-deception can be a survival mechanism, especially when powerful emotional attachments are involved. To first think of oneself as being part of the master race and, a few years later, to be faced with such violence and destruction must be a destabilizing prospect for many people. The propaganda and lies perpetrated on the German people do not just dissolve in thin air. This stuff was baked in at times of great vulnerability. We underestimate the power of tyrannical psychopaths when we are broken as the Germans were before the war.

16 Intimidation

I was now at an emotionally perilous juncture.

After years of pushing for the Nazi-era history of 16 Wallstrasse to be uncovered, I had succeeded in getting it dragged out into the light of day.

And if I had a right to feel triumphant, I nonetheless was marooned, feeling *bitterly* triumphant, as I had no partners interested in aggressively using this truth to strengthen our bargaining position against our Heim & Gerken opponents.

My whole being—mind, heart, and soul—was still roiled with revulsion over the prospect of having to reward Heim and Gerken (via their heirs) for their roles in Nazism and the Nazi theft of my family's property.

Louis Wonderly's detective work produced results so quickly, it was exhilarating. Yet by the irony of fate, his findings converged with serious offers from investors wanting to buy 16 Wallstrasse. And most of my Berglas relatives were anxious to get the building sold as soon as possible.

On January 6, 2000, Dorothea von Hülsen wrote to tell me that Clemens Lammek was threatening to sue me on the Berglases' behalf for getting in the way of the sale. Never mind that if we succeeded in eliminating Weber from the case, the Intrators and Berglases would make more from the sale of the property, as would the lawyers.

"Joanne," Louis told me after he learned of Lammek's threat, "don't fall for that. It's an intimidation tactic. The evidence is all in *your* favor and against Heim & Gerken."

Yet while it was comforting to know that Louis was supporting me, and while he might have been correct that Lammek's threat was idle, once again during this prolonged restitution case, Lammek's threat came at me in real time. My sleep, always poor, had me waking up in cold sweats. I did not have the perspective to see it just as a bullying tactic, and to this day I still do not know if it was. At a remove of years, I can view what was going on with some objectivity in understanding my reactions.

The 16 Wallstrasse case had started with the German government surreally requiring me to prove that when Nazis stole my grandfather's building from him, my grandfather was a victim of Nazi antisemitism. Von Trott had resolutely and erroneously insisted that finding documentation of Heim & Gerken's conduct during the Third Reich would be impossible. To my face, German judges had slandered my Jewish grandfather. What were the chances of my being treated fairly if I was sued by a German attorney in a German court?

One word von Hülsen used in addressing and describing the status of the restitution case, a word that especially rankled, was "character." When I would ask why she was not using Louis's research to strengthen our bargaining position vis-à-vis Johanna Weber, she would assert that information about Heim's and Gerken's character was irrelevant to the restitution law.

I viewed von Hülsen's use of the word as a red herring and ironic as a psychiatrist. The point of Louis's research was not what it revealed about the *Ariseurs'* character, though I am sure very interesting. The point was that his research documented how Heim and Gerken materially participated in, and benefited from, the Aryanization of

16 Wallstrasse. Character can describe or explain behavior, but it is irrelevant to restitution law.

The German word *Ariseur*, notably used by von Trott throughout the case, is rooted in the Nazis' high regard for the "master race" of Aryans. How polite and remote and detached from certain crimes it sounded to say "the *Ariseurs*—the people who Aryanized 16 Wallstrasse"— instead of calling them "the Nazis—the specific Nazis, the Heims and Gerkens—who Nazified 16 Wallstrasse." The terms *Ariseurs* and Aryanization are euphemisms for talking about what Nazis did when they Nazified Jewish-owned properties.

With everything Louis was turning up, it was no longer a question of connecting the dots between Heim & Gerken and the Nazification of 16 Wallstrasse. There was, rather, one big Nazi dot staring us in the face. And my own attorney wanted to disparage this mountain of evidence as an irrelevant matter of "character."

"Lammek's potential lawsuit against you," von Hülsen told me, "could only conceivably be successful in a few scenarios. This is about your determination to confront Weber and her attorneys, right? Therefore, if your persisting in that determination were to result in Weber winning her case against the State of Berlin, Lammek's case against you might succeed. It could perhaps also succeed if your actions resulted in the loss of a profitable sale of the property. In any event, the Berglases want to sell as soon as possible. I would not like to go against them alone. You should communicate with the Berglases about how to move forward."

Repeatedly in this period, Louis urged me not to be intimidated by Lammek's tactic. As an American, Louis had strong anti-Nazi sentiments. Apropos of everything he turned up on Heim & Gerken, he once told me, with great satisfaction, "This was my case waiting to happen."

"Why are Lammek and von Hülsen so dead set against showing your adversaries' Nazi past?" Louis wondered in a letter to me. "They always have a hundred arguments why this information shouldn't be used. I'm thoroughly confused as to how *not* using this crucial information is, supposedly, advantageous for you."

Louis pointed out that when we first started this investigation, von Hülsen claimed she had no information about the Webers. "But now, suddenly, she says she knows that Weber's son—whom she won't name—is doing research demonstrating how friendly the Heim family was with Jews in the 1930s. That self-serving ruse out of the Webers is laughable. Johanna Weber's father was a Nazi Party member." Louis also wondered why von Hülsen had not been more forthcoming with relevant information. "By now, she has related so many conflicting stories and strategies that I hardly know what to believe, except that having seen the evidence in this matter, I believe the facts speak loudly and clearly for you."

Though Lammek's threat thoroughly distressed me, I was hypervigilant about controlling myself around my son Benjamin. I was careful not to discuss the case in his presence. Greg, though, knew that the intelligence on the Heims' and Gerkens' Nazi past was agitating me, that I was wearing myself out, and that the threat of being sued weighed on me. If my feelings of powerlessness in the 16 Wallstrasse case, combined with my general life circumstances, were orders of magnitude less terrifying and excruciating than my grandparents' helplessness as Nazis destroyed their lives, my hopelessness and anger nonetheless were still real, still devastating for me.

Suffering insomnia, and chronically sleep-deprived, I resorted to my childhood coping strategy of going downstairs late each night, after everybody else was asleep, and dancing—frantically dancing to Prokofiev, in Martha Graham style—until I was too exhausted to think.

When I had danced myself ragged, I would collapse into a pool of sweat on a large leather sofa in our living room. On that leather surface, the sweat felt discomforting, all sticky and clammy.

Most such nights, Greg would wind up rescuing me from the sweaty leather couch. One tactic he relied on when unable to sleep was to go to the kitchen and eat a bowl of cereal. And that happened often. He would consume his therapeutic cereal and then come over and gently guide me back upstairs to bed. Finally, one morning, after yet another of those nights, Greg said: "Joanne, listen—you've had, and still have, my support in pursuing restitution, but you need help. You need to go back into therapy."

Truly furious, I lashed out at him. "Don't tell me to go to therapy because the Nazis brutalized my family. You make me sound mentally ill for wanting justice—and you, you hardly talk about the Nazis' devastation to your own German family."

The abiding undercurrent of agitation between Greg and I bore fruit in that it spurred me to consult Hans Frank, though to Greg's disappointment, not my former therapist.

"I admit," Hans said when I called, "I'm surprised that Lammek threatened to sue you. However, you should not be intimidated by it. Not in the least."

I now had both Louis and Hans encouraging me to stand up against Lammek. Hearing Hans say those words helped calm me. He continued, "I suggest that you again instruct these attorneys to send out the Kroll report on Heim & Gerken's Nazi history."

I agreed. "There's one other thing that's come up with Heim & Gerken that I'd like to run past you, to hear what you think," I said.

"Go ahead."

"I've heard that Weber's attorneys are attempting to promote a theory that Jacques Berglas went through bankruptcy in 1929. They want to allege that his 1929 bankruptcy unleashed events that precipitated the forced auction in 1938."

"Rubbish!" Hans Frank exclaimed. "That was the year of the great stock market crash. Plenty of businesses reorganized under bankruptcies in 1929 and subsequently recovered. Weber would have to prove that Jacques Berglas never recovered from bankruptcy. But we already know that he *did* recover. For one thing, had he not recovered from a 1929 bankruptcy, he would not have retained ownership of 16 Wallstrasse through 1938. I repeat my suggestion for you to again instruct the attorneys to send out Kroll's report with its damning findings."

Bluntly, without explanation, Lammek refused to use the Kroll report. After hemming, hawing, and more stalling, von Hülsen finally offered to send it to Weber's attorneys. "Why didn't you act independently of Lammek earlier? In the interest of the Intrator family?"

"I *was* acting in your interest," she responded. "Sending the Kroll report is likely to result in protracted litigation with Weber. Not getting into that protracted litigation saves you time and money." I shook my head, exasperated. I don't think it ever occurred to her to share decision-making with me. I am quite sure she was left out of von Trott's and Lammek's decisions, as I was with hers. I doubt she was aware of this pattern. I tried one more angle.

"But even if you and Lammek can't force Weber off the case altogether, by obliging Weber to accept a lower percentage of the total, you would be getting more money for both the Intrators and the Berglases, and for yourselves!" The conversation ground down. It seemed pointless.

In the beginning, if our attorneys had promptly done the work of exposing Heim and Gerken and their Nazi connections, we might have avoided this interfamily conflict. But with the intelligence collected years later and by Kroll instead of our attorneys, just as offers to buy 16 Wallstrasse were pouring in, the restitution case was coming down to a business settlement between the *Ariseurs* and the Berglases, with me on the sidelines advocating for true justice. If one part of me was still unsettled in the face of Lammek's threat to sue me, another part of me was energetically insisting that caving to Weber's demands would be cowardly and shameful.

The once fond and productive union of the Intrator and Berglas families was abandoned and forgotten, a treasure lost—like so much else—to the Nazi Reich.

On his deathbed, my father had demanded to know whether I was tough enough. I thought now about how the word "tough" had evolved for me. I *was* tough, I decided. I was tough enough to overcome the shame of my 1967 trip and not buckle in Germany; after all, I was now a doctor, wife, and mother, not an overwhelmed college girl. As my family's case dragged on, "tough" meant I had to stand up to German lawyers. "Tough" also meant finding a solution to the disrupted family union by uniting the Berglases and the Intrators against the *Ariseur* Johanna Weber.

I could not imagine my Berglas cousins not siding with me once they were made aware of everything I knew. I thought back to how our families first became related. In the 1800s in Austrian Galicia, Salomon Berglas married Fanny Intrator, and then the couple moved to Berlin, where they thrived. Because of that root connection, as it happened, *both* families were related to Max Karp. In hopes that the Berglases would choose justice over an immediate financial settlement of the 16 Wallstrasse case, I mailed them a dossier on our common relative who had been murdered at Sachsenhausen.

Within it, I highlighted the last letter Max sent to my father before Max was abducted and sent to the concentration camp. The letter references his previous ordeal being deported to the no-man's-land of Zbąszyń. An element of the letter that I thought might particularly grab the Berglases' attention, though, involved Max's ultimately futile attempts to escape to Shanghai; Jacques Berglas had been the promulgator of the Berglas Plan, a valiant if failed effort to establish a colony for European Jewish refugees in China.

While awaiting responses from them, and aware of how fast-moving the potential sale of 16 Wallstrasse might be, I asked Hans Frank to fax Lammek a request to be copied on all correspondence involving Weber and the sale of the building. In that fax, Hans said, "I will meet with Dr. Intrator to persuade her to fall in line, if that is humanly possible."

"Joanne," Hans said to me on the phone after sending that fax, "would you be available to meet with me in my apartment to discuss this matter comprehensively?"

"Yes, of course. And I very much appreciate your efforts."

"When you come, please bring the Sonex agreement with you. I want to be sure of understanding it completely."

On February 25, I met with Hans in his Central Park West apartment living room. From its wide windows in this premium location we faced the park. Hans's living room, rather like the man himself, exuded *Gemütlichkeit*. When he joined me, I observed how frail he had become. Hans was now eighty-eight, and I knew he recently had been through several illnesses. I was deeply grateful that he was still devoting energy to my case, and I watched him as he calmly and efficiently pored over the Sonex agreement. Despite his diminished physical state, Hans was mentally sharp and well disciplined.

"Do you realize," he asked, looking up, "that this agreement gives Sonex fifteen percent of the market value of 16 Wallstrasse—due from you and the Berglases—no matter how much Weber would get from you?"

"I don't understand."

"The first money paid out is the fifteen percent to the lawyers. That amount comes from the gross amount. It is independent from what you pay the *Ariseurs*."

"So the lawyers get paid from the top, meaning they have no financial incentive to work against Weber on our behalf? How was this missed by all of us?"

Hans shook his head. "A partial remedy," he said, "would be to require Lammek to get Weber to accept a flat, pre-agreed amount rather than a percentage of the sale. That way, your attorneys will still be motivated to get the best possible price for the building, while limiting your financial exposure to Weber's claim."

"You mean the lawyers and family have equal exposure."

"Yes."

Hans next reviewed Kroll's documentation of the Nazis who Aryanized 16 Wallstrasse. He already knew the gist, but I brought the materials to this meeting, thinking it might have an impact on him. I watched Hans as he meticulously inspected David Heim's and Klaus Gerken's Nazi Party membership documents, and the information about the mass production of Nazi flags in the building. All the primary historical documentation was conspicuously stamped with the Nazi swastika.

"Hans, why do you think Lammek hasn't used this in our favor?"

"That omission is curious, and I can't explain it. But I do think Lammek believes he did you a service when he got the LAROV to declare you rightful owners of the property. And you know, Weber's lawyer will be callous about this Nazi business. He's there to fight for money for his client, not to see his clients' past victims compensated."

In the following moments of silence, I sensed Hans Frank regarding me with a palpable paternal gentleness. "Joanne," he began, "I'm concerned about the emotional cost—for you—of this case. You see, I have no doubt, if you were to continue refusing to negotiate with Weber, you'd ultimately prevail at the end of all the litigation and court processes, but it wouldn't be worth the nerve-shattering strain on you. I'll be honest: there's more than one clause in this Sonex contract"— he waved the papers—"that is surprising to me, yet I wouldn't feel right if I did anything but urge you to be practical and to consider the well-being of the living. Taking an adamant stand against paying off the *Ariseur* will push resolution of your restitution case much further into the future. Not only would that be harder on you, but it would make it more likely that the originally injured Jewish parties, including your uncle Alex, would die before it is resolved."

Hans's face was framed by the winter-bare trees in Central Park beyond the windows. I spoke up. "So it's exactly as the LAROV judge confessed to me: 'They all die when they get their property back.'"

Hans raised his eyebrows. "The Nazis ran your grandparents out of their Berlin businesses and home, and your father out of the legal profession. Still other members of your family were imprisoned in concentration camps or murdered. You will never be able to make up for what horrors were done to them."

Hans had never before spoken so personally to me. The moment was intimate, reminding me of tender times passed with my father. "Joanne," he continued, "you have done the very best anybody could conceivably do." He turned to gaze out the windows at the trees in the park and then turned back towards me. "This case, this maddening battle with a horrible, immutable past, is robbing you of precious time to be spent as a loving mother and wife."

I knew he was reaching inside himself, beyond his role as an attorney, to speak with me this way. Getting up from his chair, he walked to the windows, giving me time and space to absorb his words. To stop myself from crying, I had to pinch my hand.

Hans walked slowly over to his desk and sat down. "Joanne," he said, "there's an important exercise I want to walk you through here. I know that your father was pragmatic and realistic and would want you to be too. I'm going to show you how little the final dollar difference would be between settling now, and entering into a protracted legal battle against Johanna Weber."

Hans's hand was a little shaky, but he worked steadily, doing the math, showing me how various scenarios would turn out, and what each of them would mean for me, my brother Jack, and our uncle Alex. I followed his reasoning. He then said, "Let's draft a proposal from you to Lammek. The relationship between the two of you has become so contentious and adversarial that doing something to demonstrate good will, instead of backing him into a corner, will likely prove helpful."

As Hans worked on the draft, he explained what he was including in it. "The latest offer for the property is eight million deutsche marks," he said, "and we are going to propose that Weber receive a flat amount of five hundred thousand marks. If Lammek gets a better offer, you will wind up with more money, but Weber won't. Her payoff amount will be contractually fixed and limited."

When the draft was finished, Hans asked, "May I fax this now?"

I nodded.

≈

Several days later, my phone rang. The relative calling was Alfred Berglas's eldest daughter, Ellen Ruth Einhorn. "Joanne, you have my absolute support," she said. "What happened in the 1930s, and what's happening now with this, is terribly upsetting. Those Nazi heirs shouldn't see a pfennig. Not one red cent."

"Thank you so much for saying these things, Ellen. It's gratifying to feel the families coming together a little like this. But may I ask you something?"

"Of course."

"Have the Berglases been looking at me as the only one holding things up?"

"Some of the Berglases have been saying that, yes."

I did not ask which relatives. It was now time for reconciliation, not more conflict.

"But Joanne," Ellen went on, "I want you to know that my brother David and my sister Gaby are both firmly on your side too."[1] David's call came the next day.

17 Soul Murder

"Joanne," Louis told me one day on the phone, "the evidence that we've already gathered on Geitel has me strongly suspecting we're likely to turn up a great deal more on the company as our investigation continues. A business like Geitel's, located in central Berlin, wouldn't have been able to score huge Nazi government orders for 'national flags' without demonstrating ironclad loyalty to the Führer's goals, along with exploiting deep connections inside the Nazi hierarchy."

"Go for it, Louis," I responded. I wondered what he might find next. Something already gnawing at me was that my family had operated a large-scale textile business from inside 16 Wallstrasse. Though I lacked direct proof their textile production machines were commandeered by Geitel and subsequently used to turn out swastika flags, logic suggested that could well have been the case.

These days, an Internet search for this Geitel enterprise by its original name, Berliner Fahnenfabrik Geitel & Co., reveals photos of Nazi flags with the Geitel name stamped on a fabric border. Geitel and Company, however, grew so notorious for their Holocaust-era activities they camouflaged their company name, changing it to BEST, Berliner Stoffdruckerei GmbH, in 1948.

I soon received a fax from Louis, who had spoken with Rolf Geitel, who was seventy-eight and still going to work every day to run his family's flag-making company. Louis reported that he said the only thing he knew about his family's Holocaust-era swastika flag business was that it was located at 16 Wallstrasse. Rolf adamantly denied that his father was a Nazi Party member.

When Louis explained the 16 Wallstrasse case to Rolf, Rolf said it would be "*Unverschämtheit*," or intolerable, for our family to be denied any part of the building. He allowed that the Nazi regime was "criminal."

Waiting for a patient to arrive one morning in the late spring of 2000, I received profoundly upsetting news from Louis. On September 1, 1941, Reinhard Heydrich signed a decree compelling all Jews in the Reich to wear a cloth yellow Star of David on their chests. What Louis had discovered was that, in conformity with Heydrich's decree, the Nazis placed a rush order—with Geitel—for almost one million antisemitic patches. That order was produced inside 16 Wallstrasse.

The Nazis not only compelled Jews to wear them but also forced Jews to pay for them. The Nazis threatened Jews with deportation to concentration camps if they were caught without them, yet they were designed and fabricated in ways that guaranteed the stars would quickly fray at the edges when worn. The Nazis then toyed with the hapless Jews further by prohibiting them from making any sewing repairs to their patches. The German word for Jew, *Jude*, was produced at the star's center in mock Hebrew letters. Public posters with images of the patches announced, "If you see somebody wearing this patch, you are looking at an enemy of our people." An average Aryan in the street, spotting a Jew wearing one of these *Judensterne* made inside 16 Wallstrasse, could, with total impunity, spit on and then severely beat him or her.

The top-level owners and managers of Heim & Gerken and the Geitel company were all Nazi Party members before the forced auction of my family's building. As owners, Heim & Gerken profited off Geitel's mass production of yellow Stars of David, as nearly the entire floor space was rented by Geitel. It is certain that when outside during their last month in Berlin, my grandparents had been forced to wear the same ostracizing, antisemitic yellow stars manufactured inside the building that the Nazis had stolen from them.

There, in my office, awaiting a patient, I fought tears of rage. I thought, *Had I known this before I signed an agreement to settle the 16 Wallstrasse case, I would never have signed! I would have fought the case for the rest of my life! How could this have happened?*

My patient arrived. Compartmentalizing, walling myself off as best I could from Louis's shattering revelation, I pulled myself together. Later, after work, the terrible irony of how the whole obscene process of the Holocaust started in places like 16 Wallstrasse struck me more forcefully than ever.

That Johanna Weber had indirectly profited off Geitel's mass manufacturing of yellow *Judensterne* inside 16 Wallstrasse made no substantive difference in my case. Our contract with the *Ariseurs* had already been signed. Adding to my moral outrage was that—as with most everything Louis discovered—the damning information was available years before I met von Trott.

For example, in 1988, Holocaust scholar Konrad Kwiet published an article in *Der Spiegel* detailing Geitel's large-scale production of the yellow patches.[1] Kwiet did not specify that Geitel was located in 16 Wallstrasse, but that was the sort of research our attorneys, and not Louis, should have been doing to fulfill their contractual obligation to "locate" our property. An earlier article by Hermann Simon, the director of the New Synagogue in formerly East Berlin, identified 16 Wallstrasse as the site where the stars were fabricated.

Learning about the mass production of nearly one million

Judensterne inside 16 Wallstrasse left me feeling as if nothing I had accomplished in the case meant anything. Why was it so much easier for me to feel sad and hopeless than to scream out in rage for the lack of help I received from the lawyers? I must have sensed that my anger was so ancient that it would unhinge me, so I took the bruising upon myself. My tendency towards self-blame was ingrained in me during childhood, originating in my strongly ambivalent feelings towards my mother. Then, as a child, I had done it to protect myself against the risks of challenging those who were responsible for taking care of me, and were failing in their duties, fearing retaliation for speaking my mind.

Intense distress often rests on a knife's edge between loss of perspective and deepest insight. I could now more easily understand the hope and confusion of my grandparents and of similarly situated Jews in believing they remained a part of Germany even as Nazi power grew to encompass every aspect of their lives. They imagined they could rely on other Germans to protect them against the Nazis' implacable hatred.

I recalled those letters from the Reichsbank to my grandfather, written in the politest, most formal German while extorting him for money on antisemitic legal grounds. These proper, decorous, respectful-sounding words sadistically peeled away a person's savings and possessions, as well as that person's sense of community.

Each time my grandfather had to surrender extorted money, he probably hoped against hope that it would be the last. Likewise, with his every attempt to obtain a visa, his hope was followed by frustration after frustration until, towards the end, he descended into a state of nearly complete helplessness and hopelessness.

∽

I decided to return to therapy.

At the session, as I explained to my analyst what had led me back to her office, I could see and sense that she was intently absorbing everything I said. When I finished, she paused, then said, "When you aren't raging against yourself, you're mentally raging against the Germans for their passive-aggressive conduct, bureaucratic road-blocks, the ways they make it impossible to achieve justice, and their overall lack of interest in your family. And I recognize that you hate yourself for failing to magically repair your father's life."

I was listening.

"Previously, you found a way to hold two opposing thoughts about your mother—namely, your hatred of her for tormenting you and your love for her. It would be best if you did something similar with this 16 Wallstrasse case. On the one hand, nobody could have tried harder than you have to reclaim your family's patrimony. On the other hand, though, the task you set for yourself is impossible."

The next thing the analyst told me reminded me of something Hans Frank had said. "Your life is in New York, not Berlin. Nothing anybody says or does here, or there, can take the pain away from your grandparents or your parents, or undo what the Nazis did to Jews. There is no justice. There can never be any real justice in this."

"And?"

She took a deep breath, then leaned back in her chair. "I call what you're doing to yourself, in this case, 'soul murder.' You should find a way to stop."[2]

Soul murder—what was she talking about?

In response, I leaped to my feet, sweeping up my jacket and purse. "Who but an American would recommend I step back?" I said contemptuously. "After all, isn't that what most American Jews in the

1930s and '40s did when it came to the life-or-death plights of their European brethren?"

With that, I walked out on her. It took time for me to comprehend her wisdom and to accept that the justice I wanted was coming at a sacrifice of my own life. That was soul murder.

In the negotiations with the *Ariseurs*, Weber's attorney sent many letters to Lammek that he doubtless considered professional and polite but to me were insulting and offensive. In one, the attorney alleged that his client, Weber, understood how much Jews suffered under the Nazis and how difficult it must be for Jews to deal with "heirs to the generation of perpetrators." Truth: Johanna Weber was an *adult* during the Holocaust, and an heir perhaps—but heir of *what*?

Still, with circumstances backing us into a corner, we agreed to let them have one million deutsche marks.[3]

I thought and thought about what I could do. Might an imperceptible nudge from an ancestor—my Opa Jakob, or Max Karp, perhaps, if not my instincts—lead me to another inspired turning point, as happened when I took the flash photo of that LAROV judge? I badly wanted to expose Johanna Weber and her family's shameful secrets. She might get her one million marks, but I wanted the moral satisfaction of publicly confronting her aggressive denials with the incriminating facts.

Opportunity knocked for me in the person of journalist Christopher Schwarz. For *Wirtschaftswoche*—roughly, the German equivalent of *BusinessWeek*—Schwarz published an article about Kroll and its most recent investigative activities. Without identifying 16 Wallstrasse or the people involved, he included in his piece a few paragraphs about the case.

"I'm going to make sure this article gets called to Lammek's attention," Louis told me. "The idea is to send a message to these attorneys and Frau Weber that the 16 Wallstrasse story is newsworthy." Not long after that, I received a call from Schwarz.

"Dr. Intrator," he said, "I'm intrigued by your restitution case and want to publish a full-length feature on it. Would you and your uncle Alex be available for interviews?"

One month later, I picked up Schwarz at the White Plains Train Station near my uncle Alex's home. Alex's wife, Bella, prepared fresh coffee and a lemon pound cake; anyone just meeting her would not know that Alzheimer's disease was slowly affecting her mental acuity. At first, my uncle was distant, formal, and palpably distrustful. He made clear his profound disappointment in the restitution process. I tempered my outrage about the case, afraid that once I started showing how upset I was, I might completely lose my composure. Schwarz's manner was professional but engaging, and eventually Alex loosened up.

The article on our 16 Wallstrasse case appeared in the December 2000 issue of *Wirtschaftswoche*. Spread over four pages, the piece featured impressive photos of the building, along with images of me and my father. The title, taken from Primo Levi, was "Victims and Perpetrators." The article began with my uncle Alex's anecdote of witnessing Adolf Hitler, before he came to power, sitting leisurely in the Hotel Kaiserhof in Berlin enjoying music performed by a Hungarian string orchestra. It gave a detailed overview of the facts of the case, Louis's shocking discoveries, and the disputations between the adversaries. It ended with me imagining my father, Gerhard, telling me to enjoy life and have a schnapps. That vision came from my head. He would have said, "Enough."

In response to the article, I received many letters from longtime friends and colleagues. My synagogue invited me to deliver a talk about my experiences to the congregation. But if the article had any substantive effect on my attorneys or the *Ariseur*, I never knew it. I had been hoping for public outrage over the one million *Judensterne* produced in 16 Wallstrasse. I wanted the cursed deal with the *Ariseurs* to fall apart. I wanted the *Ariseurs* driven off the restitution claim.

My next 16 Wallstrasse–linked media exposure came through *Deutsche Welle*, which broadcasts to German speakers worldwide. The opportunity for a filmed interview arose with Louis traveling to New York City for a Kroll International meeting. Though Louis and I had conducted intense communications with each other by fax, phone, and email, this was the first time we were to meet face-to-face. Knowing that, *Deutsche Welle* wanted to memorialize our meeting.

Before the filming, Louis, his German wife, Maria, and I had our first in-person meeting. We could not stop smiling at one another. "It's as I've said before," Louis said. "The 16 Wallstrasse was my case waiting to happen. I remain incensed that greater justice hasn't been achieved."

The first part of our filming with the *Deutsche Welle* team was fun. To get the shots just right, the cameraman and his crew had me open the door and greet Louis a dozen times. To my dismay, though, that "fun" thing was the mood the filmmakers wanted for the entire segment. They were interested most in the upbeat angle of a first-generation American's impressions of her father's German hometown. So they were focused on my initial infatuation with Berlin, demonstrating, at best, polite tolerance for the weightier, darker details of my visits.

Had they forgotten the context of their interview? Exactly what work did they think Louis Wonderly had done in the matter? And what would be *my* excuse for not pushing harder to tell them the 16

Wallstrasse story? Lurking in my subconscious was my lingering fear of Lammek—or some other German—suing me. I feared it would be too dangerous to vent my true feelings. Not that it particularly mattered; what little I said apropos of my nightmare *tsuris* in Berlin wound up on the *Deutsche Welle* cutting room floor. The segment, besides being a huge disappointment, seemed another denial of the dark underbelly of the so-called *Wiedergutmachung*.

I had hoped for the magazine and television stories to produce tangible results. I had not thoroughly learned the lessons of my experiences in Berlin, though, and therefore overestimated what I could achieve. Time and again, I felt I had failed my father and myself. Intellectually, I knew this was not my failure. But as I have so often pointed out to my patients, "Intellectual understanding often falls dramatically short of true acceptance. The emotional brain requires a lot more than just cognitive intelligence."

18 Cornered

In the warp and woof of my relationship with the attorneys, one recently introduced thread was curious. In early 2001, I learned that von Trott's law firm had been reorganized under the umbrella of a global concern, White & Case LLC.

"What does this mean for us?" I wondered.

"There will be no change, absolutely no change in our handling of your case," von Hülsen said, perhaps not appreciating that she was not in the least resolving my puzzlement over the situation, or making me feel more confident in her, Lammek, and von Trott.

For my part, though, I was determined to accomplish a few things. Among them was getting the attorneys to reimburse me for the Kroll research. Lammek bristled at my demand, as did von Hülsen. I wasn't surprised.

"We did not authorize you to hire Kroll," von Hülsen argued.

I was ready for that. "But you suggested I might hire a private detective."

Lammek said, "If you approve, I'll speak with the Berglas family and see whether they'd be willing to split the Kroll costs with you." Lammek was handling my request by shifting my Kroll expenses onto another branch of our family.

I resolved not to give in. Von Trott would have to pay my Kroll expenses, though I dreaded taking my demand to him. I knew I held the morally superior position and was confident of prevailing eventually; still, the prospect of confronting him stirred up unpleasant emotions.

On March 27, 2001, I made the call. "Hello, Herr von Trott, this is Doctor Intrator." I consciously projected self-assurance, but before I knew what was happening, von Trott had proffered some pleasantries before asking if I could call back in early April.

"I am exceedingly busy this week," he said.

Before I called von Trott again, on April 3, I steeled myself against small talk, resolving to get to the point. "Herr von Trott," I said firmly, "I want to know more about Sonex. I only met with the owner, Joseph Weinfeld, once in 1993 in Berlin over a cognac. I sympathize with what he suffered in the Holocaust, but to tell you the truth, I can find very little about this company Sonex. What is your relationship to it, and to Weinfeld? Are *you* a public face of Sonex?"

There was a pause. I hoped I was not coming off as paranoid, even though I was rationally wondering if this Sonex was not just some sleek money-making outfit.

"I don't work for the claimants. I work for Sonex," von Trott confessed.

This time, the brief pause was on my end of the conversation. In it, my thoughts clicked into place. Von Trott worked for Sonex, not for us. As clients of Sonex, we had no real German legal representation. Von Trott and Lammek and von Hülsen were working for Sonex, not for the Berglases and not for the Intrators.

Von Trott knew how exasperated I was, even if I didn't express my sentiments overtly. "I have a suggestion," he said. "We three attorneys could split the Kroll expenses with the Intrator and Berglas families."

At last, I had gotten this hard-nosed German lawyer to budge. "That's not good enough," I replied. "I refuse to accept it. Sonex must pay every penny of the Kroll expenses."

"But I brought you and Sonex together," von Trott said. "For that matter, I brought you and von Hülsen together."

First, von Trott had presented himself to me as the Berglases' attorney. He told me von Hülsen would have to be my attorney to avoid a conflict of interest with the Berglases. Now neither von Trott nor Lammek were our attorneys at all, and I felt certain von Hülsen worked for Sonex too. Instead of asking von Trott about that, I said, "I heard that during the negotiations, Lammek used the Kroll findings to exert moral pressure on Heim & Gerken's attorney. What was that attorney's name again? Löw. Albert Löw in Munich. If Lammek really did use the Kroll findings in negotiations with Löw, wouldn't that mean Sonex had a financial advantage out of the Kroll findings for which I paid?"

Following a more prolonged pause, von Trott responded, "Give me another week to think about this."

One week later, I was on the phone with von Trott again. "Mrs. Intrator," he said, persisting in not using my professional title, "I might be prepared to pay a somewhat higher percentage of the Kroll expenses, but I can tell you right now that we are not going to pay one hundred percent of those costs."

"Oh, but you are. I'm going to insist. You *are* going to pay one hundred percent of the Kroll expenses."

"You know that the Kroll research is really not so important to this case."

"What?"

"The findings regarding what happened inside 16 Wallstrasse after Heim & Gerken took possession of the property are merely of historical interest."

I was fuming. Von Trott recognized that Kroll's research, which exposed Heim & Gerken's connections to the Nazi Party and

Aryanization, was part of the documented history of the building, yet he was dismissing it all as being "merely of historical interest."[1]

Double-talk on top of more double-talk out of Jost von Trott zu Solz!

"I want to clarify," he continued, "that neither I nor my colleague Mr. Lammek are your attorneys. Dorothea von Hülsen is."

"Just recently, you indicated that none of you are my attorneys."

Von Trott was silent. Right after that conversation ended, and knowing I was soon scheduled for yet another phone call with him, I fired off a fax, telling him exactly what I thought about his insulting "merely of historical interest" comment. What did that mean? Wasn't he both validating the historical truth at the same time as denying its importance? Was this double-talk—the words "merely" and "historical" in the same sentence? What a manipulation! Historical truth becomes "merely"?

"Hello?" von Trott said at the beginning of our next call.

I was in no mood for opening pleasantries. "You can count me as a dissatisfied client," I said. "I am preparing to talk with various Jewish community heads in the United States. I'm interested in their thoughts about our predicament with you, and Heim & Gerken."

"*Ach so?*" His voice had an edge of sarcasm.

"Let me remind you, Herr von Trott, of why I felt compelled to hire Kroll. You and the LAROV judges had prior knowledge that 16 Wallstrasse was used to manufacture Nazi flags and paraphernalia. This case might have come to a more satisfactory end years earlier had you been more forthcoming with that, and related information."

"Well, I will talk with Sonex about your request for us to pay a higher percentage of the Kroll expenses."

"Don't you have the authority to make these decisions?" I asked.

My next call with von Trott took place on May 8. "We are *not* going to pay the full Kroll expenses," he said. "I repeat—we are not going to pay the full expenses. And that's that. I have nothing more to offer you."

I took a deep breath and quietly exhaled. "Herr von Trott," I replied, "you say you have nothing more to offer me, and trust me, I believe that. However, I have not forgotten your firm's relationship with White & Case, whose offices are right around the corner from me here in New York. You are White & Case's representative in Germany. Don't you agree that White & Case could help? Why should I not ask White & Case what we should do?"

From von Trott, a lengthy silence. I waited. Eventually, the cornered attorney said, "We will pay the Kroll expenses in full. And I'll tell you what. I would very much like to be able to settle things, such that, at some time in the future, it would not be uncomfortable for us to sit together and enjoy a glass of wine."

I made no reply.

"I'll arrange for Sonex to release the funds and wire them into your account," he said. So I had my flashbulb moment. Once again shame led to movement, though it gave me little pleasure.

19 Flowers from Uncle Alex

Very shortly after the 16 Wallstrasse case officially wrapped up, I received a fragrant, sumptuous floral bouquet.

How beautiful! Who sent this? I wondered.

Inside a white envelope sticking out of the bouquet was a note from my uncle Alex.

> *Dearest Joanne: Please accept these flowers as a token of my heartfelt gratitude for everything you've achieved for us in recent years. I know what you've sacrificed in order to help me, and I am the world's proudest uncle besides.*
>
> *With all my love, Alex*

I had a lump in my throat. As I selected a spot in our home for the flowers, I felt proud of myself for having gotten money out of the 16 Wallstrasse case for Uncle Alex, who, after all, was a direct victim of Nazi persecution.

A few nights later, I picked Alex up to take him to dinner at one of his favorite haunts in White Plains. Midway through our drive to the City Limits Diner and Grill, he started humming a jaunty, pitch-perfect rendition of the main melody from the final movement of the Brahms Violin Concerto. Perhaps his bohemian attitudes and devotion to the religion of classical music contributed to his reaching so advanced an age in good health, despite his being a refugee from the Third Reich.

Inside the restaurant, Uncle Alex received a cherished regular's VIP treatment. Once we were seated and had given our orders, we started talking. "To tell you the truth, Uncle Alex," I said, "the end of the case feels anticlimactic for me. I'd do it all over again, if I had to, but it seems to me that, quite apart from the monetary settlement, there's unfinished business at 16 Wallstrasse and in Berlin."

"There's certainly the Intrator-Schimmel case," he said. "Your father might have been right when he said we'd never see a penny from it."

Uncle Alex was talking about the pending case involving the wholesale egg business that Nazis had stolen from our family. I replied, "When I saw the historical documentation of Nazi-era advertising saying, 'Now you can have Aryan eggs again for Easter!' I was astonished and disgusted."

"*Ach ja*," said Uncle Alex, his voice tinged with sarcasm. "Aryan eggs, *natürlich*, Aryan eggs!"

I smiled. Alex gave an elegant little shrug of his shoulders and continued, "Richard Wagner's widow, Cosima Wagner, aggressively tried to keep Jews out of Bayreuth after the composer's death, but her own maternal grandmother was from a Jewish family."

"The hypocrisy! I still intend to help you see something out of that eggs case, if I can, Uncle Alex. But I admit, I don't have the same idealistic view of restitution I had before I got involved with 16 Wallstrasse. I'm more hardened and cynical. And I'd be lying if I denied sometimes feeling depleted, worn down, kaput."

"Joanne," Alex said, "take a moment to relax and enjoy your Cobb salad."

Soon enough, though, Uncle Alex was waxing philosophical. "I remain convinced that what will always prevent catastrophe in the United States is the Constitution. For all their faults, the Founding Fathers were very wise about the underpinnings necessary to freedom and stability. Above all, the First Amendment, that guarantee of free speech, will always protect us, and keep certain kinds of negative pressures from building up and coalescing."

I thought about Kerstin's reality of growing up in a place where free speech was unknown. For those raised within the stultifying confines of Communist East Berlin, decades of authoritarianism had embedded a lifetime's worth of caution and wariness about speaking out. She had perfected the art of keeping her thoughts to herself, especially comments critical of authority. I thought about how my bold actions during my visits to Berlin had scandalized my young German friend.

"Is everything here OK, Mr. Intrator?" a waiter asked.

"As usual, excellent!" Alex replied with a smile.

"Tell me, Uncle Alex. Do you think Gerhard would approve of how I handled the 16 Wallstrasse case?"

"I'm certain your father would have been at least—and I repeat—*at least* as proud of you as I am. And I am immensely proud of you."

"You do know, though, the questions he posed to me on his deathbed. I am still unsure he was expressing confidence in me there. 'Are you tough enough yet? Do they know who you are?' Since I first heard them, those questions have been ringing in my ears."

"Joanne, dear," Alex asked, "remember when you first started your postgrad premed studies? How you were so anxious over your mother's possible negative reactions that you kept it secret from her but let your father in on what you were up to?"

"Yes," I replied.

"Your father believed in you, and I know that from lots of things he said to me. His deathbed questions weren't expressing doubts about you. They were to prod you, to encourage you."

"Thank you very much for saying that, Uncle Alex." I paused to collect my thoughts before continuing. "I often hope and believe that I did what my father needed me to do. As a sort of spiritual, if belated 'Thank you!' from me to him, for all the ways he propped me up and served as an antidote to my mother's harsh expressions of disappointment in me. My greatest sadness, of course, is that restitution came too late for him to benefit from it."

"My younger brother," Alex said ruefully. "His memory is a blessing."

I smiled at my dear uncle, thinking of his brother, and of my extended family. Uncle Alex didn't know it then, but his beloved wife, Bella, would soon need to move into a memory care center, and he would have to part with the house they had lived in. The money he received from the restitution case would provide him financial stability when he moved into assisted living. There Alex would remain, comfortable and safe, until he died in 2004.[1]

Nobody would deny the material benefits of receiving monetary restitution. However, discovering and understanding what had happened to my family in the Nazi era was, for me, priceless. Agonizing and prolonged as the process had been to honor the challenge my father extended in the waning hours of his life, my quest for restitution had resulted in the peace of closure. Our story, *my* story, finally had coherence.

I knew that my father's deathbed questions to me had been his final, most precious gift.

Epilogue

When I set out to recover my family's property, I had no idea of the toll it would take on me, my professional practice, and my personal life over the nine years it lasted. Though I soldiered on with my practice, my marriage eventually faltered, the stress of the 16 Wallstrasse case playing a part in its dissolution. Ben, fortunately, went on to Columbia College, scathed of course from the divorce as many such children are.

I had no sense of the rage that would fuel me over those years, no knowledge of the deep need that would propel me—sometimes beyond ordinary logic and reason—through the years of legal wrangling. I could not see into the future to know the good Germans I would meet; nor could I have foreseen those who would perpetuate the crimes of their country by slow-walking rightful restitution. I knew none of that, but I knew what my father had wanted. Claiming my family's piece of our German past forced me to come to terms with the ghosts that had haunted me through a psychologically troubled childhood and early adulthood. I may not have been able to eliminate my free-floating anxiety, but by facing my fears and the darkness, I stopped living inside my head, found my voice, and spoke up.

The process of restitution allowed me to excavate my family's story, to read their words, tucked away for decades in letters of anger, desperation, and futility—of lives uprooted and destroyed through the systematized hate of the Nazi regime.

The looting of my family, the Nazis' sadistic impoverishment of my grandparents, and the breaking of my father—and by extension, very nearly me—is a story I have been compelled to tell. The Holocaust was not simply murder. It was also a humiliation, and a systematic attempt to despoil an entire people of everything they owned and held dear.

In an unusual turn of events, my engagement with the history of 16 Wallstrasse has evolved through the present day. In 2005, Aubrey Pomerance of the Jewish Museum Berlin contacted me about acquiring my family's letters. When he first approached me, I had conflicting feelings about giving the collection away. I treasured the physical presence of my family's letters; I did not need to touch or read them to take comfort from their being within reach.

Aubrey's patient persistence eventually led me to see the wisdom of donating the collection to the museum, where it would be professionally reviewed, conserved, and made available to scholars and the public. In 2012, after the museum had received the full collection, Aubrey contacted me to say they were planning a special online exhibit about the year 1933, a year viewed as "the beginning of the end of German Jewry."

On April 7, 2013, the museum posted the sinister letter that the Nazi government sent my father on April 7, 1933, telling him that if he was Jewish, he had to reply with a request for an indefinite leave of absence from his position, as well as provide a declaration that he was not retaining any of the books or papers that had been given to him on the job. Aubrey wrote a moving summary of how that letter fits in with the additional Nazi persecution of my family.

Shortly after the exhibition went live online, Aubrey told me that a prominent German scholar wanted a photograph of my grandfather Jakob for an upcoming exhibit in Berlin. That scholar was Dr. Benedikt Goebel.

Benedikt has since become a cherished friend. Born in the German city of Münster, he is now, in my mind, a Renaissance man of Berlin, steeped in all aspects of the city's history and committed to taking an active part in its ongoing development. His wife, Dr. Gesa Kessemeier, also a distinguished historian, has as one of her specialties the history of Jews in Berlin's textile and garment production industry, which is to say that it is her business to know all about my family's history and that of similarly situated Jewish families in Berlin.

The reason Benedikt wanted a photo of my grandfather was that he had thoroughly researched the Nazi-era history of Jews in Berlin's Mitte district and wanted to include my family in an upcoming exhibit to be called *Geraubte Mitte*—Stolen Mitte.

After nearly a decade at loggerheads with German attorneys who showed they couldn't have cared less about the details of the Nazification of my family's building, a brilliant German humanist wanted to mount an entire exhibition on the subject, in Berlin!

After I sent photos of Jakob to Benedikt, he and I began communicating about the planned *Geraubte Mitte* exhibit. What most impressed and excited me was how passionate Benedikt and his co-curator, Lutz Mauersberger, were about memorializing the history of the Jews of Mitte. Because the district had been divided by the Berlin Wall, much of its history had fallen through metaphorical cracks and then been forgotten. Benedikt, Lutz, and the others involved did heroic work to uncover this history.

When I went to Berlin for the opening of *Geraubte Mitte* in September 2013, Benedikt drove me to 16 Wallstrasse for a German television news filming about the building. The building was no longer in limbo; it had been refreshed and was being used for normal commerce, giving me a more physical sense of its purpose in the pre-Nazi period, when my grandfather and his nephew were able to flourish there.

The exhibit was housed in the Ephraim Palace in Mitte, originally built in the time of Frederick the Great and named for Veitel Heine Ephraim, a Jewish man prominent in the period. The Nazis destroyed the rococo structure in 1936, but a 1985 reconstruction brought it enchantingly back to life. Today, it houses the City Museum of Berlin. That my family's history was being highlighted in the City Museum of Berlin, in itself, made me feel proud. Yet I could not have anticipated how magnificent and impactful this exhibit was. Photos of Mitte in the Nazi era were enlarged to full-room size, giving me a spatial and emotional sense of the environment at the time. The displays were all meticulously thought-out and detailed, yet accessible. Words cannot express my deep gratitude to Benedikt and his collaborators. When I found myself before a display of the *Judensterne* produced inside 16 Wallstrasse, I sensed that this was all surreal. I understood intellectually that my family had been persecuted and their stolen property had been used to mass-manufacture Nazi symbols. Still, part of me found it impossible to register it fully.

As my Berlin visit coincided with the Jewish High Holidays, I attended a service in the Fasanenstrasse Synagogue, where my grandparents had taken my father and uncle for High Holiday services so long ago. After being destroyed during Kristallnacht, it was restored in 1959. Afterwards, I had dinner with the friendly, welcoming people of the Fasanenstrasse Synagogue and felt great joy over witnessing Jewish life rekindled in Berlin.

After I returned to New York from my *Geraubte Mitte* exhibit trip, Benedikt helped me arrange for *Stolpersteine* to be laid for Jakob and Rosa in the sidewalk outside their apartment building at 185 Kurfürstendamm. Literally translated, a *Stolperstein* is a stumbling stone. In 1992, German artist Gunter Demnig began his work on a decentralized memorial for the victims of Nazi terror. Each *Stolperstein* is a brass plaque atop a cement cube. The plaque bearing the name and other information about the victim is placed outside the victim's last freely chosen residence or workplace before their being victimized by the Nazis.

The laying of the *Stolpersteine* for my Opa and my Oma was scheduled for March 24, 2014. During my time in Berlin, I stayed at a bed and breakfast across the street from my family's former apartment. The weather was persistently drab, cold, and rainy; I remember feeling the cold working its way into my bones.

I held it together to lay the *Stolpersteine*, but the experience, while tremendously meaningful, was emotionally wrenching. Some of that difficulty was softened by the presence of many wonderful, supportive people, including my research buddies Peter and Kerstin, as well as Benedikt, Aubrey, and a rabbi. On this occasion, I met Gunter Demnig, the extraordinary artist with a moral conscience behind the entire *Stolpersteine* monument throughout Europe.

Also present for the solemn laying of my grandparents' *Stolpersteine* was Reinhard Naumann, deputy mayor for Charlottenburg-Wilmersdorf. That he would come to honor me—a non-constituent—and my grandparents struck me as profoundly decent. And I was also deeply honored that passersby—total strangers—stopped in solemn observation of this *Stolperstein* ceremony.

Back in New York, I opened discussions about a possible English-language adaptation of the *Geraubte Mitte* exhibit with my friends at the Leo Baeck Institute. Today, the Leo Baeck Institute, with branches in Berlin, Jerusalem, London, and New York, is the custodian of the world's largest collection of books, documents, and art of German-speaking Jewry. I have long been nourished through the cultural programs and personal support of the people at LBI, as its community refers to the organization.

In 2016, with LBI's help, the adaptation of the *Geraubte Mitte* exhibit—called *Stolen Heart* in English—opened inside the Center for Jewish History at 15 West Sixteenth Street in Manhattan. (Because Mitte was the "heart" of Berlin, *Stolen Heart* was an appropriate translation of the show's German title.)

As our exhibit reminded me, in 1932, about 25 percent of the 1,200 buildings in Mitte belonged to Jews, and the Nazis stole every last one of those Jewish-owned properties. But only about 5 percent of the Jewish owners or their descendants ever received restitution. I was in that 5 percent. The other 95 percent of the victims never saw an iota of justice.

The *Stolen Heart* exhibit was written up in many publications, including the *Forward* and the *Wall Street Journal*. A packed opening night program was held in the Center for Jewish History's elegant, wood-paneled auditorium. I shared the stage with Benedikt; Dr. William Weitzer, director of the Leo Baeck Institute; and Princeton University professor Harold James.[1] I was very appreciative that a representative from the German Consulate delivered an address to the audience.

Professor James, an economic historian, gave a brilliant talk on the Nazis' expropriation of Jews. One point he emphasized hit home for me: how the Nazis meticulously robbed Jews of everything they had, so that even if they were able to escape to another country, they would arrive humiliated and impoverished and, therefore, more likely to be met with scorn, considered despicable in their new refuge. How that hit home personally but more importantly for the massive refugee crisis I am sure he was also referring to.

Returned to Berlin, Benedikt began arranging for a *Stolperstein* to be laid for Max Karp. I was pleased, though I felt a certain foreboding. The prospect of attending a *Stolperstein* ceremony for my relative murdered by the Nazis stirred up profoundly disquieting emotions.

When I arrived for Max Karp's *Stolperstein* ceremony in Berlin on December 4, 2017, the weather was again cold and gloomy. Benedikt gave me an insider's tour of the area around 70 Holzmarktstrasse, where my doomed relative had last freely lived. The neighborhood was still dominated by drab Communist-era structures. Still, here and there on the tour, I would see a recently built children's playground with *kinder* happily running around, and I would think, *This is like seeing grass grow up through concrete—there are signs of new life.*

At Max Karp's *Stolperstein* ceremony, I was comforted by again seeing Gunter Demnig. During the solemn event, I kept thinking about Max's letters to my father, with his desperate pleas for help. I recalled how prisoners at Sachsenhausen were tortured, and my heart ached. Yet emotions can come in layers. Berlin newspapers noted Max's *Stolperstein* ceremony, and I was grateful and comforted by that, as well as by the presence of the good people who witnessed the ceremony.

Still, there it was. Mendel Max Karp's *Stolperstein* honoring his memory by noting his murder in Sachsenhausen.

When mounting the *Geraubte Mitte* exhibit, Benedikt had often remarked—including to German media—that in all of Mitte, there was not one public marker of what the Nazis wreaked on Jews. And so he got to work, pushing for a memorial plaque to be placed at 16 Wallstrasse. He organized the effort in part through the Aktives Museum, which carries out scholarly and educational work on the history of fascism and resistance.

I was, of course, boundlessly appreciative of Benedikt's efforts.

The German saying for "Patience is a virtue" is *Geduld ist eine Tugend*. Benedikt needed (and had) plenty of *Geduld*. First, the city of Berlin needed to approve the plaque's placement. Once that was achieved, the new building owner had to agree to the plan.

It turned out that 16 Wallstrasse had been acquired by the European Organization for Nuclear Research, known by its French initials, CERN. It was at CERN in 1989 that the British scientist Sir Timothy Berners-Lee invented the World Wide Web. Martina Morawietz, an investigative reporter with the German network ZDF, led some terrific behind-the-scenes efforts to encourage CERN to move ahead with the plaque.

After much effort, Benedikt's efforts were successful, and an unveiling ceremony was scheduled for October 26, 2018. On the day of the ceremony, I stood in one of 16 Wallstrasse's interior courtyards. As the crowd gathered for the unveiling, I mingled with people and found myself increasingly moved that they had each come to bear witness to the dedication of this commemorative plaque.

As the program opened, words spoken by CERN's Charlotte Warakaulle had a special resonance for me. Of CERN, she said, "We owe our existence to the foresight and determination of scientists and politicians from many nations, who shared a vision of reconciling a war-torn continent through culture, including science. We continue to live by this vision and to be inspired by it."

Benedikt delivered a speech contextualizing the history of 16 Wallstrasse within the Nazis' broader dispossession of the Jews of Mitte. Among other notables who spoke at the unveiling was Berlin deputy mayor Stephan von Dassel.

When it became my turn to speak, and I was standing with a microphone in hand, the crowd suddenly looked much larger than it had. I froze. But then, if only in my imagination, I had a vision of my father gently encouraging me to begin.

"Go ahead, you'll be fine!"

I started by telling the attendees about my father's deathbed questions. In one pause, I made eye contact with Louis, who had done so much to uncover the heinous things perpetrated on my family at this address. As I hit my stride in the speech, I dearly wished Gerhard Intrator could be there, for real, to hear me bearing testimony for our entire family.[2]

Seeing the Aktives Museum plaque on a wall at 16 Wallstrasse was immensely satisfying. The plaque declares that the Nazis' *Judensterne* were produced inside the building in 1941. My grandfather's name and his Berglas nephew's name are honored in descriptions of crimes the *Ariseurs* committed against them. And the murderous outcomes from the Nazis' hellish perversions of the Star of David symbol are unflinchingly described.

Inside my head, I was shouting, *Finally! Finally! Finally!*

Author's Note

Truth will ultimately prevail where pain is taken to bring it to light.
—George Washington

The most consequential action I took during the 16 Wallstrasse case was insisting on the facts.

As I compose this note, the world continues to remind us how imperative it is to understand facts and act based on facts, not on rumors or lies. Unfortunately, when you read this, I have no doubt we will still be facing a "firehose of falsehood" from various directions. We remain vulnerable to lies from so-called strong men, charismatic types, trying to dismantle democracies or sabotage nascent ones. Why is this so?

It is an innate human desire to feel safe. Sadly, assured safety is impossible, given we know we will die and have little control over when. If we are fortunate, we have had chunks of time when we can distract ourselves from these thoughts because we have been engaged in our life's activities. But in times of danger—such as the pandemic, economic reversals, the worldwide effects of climate change, or war—it is harder to be diverted from our fears. I say this as a psychiatrist and as an ordinary human being. We are vulnerable to lies when we are afraid.

When I was in Berlin, I was susceptible to lies or partial truths because of the recent loss of my father and my psychological weaknesses emanating from my unprotected childhood, partially due to the impact of the Holocaust on my parents. Naively, I wanted to be in safe hands in Berlin, helped by people with my best interests in mind, people working to contribute to the repair of the world through restitution. Raised in a Germanic household, I so easily fell into line in Berlin, embracing the role initially of a dutiful and grateful client, even inhibited from challenging my lawyers or deeply questioning their methodology when my gut told me otherwise. I wanted to believe the word *Wiedergutmachung*, "to make good again," the word most often used in describing restitution.

Believing the word propelled me to Berlin. Exposing its shallowness led me to succeed in finding the truth. But it took me a long time.

The details of my family's everyday life under Nazi rule had personal meaning for me, but the lessons from their experience and my own in Berlin in the 1990s apply to us now. We must be vigilant in pursuing the truth, especially during rough times. We need to be aware of the ease with which the truth can be manipulated. We must face our susceptibility to exploitation.

Tyrants posing as quasi-parental figures, who see themselves as saviors of their fabricated reality, toy with the truth to generate chaos, thus gaining power. They are exquisitely gifted at playing the victim card, claiming to be misunderstood and sidelined. Their well-honed manipulative skill forges a bond with their followers, who experience the same slights. To bake this in further, the tyrant offers up someone or some group to blame as the cause of the failures or insufficiencies that their followers are experiencing. As I write this, antisemitism is on the rise, as are other hateful and malicious slurs towards non-white people.

Hitler blamed the Jewish bankers for World War I. He stoked the fires of antisemitism in Germany, thus coalescing his power and establishing the Jew as the outsider. This forged his followers into a fiercely unified insider group. Grandiose myths spun out of Nordic fables proffered them the illusion of Aryan superiority. The Nazis created euphemisms to facilitate and hide the Nazi intentions to murder. Amongst hundreds of words utilized during the supposed thousand-year Reich, the word "liquidate" was, for me, the most horrifying.

The manic excitement deliberately provoked by tyrants leads to violent solutions to their followers' perceived victimhood. The violence is purposeful and enlivening. It wrests revenge for feelings of diminishment and offers a physiological antidote through its instantaneous adrenal rush. When adrenaline is used up and the perpetrator's enlivened psyche crashes, violence is needed again; otherwise, depletion and diminishment take hold. Violence is addicting.

The giddy-like brutality seen in Nazi footage, as Jews were killed for sport, speaks to the energetic charge and exhilaration of the murderers. For an incident closer to our own times, I am reminded of when the previous president called the 2020 election "illegitimate," provoking the January 6th insurrection. We witness the mob's use of violence to assuage their anger for feeling sidelined politically, economically, and culturally. Russian president Vladimir Putin, once the KGB king of a massive USSR, is now relegated to a country whose economy is no bigger than that of Texas. Desperate, paranoid, and sidelined, fear intensifies and the aging tyrant becomes an even greater danger. These are our times and likely will be so when you read this.

So why is a psychiatrist ending a memoir titled *Summons to Berlin* in such a fashion? I feel it's my duty to alert people, to help them be their better selves, so they can negotiate the world as it presents itself. It means that I must provide an atmosphere in my practice that feels safe, without judgment, giving my patients psychic space to know their truth—about themselves, their family, their work, their friends, their relationship with the world. We look at what is missing. We name it. Putting feelings into language takes the power of emotion down a notch. We ask if there is a pathway for reclamation or if it is something that must be mourned. We need to balance the starkness of the loss with the use of our physical body. By walking, dancing, gardening, or cleaning the house, engaging our body siphons the damaging mental and physical effects of the associated stress. Even standing in place, feeling the strength of our legs in contact with the ground while at the same time taking some mindful breaths can help. If we can live in moments, now and then, which I know is no small task, we might be able to catch ourselves from fast-forwarding and tormenting ourselves. Even by pausing for one moment, we might avert losing a day in the present.

We need to look realistically at the world as it is and find individual solutions that are not impulsive or harmful to others. Maybe there are safe spots in our lives, a tree or a dog or a poem or a bath. Or, if we are truly fortunate, we find those safe spots in our relationships and work. Writing this memoir has been crucial for me, as it is a way of grounding what I accomplished in Berlin. Will it help me manage all that is to come? I don't think so; what will is my nascent ability to tolerate as best I can my innate anxiety and face things with courage, not denial. No small task.

Acknowledgments

Kathrin Seitz, my friend of over forty years and my first writing coach, inspired me when she said my story had the quality of a hero's journey. It was clear to both of us that my father's last words should begin the book. My private life interrupted, so it took a few years to start writing. There was much to organize. Many of the letters from the black file cabinets needed to be photocopied and the originals protected. For that special task, Hermann Simon, with whom I shared some meals in Berlin and New York, suggested his colleague Sonja Longolius, who was coming to New York for a MOMA internship. We spent many a weekend day sitting on the floor of my office organizing the letters. Her presence brought calm to a spot that was overrun with Berlin notes, legal letters, and patient files. At a later time, another Berlin helper joined me. Thanks to Jeffrey Himmel, who introduced me to Max Wolter, translator of the crucial letters between my father and his dissertation advisor, Professor Kern. Both Jeffrey and Max, like my father, were Freiburg alumni. Tanje Hoehne, a cellist and puppeteer also from Berlin, worked as an invaluable translator for some of the harder-to-read letters. Malgorzata Bakalarz, a scholar of Polish restitution and sociologist also sent from LBI, offered many insights during the Sundays we spent together.

I didn't start writing the book until 2010. It took being invited to Munich by Louis Wonderly and his wife, Maria, to help me get going. The former journalist, in his matter-of-fact good-sense way, over three intense coffee-filled days, helped me sort the hundreds of pages of notes I had brought with me into a dozen boxes, each with a chapter title, which became the beginning of my very first draft. Louis continued doing research at his own expense well after the case was finalized. My office mate, Dr. Jocelyn Charnas, read this first draft and was extremely enthusiastic yet aware of the immense work ahead.

Then, after a long while and a couple rewrites, Scott Rose became an invaluable researcher, translator, and editor, with a now and then brilliant turn of phrase. At the Leo Baeck Institute's *Stolen Heart* exhibit, I met Sarah Wildman and read her book, *Paper Love*. So moved by her memoir, I asked her to evaluate mine. She recommended an edit, and we worked together for a year. More interruptions and rewrites followed, until my oldest friend, Dean Pitchford, a lyricist, screenwriter, and producer, spent many days reviewing it and giving me extensive notes. Nancy Bachrach, my brilliant college friend and witness to my behavior in the infamous German thought class at Connecticut College, read the latest draft in early 2021, then asked me with a wry smile over Zoom, "Do you still have any energy left?" Who was I to say no to Nancy? Thus, she guided me to Amy Spungen, who took me in hand and did the developmental edit that Dean had gently pressed for. It was a wonderful and challenging year working with her. After my work with Amy, the manuscript went on to Kristen Tate, another fine editor.

Several friends and colleagues were kind enough to read the book and offer useful comments. Fredric Price encouraged me to utilize my knowledge of German history and personality to approach the vast subject of restitution. Dr. Marianne Legato, who first taught me at medical school in 1977 and is now a close friend, urged me to do as much psychiatric commentary as possible in the book. Dr. Robert

Hare was kind enough to review the portion on psychopathy and our research. My brother, Jack, filled in some important details.

John and Lexie Intrator, Uncle Alex's son and daughter-in-law, gave it a thorough read, as did Cathy Halstead, a college friend and benefactor of the *Stolen Heart* exhibit. Benedikt Goebel and Elisabeth von Haebler were very helpful. William Weitzer and Frank Mecklenburg from LBI each made valuable suggestions and offers of help. Christina Kautz and Kerstin Brichtswein Kujath, as well as Benedikt's family, took particularly good care of me on several of my trips to Berlin.

Alon Brav filled in crucial details about Edith Intrator Brav, the twins, and his great-uncle Ignaz Brav, who was murdered in Lvov. Götz Aly filled in the details about Max Karp and wrote an article mentioning my coming to Berlin for Max Karp's *Stolperstein*. My trip to see David Berglas in England provided anecdotes of our family life in Berlin before the war and validation about some of the issues regarding the case. Martina Morawietz, who had interviewed me for ZDF television when I was in Berlin for Max Karp's *Stolperstein*, helped considerably, especially in making sure the plaque from CERN was finalized. She, too, remains a personal friend like so many others I have met in Berlin.

Other colleagues, friends, and scholars have been recognized in the book and are much appreciated.

My former husband, Greg, now deceased, played an important part until he could no longer work due to severe heart failure. The drafts of chapters I wanted him to read would be spread out over two adjoining tables at a Columbia University hangout many Friday afternoons through lunch and dinner. We talked about the case, about our own failed marriage, and about our son. Greg read what I had written, drafted some paragraphs, and edited parts to the best of his astonishing ability. For a few short years, our little family reunited in caring for Greg until he died in August 2019.

Notes

Chapter 1: The Intrators

1. Between 1880 and 1914, approximately 5,000 Jews died annually of starvation in Galicia. See Martin Gilbert, *The Routledge Atlas of Jewish History*, 7th ed. (London and New York: Routledge, 2006), 79.

2. Moses Mendelssohn (1729–86) was a leading intellectual in the Berlin of the 1700s, a pathbreaker for Haskalah, the Jewish Enlightenment. He combined his love of Judaism with broad reading and writing on secular topics, achieving wide recognition throughout Europe for his thinking. Additionally, Mendelssohn was a skillful businessman who enjoyed success in textiles. He was a grandfather to the composer Felix Mendelssohn. The Nazis destroyed Moses Mendelssohn's grave in the Jewish Cemetery of Berlin. After German reunification, Mendelssohn's tombstone was reconstructed and named an *Ehrengrab*, a burial site of special honor.

3. Approximately 100,000 German Jewish personnel served in World War I; about 12,000 of them were killed in action. See Gilbert, *The Routledge Atlas of Jewish History*, 89.

Chapter 2: My Father Leaves Berlin

1. Alfred Intrator to Gerhard Intrator, 24 March 1938, Intrator Family Collection, Jewish Museum Berlin.

2. Jakob Intrator to Gerhard Intrator, 19 June 1938, Intrator Family Collection, Jewish Museum Berlin.

3. Dorothy Thompson coined the term *cold pogrom* to describe the legal and administrative measures used by the Hitler regime to bring about the economic ruin of German Jewry. As chief of the Berlin bureau of the *New York Post* in the late 1920s and early 1930s, Thompson witnessed the rise of Nazism and reported extensively on the mistreatment of Germany's Jews. In 1934, she became the first American journalist to be expelled from Nazi Germany. See David Wyman et al., eds., "Thompson, Dorothy," Encyclopedia of America's Response to the Holocaust, accessed March 3, 2022, http://enc.wymaninstitute.org/?p=517.

4. Jakob Intrator to Gerhard Intrator, 18 June 1938, Intrator Family Collection, Jewish Museum Berlin.

5. Alfred Intrator to Gerhard Intrator, 13 November 1938, Intrator Family Collection, Jewish Museum Berlin.

6. Jakob Intrator to Gerhard Intrator, 23 November 1939, Intrator Family Collection, Jewish Museum Berlin.

Chapter 3: The "Polish Action"

1. Jakob Intrator to Gerhard Intrator, 18 December 1938, Intrator Family Collection, Jewish Museum Berlin.

2. Jakob Intrator to Gerhard Intrator, 10 May 1940, Intrator Family Collection, Jewish Museum Berlin.

3. Ignaz Brav to Gerhard Intrator, 12 June 1941, Intrator Family Collection, Jewish Museum Berlin.

4. Victor Klemperer, *The Language of the Third Reich: A Philologist's Notebook* (Berlin: Verlag, 1957), 149–50.

5. Documentation from Blecher was found through the Central Tracing Bureau and British Red Cross on July 24, 1946.

6. Max Karp to Gerhard Intrator, 17 November 1938, Intrator Family Collection, Jewish Museum Berlin. See also www.jmberlin.de/en/max-karp-polenaktion, a virtual exhibition at the Jewish Museum Berlin.

7. Jacques Berglas pursued his business connections in China beginning in 1935, as affidavits and visas were not required there for emigration. He originated a proposal to allow thousands of German Jewish citizens to settle in the southwestern portion of Hunan province. The "Berglas Plan," as the newspapers named it, was given serious consideration until the war in Asia made it impossible to implement because of the Japanese occupation of Shanghai and the curtailment of transportation from Europe to Asia.

8. Max Karp to Gerhard Intrator, 8 August 1939, Intrator Family Collection, Jewish Museum Berlin.

9. Jakob Intrator to Gerhard Intrator, 28 October 1939, Intrator Family Collection, Jewish Museum Berlin.

10. Max Karp to Jakob Intrator, 31 October 1939, Intrator Family Collection, Jewish Museum Berlin.

11. Jakob Intrator to Gerhard Intrator, 8 January 1940, Intrator Family Collection, Jewish Museum Berlin.

12. The German historian Götz Aly conveyed his opinion about Max Karp's fate to the author in a letter dated June 22, 2020. Aly came upon the letters of Jakob and Gerhard Intrator in the Jewish Museum in Berlin, which prompted him to study and write about Max. He wrote, in part, "Since Max Karp was arrested during the first weeks of the war, his relatives were still treated with a certain amount of caution by the authorities. I assume that your grandfather repeatedly asked the Gestapo in Berlin about his nephew. They must have informed him that Max Karp had been taken so called into protective custody (*Schutzhaft*) as an enemy

alien (because he was a Polish citizen). When Max's situation worsened, or at a time when he was already dead or murdered, your grandfather will have been informed by letter, or probably even by telegram, that his nephew's condition had deteriorated considerably due to a serious infection. A short time later, Max's death will have followed. All this was part of a cover-up strategy that still seemed appropriate to the Nazi authorities at that time. It is certain that the body of Max Karp, like that of many prisoners in Sachsenhausen, was cremated in the municipal crematorium in Oranienburg . . . . However, I regret to say that the ashes in that box were most probably not the remains of Max Karp but a combination of very different people that were brought to death in the same way in the Sachsenhausen concentration camp. I am very sorry to give you such a devastating answer. While no exact documents are available, many factors indicate that the death of Max Karp, who was almost certainly murdered, must have happened in this manner."

In the opening pages of his book *Europe Against the Jews, 1880–1945*, Aly provides details of Gerhard Intrator's strenuous but doomed efforts to rescue his cousin Max Karp from the Nazis. As a prototypical example of the depraved hostility many Nazi-era European governments evidenced towards their Jewish populations, the author cites details surrounding Karp's death at Sachsenhausen.

13. Typically the letters from Jakob were in pale-blue onionskin envelopes. On the back, written in his elegant German cursive, would be my grandfather's name and return address. On the center-upper region between Jakob's first name and last was the Nazi-mandated, stigmatizing designation "Israel" to identify Jakob Intrator not as a citizen who fought for Germany in WWI but as

a Jew—and therefore an enemy. Across the bottom of the back of
the envelope would be an officious white adhesive band with seals
of the Oberkommando der Wehrmacht—the High Command
of the Nazi Armed Forces, ornamented with an eagle extending
his wings, his talons grasping a wreath surrounding a swastika.
Separate from the seals, printed in ominous thick black letters,
was *Geöffnet*—"opened." The High Command of the Nazi Armed
Forces insultingly, abusively, announced that they were opening
my grandfather's letters. I realize now, as my father and grandparents did then, that to convey on paper their most candid and
intimate thoughts about the Nazis' ongoing crimes would have
invited death.

Chapter 4: The Rothschilds

1. Helen Epstein, *Children of the Holocaust: Conversations with Sons
   and Daughters of Survivors* (New York: Putnam, 1979). Another
   book that offers a rich perspective on this subject is Ira Brenner,
   ed., *The Handbook of Psychoanalytic Holocaust Studies* (Milton
   Park, UK: Routledge, Taylor and Francis, 2019), 90–95.

2. For more on the USC Shoah Foundation, visit https://vhaonline.
   usc.edu.

3. For a discussion of both German and Nazi child-rearing, see Anne
   Kratzer, "Harsh Nazi Parenting Guidelines May Still Affect German
   Children of Today," *Scientific American,* published January 4, 2019,
   https://www.scientificamerican.com/article/harsh-nazi-parent-
   ing-guidelines-may-still-affect-german-children-of-today1/.

Chapter 5: The Inheritance

1. Jakob Intrator to Gerhard Intrator, 13 November 1938, Intrator
   Family Collection, Jewish Museum Berlin.

2. Jakob Intrator to Gerhard Intrator, 8 January 1940, Intrator Family Collection, Jewish Museum Berlin.

3. Jakob Intrator to Gerhard Intrator, 22 September 1941, Intrator Family Collection, Jewish Museum Berlin.

4. Jakob Intrator to Gerhard Intrator, 7 January 1942, Intrator Family Collection, Jewish Museum Berlin.

5. The form, dated March 10, 1943, was issued by "The Republic of Cuba, City and Province of Habana, Embassy of the United States of America."

6. Broken heart syndrome is a true medical catastrophe. Known by its medical name, takotsubo cardiomyopathy is a temporary heart condition featuring weakening of the left ventricle due to severe emotional or physical stress, ultimately causing heart failure.

Chapter 6: Von Trott

1. Subsequent generations of Germans discussed the controversies surrounding moral motivations in the Operation Valkyrie murder plot. The discussion reemerged in media in 2008, when the movie *Valkyrie*, starring Tom Cruise, was released. Apparently, Colonel Claus von Stauffenberg was not perceived as a hero until the late 1960s, and the first monument commemorating him was not erected until 1980. Conspirators in the Operation Valkyrie plot came from such diverse political backgrounds that it's impossible to establish one clear motivation—and the motives mentioned by historians have very diverse interpretations. For example, the urge to kill Hitler in order to gain a better position to negotiate with the Allies was seen as an act of patriotism that would end civilians' suffering—or, alternatively, as a cynical calculation of traitors.

2. Magical thinking is a cognitive thought process that occurs between the ages of four to seven, when unrelated events are

connected despite any logical link. The process can occur in adulthood during times of great stress.

3. Katie Hafner, "The House We Lived In," *The New York Times Magazine* (November 10, 1991): 32.

4. Bessel van der Kolk, *The Body Keeps the Score: Brain, Mind, and Body in the Healing of Trauma* (New York: Penguin, 2015).

5. Contingency arrangements ("no win, no fee") were forbidden in Germany until 2008. They are still rare there. The concern was and is that these arrangements have the potential for undercutting fees and creating undo incentives. See Bernhard Schmeilzl, "No Win No Fee Agreements Are Void in Germany," Cross Channel Lawyers, published July 26, 2016, https://www.crosschannellawyers.co.uk/no-win-no-fee-agreements-are-void-in-germany.

Chapter 9: Deutschland

1. James Joyce, *Ulysses* (Paris: Shakespeare and Co., 1922).

2. Coming to power, Hitler appropriated the idea of building a national system of highways (the *Reichsautobahn* system) and presented it as a way to fight unemployment. The highways were termed "Adolf Hitler roads" ("*die Strassen Adolf Hitler*"). By 1941, only half of the project was completed.

3. A plaque on an exterior hotel wall at 27 Kurfürstendamm, Berlin, reads: "Beginning in 1928, a Kempinski restaurant stood on this site, a world-famous symbol of Berlin hospitality. Because the owners were Jewish, the celebrated restaurant was 'Aryanized' in 1937, with the Jewish owners forced to relinquish their property under duress. Some members of the Kempinski family were killed; others succeeded in fleeing. The Kempinski Bristol Hotel that opened here in 1952 intends for the fate of its founding family

never to be forgotten." (Ownership has since changed hands, and the hotel now is known as the Hotel Bristol Berlin.)

4. For more on the anti-Jewish riots, see "Anti-Jewish Incitement and Riots in the Summer of 1935: German Situation Reports and Articles in the German Jewish Press," from the Yad Vashem Shoah Resource Center collection, https://www.yadvashem.org/odot_pdf/Microsoft%20Word%20-%203826.pdf.

5. Jakob Intrator to Gerhard Intrator, 25 March 1938, Intrator Family Collection, Jewish Museum Berlin.

6. It turns out that legally and biologically, Jost von Trott zu Solz was *not* closely related to Adam von Trott zu Solz. They were from different branches of the very extended family tree for the name von Trott zu Solz. Jost ultimately came from the Solz branch and Adam from the Imshausen branch.

7. Stasi headquarters was known as the Commercial Coordination, or KoKo. Its head was Alexander Schalck-Golodkowski, the infamous foreign currency trader. After he escaped to West Germany in 1989, there was a nationwide televised police raid at 17 Wallstrasse to remove the enormous number of stolen goods Golodkowski planned to sell, gaining foreign currency needed by the German Democratic Republic. While active, he provided over 50 million deutsche marks for the GDR each year. Golodkowski died in 2015.

8. These book burnings were the "Action against the Un-German Spirit," orchestrated by the Nazi German Students' Association across the country. They happened at most of the universities in Germany, including Gerhard's.

Chapter 10: Eggs and Kafka

1. See Christoph Kreutzmüller et al., *Final Sale: The End of Jewish Owned Businesses in Nazi Berlin* (Berlin: Aktives Museum, 2010).

Chapter 11: Deceptions and Cruelty

1. Books on the subject include Robert Jay Lifton, *The Nazi Doctors: Medical Killing and the Psychology of Genocide* (New York: Basic Books, 1986) and David G. Marwell, *Mengele: Unmasking the "Angel of Death"* (New York: Norton, 2020). For an interview with Marwell on the author's blog, see "David Marwell's Outstanding Book on Mengele," published December 3, 2020, https://joanneintrator.com/2020/12/03/david-marwells-outstanding-book-on-mengele/.

2. A central source for information about the forced singing at Sachsenhausen is Juliane Brauer, "Musik im Konzentrationslager Sachsenhausen," *Metropol Verlag*, 2008.

Chapter 12: Movement

1. Joanne Intrator, "A Brain Imaging Study of Semantic and Affective Processing in Psychopaths," *The Journal of Biological Psychiatry*, no. 42 (1997): 96–103. According to an email communication from Robert Hare to the author on February 10, 2022, "the SPECT study has some 330 citations."

2. The term "sociopath" is outdated and reflects the sociological factors that influenced antisocial behavior. Though the words "psychopathy" and "sociopathy" are colloquially used interchangeably, "psychopathy" is the term used in brain-based research.

3. Robert Hare was influenced by the psychiatrist Hervey Cleckley, who wrote *The Mask of Sanity* (St. Louis: C.V. Mosby Company, 1982).

4. Henry V. Dicks, *The Columbus Centre Series: Licensed Mass Murder* (New York: Basic Books, 1972). A psychosocial study of eight Nazi SS murderers.

5. It was not until the first decade of the twenty-first century that historians started examining the postwar German judiciary. The Rosenburg Files project reveals the high degree of continuity between the personnel of the Nazi judiciary and the Justice Ministry in the postwar Federal Republic. Of 170 postwar jurists, 90 had been members of the Nazi Party. The Leo Baeck Institute in New York hosted the panel presenting the progress of The Rosenberg Files project in 2016.

6. These statistics were in correspondence from Dorothea von Hülsen to the author dated February 15, 1996.

Chapter 14: Stalled

1. William L. Shirer, *The Rise and Fall of the Third Reich* (New York: Simon & Schuster, 2011) and William L. Shirer, *Berlin Diary: The Journal of a Foreign Correspondent, 1934–1941* (New York: Alfred A. Knopf, 1941).

2. Martin Franz Julius Luther (1895–1945) was a Nazi diplomat with especially close ties to Heinrich Himmler. In his notes from a lecture on December 4, 1941, Luther wrote, "We must act on the opportunity the war presents to achieve a final resolution of the Jewish question in Europe." See Ernst Klee, *Das Personenlexikon zum Dritten Reich* (Fischer Taschenbuch, 2005), 384. As a deputy foreign minister, Luther pressed for all Nazi-aligned and/or occupied countries to betray their Jewish populations by turning them over to the Nazis. After attempting to oust Joachim von Ribbentrop as minister of foreign affairs, in 1943 Luther was arrested and sent to the concentration camp at Sachsenhausen.

Had Luther not died of a heart attack shortly after the war ended, he would have been a defendant in the Ministries Trial of 1947–48 for his role in carrying out the Holocaust.

3. *Die Wannseekonferenz* is a 1984 German TV film. Of note: In 2001, *Conspiracy* was an American made-for-television film about the Wannsee Conference.

4. See, in particular, Max Weber's writings on the topic, including his 1921 essay "Bureaucracy": https://tinyurl.com/m63yjh8h.

5. Erwin Schrödinger (1887–1961) was an Austrian-born, Nobel Prize–winning physicist. In a 1935 exchange with Albert Einstein, Schrödinger devised the Schrödinger cat thought experiment to underscore—one might say, to satirize—what he considered an absurdity in the so-called Copenhagen interpretation of quantum mechanics, wherein a particle is hypothesized to exist in all its possible states, simultaneously, until it is measured. That hypothetical condition is referred to as "quantum superposition." Schrödinger's thought experiment involves: i) a cat inside a metal box, together with ii) a radioactive source that has a fifty-fifty chance of decaying, iii) a Geiger counter, and iv) a flask containing more than enough poisonous gas to kill the cat. If the Geiger counter detects radioactive decay, it triggers the fall of a hammer to break the flask of poisonous gas, killing the cat. If there is no radioactive decay, the cat remains alive. But how is anybody outside the metal box to know whether the cat is still alive or has died? In Schrödinger's thought experiment, applying the Copenhagen interpretation of the quantum mechanics of particles to the cat in the box, the cat would simultaneously be dead and alive until somebody opened the box to see what was going on. Outside of quantum physics, in popular parlance, any paradoxical or facially

preposterous assertion might provoke the satirical exclamation: "It's like Schrödinger's cat!"

Chapter 15: Discoveries and Duplicities

1. The verse is from Johann Wolfgang von Goethe's poem "*Harzreise im Winter*" ("Winter Journey in the Harz Mountains").

2. Nasrin Büttner, "I Survived the War and Russians in the Garden," *Berliner Morgenpost*, December 30, 1999.

Chapter 16: Intimidation

1. Joanne met David Berglas once during the case in Berlin and then afterwards, in 2015 in London. He fled Nazi Germany for the United Kingdom when he was eleven. In the 1950s, David began a career as a professional magician and mentalist. First in radio, then in television, his flair for elegant showmanship led him to the zenith of his field; he is considered the "Dean of British Magicians." See David Segal, "The Mystery of Magic's Greatest Card Trick," *New York Times*, May 23, 2021, https://www.nytimes.com/2021/05/23/style/berglas-effect-card-trick.html. Sadly, Gaby Shapiro died before the case was finalized. Gaby was well known in South Africa for her political activism against apartheid.

Chapter 17: Soul Murder

1. Konrad Kwiet, "Schrei, was du kannsr," *Der Spiegel*, September 25, 1988, https://www.spiegel.de/spiegel/print/d-13531193.html. Hermann Simon was actually the first to identify 16 Wallstrasse as the site; an article he wrote that referenced it was published in East Germany before the wall came down, in Ludwig Geiger, "Geschichte der Juden in Berlin 1871," *Nachdruck Leipzig* (1988: XXVIII). Simon is also the author of an outstanding book on

Berlin Jews, *Jews in Nazi Berlin: From Kristallnacht to Liberation* (Chicago: University of Chicago Press, 2009). In it, 16 Wallstrasse and the flags produced there are given several pages (94–98). Kwiet's work, however, was what Louis found.

2. For more on the concept of soul murder, see Leonard Shengold, *Soul Murder: The Effects of Childhood Abuse and Deprivation* (New York: Fawcett Columbine, 1991).

3. One million deutsche marks was equivalent to about $450,000 at the time.

Chapter 18: Cornered

1. Jost von Trott held an archive of letters written by Friedrich de Porbeck, a Hessian military man; the von Trotts apparently became related to the Porbecks through marriage sometime in the 1700s. During the American Revolutionary War, the British established and maintained control of Savannah, Georgia, from 1778 to 1782—and von Trott's ancestor was involved on the British side.

   The Fall 1979 issue of the *Georgia Historical Quarterly* includes the article "A Note on the Victor at Spring Hill Redoubt." Von Trott's ancestor, Porbeck, had written notes on the back of a map about a Spring Hill battle (Spring Hill was the site of a British fortification in Georgia). Those contemporaneous notes Porbeck made in 1779 included information new to historians as of 1979. The author of the article wrote in his first paragraph, "This beautifully executed and well-preserved map, apparently the work of a German cartographer, has been passed down to one of Porbeck's descendants, Dr. Jost von Trott zu Solz, who has graciously allowed it to be photographed for the Georgia Historical Society."

I wondered if von Trott considered his ancestor's notes about an American Revolutionary War battle "merely of historical interest," the way he seemingly viewed Kroll's discovery of Heim's and Gerken's Nazi Party memberships, dismissing them as irrelevant to my 16 Wallstrasse restitution case.

Chapter 19: Flowers from Uncle Alex

1. Following Alex's burial, the author invited those in attendance to her home. Manfred's son, Jason Stanley—Alex's grandson—came and became a good friend. Stanley, a philosophy professor at Yale University, wrote *How Fascism Works* (New York: Random House, 2018), which describes how the democratic government of the United States is vulnerable to the incursion of fascism. Alex, who so admired the Constitution's First Amendment, would never know that his grandson would write about it; very likely, Alex would be sad and surprised that such a book was necessary in the United States.

Epilogue

1. To see the *Stolen Heart* talks by Professor Harold James, Dr. Benedikt Goebel, and myself (introduction by Dr. William Weitzer), visit https://www.youtube.com/watch?v=73LiRG5qmxc.

2. I was grateful that two of Alex's sons, John and Tom Intrator, and their wives came from Geneva to represent our family.

Bibliography

Brauer, Juliane. "Musik im Konzentrationslager Sachsenhausen." *Metropol Verlag*, 2008.

Brenner, Ira, ed. *The Handbook of Psychoanalytic Holocaust Studies: International Perspectives*. Milton Park, UK: Routledge, Taylor and Francis, 2019.

Büttner, Nasrin. "I Survived the War and Russians in the Garden." *Berliner Morgenpost*, December 30, 1999.

Dicks, Henry V. *The Columbus Centre Series: Licensed Mass Murder*. New York: Basic Books, 1972.

Epstein, Helen. *Children of the Holocaust: Conversations with Sons and Daughters of Survivors*. New York: Putnam, 1979.

Gilbert, Martin. *The Routledge Atlas of Jewish History*. 7th ed. London and New York: Routledge, 2006.

Hafner, Katie. "The House We Lived In." *The New York Times Magazine*, November 10, 1991.

Intrator, Joanne. "A Brain Imaging Study of Semantic and Affective Processing in Psychopaths." *The Journal of Biological Psychiatry*, no. 42 (1997): 96–103.

Intrator Family Collection. Gift of Joanne Intrator. Konvolut/133. Jewish Museum Berlin.

Klemperer, Victor. *The Language of the Third Reich: A Philologist's Notebook*. Berlin: Verlag, 1957.

Kratzer, Anne. "Harsh Nazi Parenting Guidelines May Still Affect German Children of Today." *Scientific American*. Published January 4, 2019. https://www.scientificamerican.com/article/harsh-nazi-parenting-guidelines-may-still-affect-german-children-of-today1/.

Kreutzmüller, Christoph, et al. *Final Sale: The End of Jewish Owned Businesses in Nazi Berlin*. Berlin: Aktives Museum, 2010.

Kwiet, Konrad. "Schrei, was du kannsr." *Der Spiegel*, September 25, 1988. https://www.spiegel.de/spiegel/print/d-13531193.html.

Lifton, Robert Jay. *The Nazi Doctors: Medical Killing and the Psychology of Genocide*. New York: Basic Books, 1986.

Marwell, David G. *Mengele: Unmasking the "Angel of Death."* New York: Norton, 2020.

Shengold, Leonard. *Soul Murder: The Effects of Childhood Abuse and Deprivation*. New York: Fawcett Columbine, 1991.

Shirer, William L. *Berlin Diary: The Journal of a Foreign Correspondent, 1934–1941*. New York: Alfred A. Knopf, 1941.

———. *The Rise and Fall of the Third Reich*. New York: Simon & Schuster, 2011.

Simon, Hermann. *Jews in Nazi Berlin: From Kristallnacht to Liberation*. Chicago: University of Chicago Press, 2009.

Van der Kolk, Bessel. *The Body Keeps the Score: Brain, Mind, and Body in the Healing of Trauma*. New York: Penguin, 2015.

Wyman, David, et al., eds. "Thompson, Dorothy." Encyclopedia of America's Response to the Holocaust. Accessed March 3, 2022. http://enc.wymaninstitute.org/?p=517.

About the Author

photo credit: Agnes Fohn

Joanne Intrator's life has been shaped by being the daughter of two German Jewish refugees. Since childhood, she has pondered why people perpetrate atrocities on their fellow human beings. After studying German history at Connecticut College, she received an MD from Columbia University and became a psychiatrist with an expertise in abnormal behavior. She spearheaded the first brain-imaging research on carefully diagnosed psychopaths, which was published in the *Journal of Biological Psychiatry*. Following her father's death in 1993, she took it upon herself to fight for restitution of a building in Berlin; her professional insights into the behavior of bureaucrats were critical to her understanding of how to negotiate with obstructionists. Her journey has been the subject of news articles, television interviews, and museum exhibits. Joanne practices psychiatry in New York City and writes a blog for *Psychology Today*. To learn more, visit JoanneIntrator.com.

SELECTED TITLES FROM SHE WRITES PRESS

She Writes Press is an independent publishing company founded to serve women writers everywhere. Visit us at www.shewritespress.com.

Quest for Eternal Sunshine: A Holocaust Survivor's Journey from Darkness to Light by Mendek Rubin and Myra Goodman. $16.95, 978-1-63152-878-1
Following the death of Mendek Rubin, a brilliant inventor who overcame the trauma of the Holocaust to live a truly joyous life, his daughter Myra found an unfinished manuscript about his healing journey; this inspirational book is that manuscript, with the missing parts of Mendek's story—along with his wisdom and secrets to finding happiness—woven in by Myra.

Surviving the Survivors: A Memoir by Ruth Klein. $16.95, 978-1-63152-471-4
With both humor and deep feeling, Klein shares the story of her parents—who survived the Holocaust but could not overcome the tragedy they had experienced—and their children, who became indirect victims of the atrocities endured by the generation before them.

Api's Berlin Diaries: My Quest to Understand My Grandfather's Nazi Past by Gabrielle Robinson. $16.95, 978-1-64742-003-1
After her mother's death, Gabrielle Robinson found diaries her grandfather had kept while serving as doctor in Berlin 1945—only to discover that her beloved "Api" had been a Nazi.

Jumping Over Shadows: A Memoir by Annette Gendler.
$16.95, 978-1-63152-170-6
Like her great-aunt Resi, Annette Gendler, a German, fell in love with a Jewish man—but unlike her aunt, whose marriage was destroyed by "the Nazi times," Gendler found a way to make her impossible love survive.

Newcomers in an Ancient Land: Adventures, Love, and Seeking Myself in 1960s Israel by Paula Wagner. $16.95, 978-1-63152-529-2
After leaving home at eighteen in search of her Jewish roots in Israel and France, Paula learns far more than two new languages. To navigate her new life, she must also separate from her twin sister and forge her own identity.